DISTANCE AND DOCUMENTS
AT THE SPANISH EMPIRE'S PERIPHERY

Distance and Documents
at the Spanish Empire's Periphery

Sylvia Sellers-García

STANFORD UNIVERSITY PRESS

STANFORD, CALIFORNIA

Stanford University Press
Stanford, California

This book was published with subsidized support from Boston College.

Printed in the United States of America on acid-free, archival-quality paper

Library of Congress Cataloging-in-Publication Data

Sellers-García, Sylvia, author.
Distance and documents at the Spanish Empire's periphery / Sylvia Sellers-
García.
    pages cm
Includes bibliographical references and index.
ISBN 978-0-8047-8705-5 (cloth : alk. paper)
1. Government publications—Central America—History. 2. Government publi-
cations—Spain—Colonies. 3. Geographical perception—Spain—Colonies.
4. Central-local government relations—Spain—Colonies. 5. Central America—
History—To 1821—Sources. 6. Spain—Colonies—America—History—Sources.
I. Title.
F1437.S45 2014
972.8'01—dc23
   2013021475
ISBN 978-0-8047-8882-3 (electronic)

Typeset by Bruce Lundquist in 10.5/12 Sabon

*This book is dedicated to
Martha Julia Garcia Sellers
and Stephen G. Sellers*

Contents

Figures, Maps, and Tables

Maps

Tables

Acknowledgments

Archivists at the Bancroft Library in Berkeley, California, at the Archivo General de Centroamérica in Guatemala, at the Archivo General de Indias, and at the Centro de Investigaciones Regionales de Mesoamérica opened the doors to archival research and provided me with essential guidance. I am particularly grateful to the entire staff of the AGCA for their hospitality.

A summer fellowship from the Taft Center at the University of Cincinnati allowed me to complete the first draft of this manuscript, and the generous leave offered by Boston College during spring 2012 offered the much-needed time to embark on the necessary revisions. My thanks to Jim Cronin and David Quigley for making it possible. Audiences and readers at both of these institutions, audiences at other campuses, and participants at several conferences—particularly those at the Sixteenth Century Society conference—gave valuable comments on portions of the manuscript.

I wish to thank Norris Pope of Stanford University Press for his energetic support of this project, which he has shepherded through to publication. My thanks also to Emma Harper for answering my many, many questions and keeping me on the right path. I am grateful to Judith Hibbard and Stacy Wagner for their assistance in the latter stages of publication. The anonymous reviewer who offered comments through Stanford University Press has helped to make this book more concise and, I hope, precise; I am grateful for the feedback. I am also indebted to Ken Mills for the extremely thorough and insightful comments that allowed me to see this manuscript in a much clearer light.

I am very grateful to friends, colleagues, and mentors from Berkeley and the Bay Area, including José Rabasa, Kerwin Klein, Russ Sheptak, Thomas Dandelet, Mark Healey, Linda Lewin, Richard Candida-Smith, Theresa Salazar, Carlos Delgado, Walter Brem, and David Kessler. Stephanie Ballenger, Laurence Cuelenaere, Kinga Novak, Jessica Delgado, Julia Sarreal, Brianna Leavitt-Alcántara, Beatrice Gurwitz, Marcelo Alejandro Aranda, Sarah Wells, Victor Goldgel Carballo, Heather Flynn-Roller, and Seth Kimmel all read some version of work included in this book, and I am grateful for their suggestions. Paul Ramírez has continually offered welcome challenges to the ideas, methods, and writing style of this manuscript; I have pushed further on many fronts because of his questions and suggestions. Alejandra Dubcovsky, ever a generous reader, has waded into this draft at multiple points, and I am particularly grateful for her comments on a late version of the Introduction. I especially want to thank Sean McEnroe for so whole-heartedly engaging in every aspect of this project. From the half-formed initial ideas to the more determined stylistic changes at the end, this manuscript has benefited at every turn from his advice.

From across the country or the state, Beatrice Bartlett, Jordana Dym, Randolph Head, and Bruce Castleman opened my eyes to new readings, sources, or ideas. Colleagues in the History Department at the University of Cincinnati, especially Maura O'Connor, Sigrun Haude, and Wendy Kline, supported this manuscript at key moments when it was going through growing pains (or shrinking pains). Sarah Jackson offered feedback on the Introduction just before it was finalized. I am very grateful to Julie Gibbings, Carmen Valenzuela de Garay, Arturo Paz, and Ramiro Ordoñez Jonama for their support in Guatemala. I particularly wish to thank Ramiro for his kindness in Guatemala City and for introducing me to Rivera Maestre.

Colleagues at Boston College have supported this project from the moment I arrived, not least by creating a lively and energetic environment in which talking about one's research is never an imposition. I am grateful to Robin Fleming for her guidance on both substance and practical matters. Heather Richardson, Marilynn Johnson, Virginia Reinburg, Sarah Ross, Dana Sajdi, and Prasannan Parthasarathi have offered ideas and encouragement in many ways. My warm thanks to Deborah Levenson-Estrada for her unbounded enthusiasm, for her friendship, and for the many fascinating conversations.

I am grateful to Margaret Chowning for challenging me early on to think about what historical writing should do and for offering comments particularly crucial to the organization of this manuscript. Her comments left me with a model for rigor that I will happily pursue for as long as I am writing. William B. Taylor sat down with me at the Bancroft Library in 2003 and pointed to the Inquisition case from Escuintla that became so many beginnings: the beginning of this book, the beginning of my longer investigation into distance and documents, and the beginning of my inexorable and entirely rewarding habit of historical thinking. I recall fondly how that page of eighteenth-century text came alive, a first instance of the many in which the past emerged as vivid but changeable, never wholly reconciled. I am deeply grateful for the continual inspirations, minute and monumental, that emerge from his mentorship.

Lastly, I wish to thank friends and family in the United States and in Guatemala for their continual encouragement. I am indebted to family members in Guatemala for supporting me in undertaking this project and many others, particularly Marina San Roman, Sergio Silva, and Igork San

Roman. I would not have trekked across country to study history at Berkeley if Pablo had not promised (correctly) that there was no other place like it. My mother's enigmatic stories about family history first sparked my interest in understanding Guatemala's past, and my father has weighed in with ideas, books, and ponderable questions at every stage of my learning. Oliver's boundless good humor, common sense, and wise counsel have kept me on track through many twists and turns over the last few years. My thanks to Alton for his ability to see remote things with such clarity that they are made near.

Note on Spelling

Where documents are transcribed or partially reproduced, as in tables, I have preserved the original—often idiosyncratic—spelling of contemporaries. In the text, I have updated the Spanish to reflect current usage.

DISTANCE AND DOCUMENTS
AT THE SPANISH EMPIRE'S PERIPHERY

Introduction

ON SEEING DISTANCES

We have become increasingly accustomed, over the last half-century, to the idea that the globe is shrinking. If travel is fast, communication is faster. The instantaneous delivery of messages that would previously have taken days or weeks has done curious things to our sense of distance, so that space and time, those two reliable measures of remoteness, seem at times entirely eroded. What does distance mean when such previously formidable obstacles can be so easily overlooked? Surely distance has not disappeared entirely. Despite the illusion of universal proximity, there are yet ways of being remote and distant in our day.[1] Distance, it seems, is not so much about a spatial measure as it is about the endurance of those obstacles: space and time. In some cases they endure where they have been carefully cultivated as barriers from a world perceived as fast-paced; in other cases they endure where resources are scarce and the means cannot be found to overcome them. So, even now, not every place is equally connected and distance is, undeniably, relative and flexible. In this sense, there is little difference between our conception of distance and that of people in the colonial Atlantic world. Distance was then, as it is now, less a question of measurement and more a question of perspective.

Pertinent as it is to both modern and colonial life, I did not begin the research for this book with the intention of studying the conception of distance. It seems now that nothing could be more central to the workings of the Spanish empire, stretching so far across four continents that, as the saying goes, the sun across it never set. But, in fact, I began at the margins of the topic, both spatially and thematically, and I only fully perceived distance as a central research problem after some time.

The discovery of the problem began with a series of perplexing questions that arose while reading a document, an Inquisition case from the early eighteenth century housed at the Bancroft Library in Berkeley. Four elderly women in Escuintla, a town on Guatemala's Pacific coast, were accused of witchcraft.[2] They were women of mixed race, and they were accused by neighbors, friends, and even a grandson. They had been known to perform rituals to turn themselves into turkeys; one had been seen naked about to take flight; another had made use of poisons. The local priest took the case seriously, filling page after page with testimony. The questions that came to mind while reading were too numerous to tackle all at once, and the questions that seemed most important then seem less important now. Why had a boy testified against his grandmother? How did the women know each other? What had they done to invite such treatment from the people of Escuintla? Fortunately for me, no clear answers emerged, and I was forced to turn to other questions.

The unanswered question that gradually rose to the surface concerned not the women of Escuintla and their witchcraft but the way the bureaucracy of the Inquisition managed their case. The tribunal in Mexico City had corresponded with the priest in Escuintla as the case progressed, ordering him to pursue testimony and requesting more when his first set of interrogations proved inadequate. But then the priest sent in his complete case, and the tribunal was silent. It remained silent for nine years. When the tribunal finally sent the arrest warrant for the four women, all of them had passed away. Why had the tribunal waited so long? How long had the case sat in a pile of paperwork, neglected? Had it been filed away by accident? How long had the documents taken in transit? How had the warrant actually *arrived* in Escuintla?

These questions opened up two related discoveries. First, I realized I did not know how the documents in the case had moved back and forth between Escuintla and Mexico City. Had they been carried by officials involved in the case? Had they been sent by mail? What mail service existed at the time? Without knowing how the documents traveled, I could not be sure how much of the delay had occurred in transit and how much had occurred within the tribunal. Second, I realized I did not understand how people in Escuintla viewed the distance separating their town from Mexico City. If correspondence from Mexico City could take nine years, did the place seem as remote to them as Spain? More so?

It became evident to me that however people in Escuintla viewed those distances, their conceptions of distance were contextual. What should have been an obvious point from the beginning finally became clear: the six hundred miles between Escuintla and Mexico City meant one thing to me and quite another thing to them. That distance was mediated by documents— by communication—in ways I found familiar. But here the familiarity ended. Created not only by geographical circumstances but also by political, social, economic, and cultural conditions, the conception of distance at the peripheries of the Spanish empire was one that I did not yet understand.

On Distance and the Periphery

This book is about how one idea, distance, might be better understood for the colonial period by considering it in the context of others: ideas that aren't always paired with distance in the modern imagination. A first, crucial idea that illuminates the colonial conception of distance is the notion of peripheries. Distances in the Spanish empire, I believe, looked different from the center than they did from the periphery. In his work on early-modern European borderlands, Peter Sahlins writes that most of the literature on the emergence of nations and national identities is written "from the perspective of the centre," but that "few reverse this lens, and consider the history . . . from the perspective of the periphery, of the borderland." Yet as Sahlins points out, considering the empire from the perspective of the periphery allows for reconsideration of "fundamental assumptions about territory and nationality, about nation and state."[3] This is no less true for the Spanish empire as considered from its peripheries in the Americas.

From a certain point of view, the use of the term periphery to describe a colonial place might seem anachronistic. The term acquired currency in the historiography of Latin America only in the second half of the twentieth century. Through the work of sociologists Edward Shils and Immanuel Wallerstein, "center and periphery" became meaningful for scholars of Latin America focusing particularly on economic history. In the 1960s and 1970s, centers and peripheries proved crucial to the elaboration of dependency theory, but even after the widespread critique of dependency theory, the terms have remained in use. Though infrequently deployed in the sense developed by Wallerstein, historians of Latin America routinely rely on the terms to designate spatial, administrative, and economic relationships. More recently, scholars have used them to talk about the history of empire, thereby drawing the twentieth-century terms into colonial contexts.

Comparative studies of empire and Atlantic history have found fresh uses for the center-periphery framework, and these uses have necessarily resulted in new meanings.[4] Space alone, it turns out, does not fully account for relationships between centers and peripheries, which are shaped as much by power as they are by distance.[5] Wealth, bureaucratic or administrative significance, population size, importance to the flow of information, importance to the traffic of commerce, and level of ecclesiastical influence were all qualities relied upon to determine centrality in the colonial world. These qualities not only suggest "an elaborately articulated and hierarchical relationship of center and peripheries," as colonial historians Lyman Johnson and Susan Socolow argue; they point to the fact that centrality in such hierarchical relationships was inescapably variable and relative.[6] An American city's waxing or waning commercial success, for example, could alter its peripheral status. And this status determined not only its relation to the center but to other peripheries.[7] The words "relative" and "relatively" punctuate discussions of centers and peripheries, as authors yield to the comparative frame imposed by the terms. And where there is relativity, there is the possibility for subjective orientations, an "apparent change in the position of what constitutes *center* and what [constitutes] *periphery* resulting from a change in the viewer's position."[8]

This observation—that centers and peripheries look different depending on the viewer's position—informs the postmodern critique of the center-periphery paradigm. The project of *de-centering* among scholars of Latin American studies concerns itself as much with resituating nodes of intellectual knowledge in academia today as with reconsidering the historical relationship between Spain and its colonies. Explicitly political in argument, de-centering aims most fundamentally to create Latin America as a site for intellectual and academic authority. In some formulations, this goal seemingly springs from an understanding of "the periphery" as "the margin." As such, de-centering often seems to argue more for a relocation of the center than for a dissolution of the center-periphery paradigm.[9] In fact, certain postmodern treatments of the paradigm aim to complicate and re-deploy rather than to discredit. As articulated by Enrique Dussel, for example, the center-periphery model becomes essential to challenging our conception of modernity and its origins. Dussel's thesis, that modernity is the "fruit of the 'management' of the 'centrality' of the first 'world-system'" aims not to discredit the center-periphery model but to credit Amerindia with the production of a powerful center.[10] As creator of the center's power, he argues, the periphery matters.

Postmodernist scholars and historians of empire, myself included, acknowledge the same key problem with the continued use of this framework: the term periphery identifies place pejoratively. Our approaches to this pejorative connotation, however, differ. While Dussel combats the problem by arguing that peripheries created the "value" of the center, other postmodern critics take a more indirect approach, claiming less that the center has no autochthonous value and more that the center should be relocated. Many historians of empire argue something similar. In framing the discussion of peripheral areas, historians make the implicit—or sometimes explicit—claim that these areas have been ignored by the historiography and merit attention.[11] As they make this claim, the discussions drift inevitably toward using the terms "center" and "periphery" to connote relative importance; since "peripheries" have been deemed unimportant, the author must lead the charge to secure their importance. As John Jay TePaske articulates it, "The existence of frontiers or peripheries in colonial Spanish American cannot be denied, but these peripheries all had important positions within the Spanish empire in America as component parts of an organic whole that constituted the Spanish enterprise in the Indies."[12] Again, the periphery matters.

And this, of course, is the central dilemma for anyone who studies peripheries: the more one asserts the importance of one's periphery, the more one asserts the value of the framework revolving around the center. Our accepted vocabulary subverts the argument we wish to make with it: "central" connotes importance and "peripheral" connotes unimportance. Even when used to argue for the importance of peripheries, the term "periphery" continues to connote pejoratively. As a result, we find ourselves arguing in defense of peripheries that peripheries are not peripheral at all—they are central.

This book, which focuses on a place with the dubious distinction of being as peripheral now as it was in the colonial period, faces the same dilemma. But here I suggest another approach to the dilemma. Instead of arguing for Guatemala's importance, I suggest acknowledging and then examining Guatemala's peripheral positioning. Instead of countering the pejorative connotation of "periphery," I propose considering the connotation in historical context. By so doing, Guatemala emerges as a place that can assist our understanding of broader conceptions in the Spanish empire. As it turns out, the pejorative connotation proves remarkably useful for understanding the term "distancia" in colonial usage. Though—as discussed in the ensuing chapters—"distancia" or distance was frequently quantified and described with fairly objective measures, "distancia" was also used to connote pejoratively in much the same way that "periphery" is used today.[13] The phrases "mucha distancia" and "a gran distancia," meaning literally "at a great distance," described in negative terms a place "on the periphery" or "at the margin" rather than all places that were simply "far away."

On Guatemala as a Periphery of Empire

Our modern associations with peripherality, marginality, and centrality can therefore be useful as insights into the colonial conception of distance. One of these insights is that only places considered peripheral lay "at a great distance." While the spatial distance from Spain to Guatemala was, of course, exactly the same as the spatial distance from Guatemala to Spain, officials in Guatemala did not describe Spain as "*distante*," whereas officials in Spain writing of Guatemala—and other places in its overseas

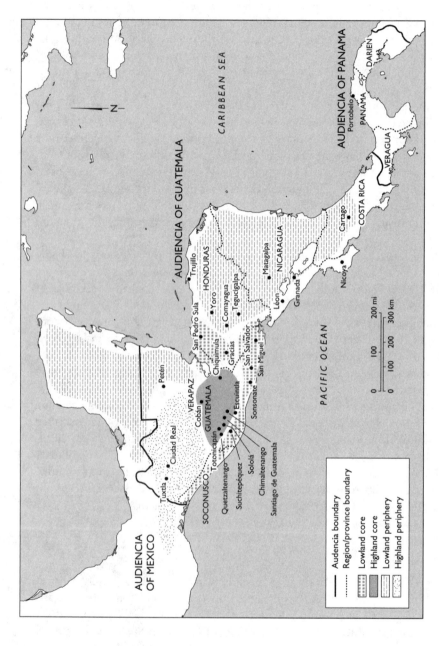

MAP I.I. The Guatemalan *audiencia* in the eighteenth century

empire—did.[14] Waldo Tobler's first law of geography, the argument that "everything is related to everything else, but near things are more related than distant things," seems to be only true from certain perspectives.[15] The Spanish monarch, the Council of the Indies, the Board of Trade (*Casa de Contratación*), and later Spanish ministries all loomed large for Guatemalan officials, important as they were to colonial American governance. Even more revealingly, Guatemala, at the periphery of the Spanish empire, had its own peripheries, and in the correspondence and reports of Guatemalan officials, "distant" is used to describe places in the provinces but not to describe important places in Mexico or Spain. So, for example, the highlands province of Verapaz at seventy miles and the southern province of Costa Rica at five hundred miles were "distante," while the Mexican port of Veracruz at a similar five hundred miles and Seville at more than five thousand miles were not.

What qualities made places peripheral to Guatemala? Spatial distance appears to have mattered, but so did distance from a crucial route, inaccessibility (temporal as well as spatial), economic or commercial status, demography, social and cultural remoteness, and administrative insignificance. Historians and geographers of Central America tend to emphasize patterns of economic and social development, as do Christopher H. Lutz and W. George Lovell, who consider the Guatemalan "resource base," landholding and settlement, economic life, and social life in identifying the peripheries of Guatemala. Building on Murdo MacLeod's conception of a ladino east and an Indian west in Spanish Guatemala, Lovell and Lutz identify highlands and lowlands as integral to a more complex designation of cores and peripheries.[16] In their conception, the core includes the colonial capital, the eastern highlands, the eastern lowlands, and the Pacific coast. The peripheries include the highland sierras in the middle of the country and the northern lowlands.[17]

Where the "core" had social and economic value, of course, it had value for Spaniards; this resulted in political and administrative structures that closely mirrored the core.[18] The Spanish organization of the region transformed several times in the sixteenth century, reflecting an early ambivalence on the part of the crown as to how the region fit into the larger overseas empire. For the first two centuries of colonial rule, Spanish America was divided into two vast viceroyalties, New Spain and Peru, which were further divided into regional *audiencias*—governing bodies with fixed territorial jurisdictions that combined legislative, executive, administrative, and judicial functions.[19] Occupying the space between the two viceroyalties, the isthmus could be considered proximate to either, and it was also closely linked to the Caribbean. When the dust settled, the *audiencia* of Guatemala stretched from modern-day Costa Rica to southern Mexico, including the jurisdictions (*gobiernos*) of Soconusco, Honduras, Nicaragua, Costa Rica, and Guatemala—which included Chiapas and El Salvador.[20]

With varied landscapes and climates, the area did not prove uniformly promising to Spanish settlers. High mountain ranges roughly parallel to the Pacific coast arched inland from southern Mexico, while sierras and cordilleras spread westward through Honduras and along a central spine through Costa Rica. Until the twentieth century, much of the region was covered by dense forest that made travel and settlement difficult. As Lovell and Lutz describe it, suffocating heat was the norm for the lowland coasts while frost was not unusual in the highlands. Spanish settlers consequently concentrated in the *tierra templada*, the valleys with more temperate climates that lay between the extremes. The first capital city, Santiago de Almolonga, was founded in the "warmer, lower altitudes in the highland core."[21] Even this favorable location was not perfect; in the mid-sixteenth century the long chain of volcanoes running parallel to the Pacific coast from Guatemala to Costa Rica proved perilous for the first time of many, and the capital was destroyed. The new capital, Santiago de Guatemala, was founded a few miles away in the valley between the *Volcán de Agua* and the *Volcán de Fuego*. Initially, as Spanish settlement spread from Santiago de Guatemala outward, the regions to the south and east of the capital were favored over the regions north and west.[22] Though the Spanish pattern of settlement overlapped to a great extent with the preexisting Indian pattern of settlement, Indian communities at the Spanish peripheries fared quite differently than those at the Spanish cores, where demands for land were most intense.[23]

Along with land, Spaniards demanded labor. Cacao provided the region with its first agricultural boom, but the later decline of the cacao plantations led Guatemalans to a greater reliance on mining, indigo production, and later cochineal production.[24] Cacao and mining were especially labor-intensive, and there is no doubt that part of Guatemala's appeal to settling Spaniards lay in its potential to provide Indian labor. Slave raids led not only to the forced migration of Indians but often to their early death.[25] Of course the greatest demographic impact on the Indian population came not from slavery but from disease, and the dramatic population decline altered the social, political, and economic landscape. The population shrank from almost 6 million in 1500 to less than 300,000 in 1680. Despite this remarkable decline, the region as a whole remained approximately 95 percent Indian in 1680.[26] There continued to exist broad swaths of territory where the population was entirely Indian or where Spaniards were represented only by the parish priest. In the same period, the black slave population in Santiago de Guatemala reached its peak.[27] Both the black slave population and the free black population reached its highest rate in Santiago in the late seventeenth century, falling into decline afterwards for several decades. Though a number of plagues and diseases took their toll in the late seventeenth and early eighteenth centuries, the falling figures for several demographic groups can also be partly explained by increasing *mestizaje*. Mulattoes and mestizos alike were identified as ladinos.[28]

A term that has shifted in definition several times, *ladino* meant something different in the colonial period in Guatemala than it has meant in the nineteenth and twentieth centuries.[29] In the colonial period, the term points to the growing number of *castas*, people of mixed race, in Guatemala and Spanish America as a whole. Eighteenth-century documents continue to identify *españoles* and *indios*, but they also identify *indios-ladinos*, *ladinos*, *mestizos*, and other categories. This growth in the mixed-race population and the consequent disintegration of the *repúblicas*—the legal spheres separating Spaniards from Indians—necessarily affected the position of specific places within Guatemalan social space. While certain regions such as Totonicapán and Verapaz remained heavily Indian, many parts of the provinces to the southeast (such as Costa Rica) grew to become predominantly mestizo.[30]

These demographic and economic factors most discussed by scholars are doubtlessly essential to determining colonial cores and peripheries, but they tend to deemphasize two key aspects that contemporaries also relied upon most in their conception of the central and peripheral. First, the spatial schema that emerges from the historiography is one that casts centers and peripheries as coterminous territories, while they were primarily understood to occupy places along routes. Routes, in this conception, are mental place-connectors; the paths themselves changed according to season and weather, but the abstracted routes, paced intervals between locations, remained constant. Second, the emphasis on economic centers and peripheries, while not incompatible with a contemporary Guatemalan understanding, reflects a view more in keeping with the perspective from the empire's center in Spain. Officials writing in colonial Guatemala considered administrative influence crucial to centrality and peripherality. Centers were understood as places with dense and effective administrative networks, both secular and ecclesiastical; distant peripheries were understood as places beyond bureaucratic control. Three examples will suffice to introduce the discussion of how routes and administrative reach mattered in the colonial conception of *distancia*.

Costa Rica is an especially revealing case. In 1768, an official in Guatemala explained the difficulty of communicating monthly with Costa Rica due to "the great distance there is to Granada."[31] Lying more than five hundred miles away as the crow flies and fifty days of travel away, Costa Rica was arguably the farthest point within the *audiencia* from the Guatemalan capital. Its social, economic, and political isolation is emphasized in the his-

toriography, and contemporaries in both Guatemala and Costa Rica seem
to have felt the distance keenly. Panama and New Granada lay just beyond
it to the south, but communication with them over land was virtually non-
existent.[32] Costa Rican officials believed the solution lay in reorganizing the
administrative structure, assigning Costa Rica to Tierra Firme. In a letter to
this effect written by the *cabildo* (local council) in Cartago in 1625, the distance of nearly three hundred leagues to Guatemala City was cast as the cul-
prit for the region's ills. The "great harm" to the province resulting from
being "so far away" (*tan lejos*) from Guatemala City affected the one hundred and twenty Spaniards and fifteen hundred Indians alike. The *cabildo*
lamented that though the arrival of the governor had been a tremendous
boon, he was present only once a year. In the interim, the four *corregidores*
(district magistrates) assigned by the *audiencia* in Guatemala committed excessive abuses against the Indian population, but the *corregidores* knew they
were beyond the governor's reach and the Indians were too poor to travel
the three hundred leagues to protest the injustices committed against them.[33]

It is worth presenting the content of the *cabildo*'s complaint more at
length—here summarized by an official in Spain—as it emphasizes the importance of distance to the inhabitants of Cartago.

In the city of Cartago in the province of Costa Rica, and in the name of said province and its residents, it is stated that the province lies 280 leagues from the city
of Guatemala, where the *Audiencia* is located. To reach the city it is necessary to
travel to Nicaragua, and of the 100 leagues that lie between Costa Rica and Nicaragua, 80 are uninhabited, and there are many wide rivers that are difficult to cross
during most of the year, and as a result there are many people who either drown in
the rivers or lose their farms after embarking on such a long journey along swampy
routes that during much of the year are impassable. The residents who are obliged
to travel to the *audiencia* for official business suffer great trials and discomfort
and risk their very lives both because of the poor road and because it is impossible to leave their crops unattended for so long, and they have no money or other
recourse, nor do they find anyone to help them in Guatemala City for it lies so far
away. . . . And there is another even worse problem in that province, and this is
that the *naturales* of this region are assigned by the President four district magistrates from the Guatemalan *audiencia* and though the *naturales* suffer a thousand
injuries at their hands it is impossible for them to go beg for justice for they are
so poor and the majority of the them go about naked. These difficulties and many
others besides would cease if Your Majesty saw fit to assign the province of Costa
Rica to the *audiencia* of Panama since it lies so close to it.[34]

The portrait of remoteness painted here is extreme. By the late seventeenth century, Costa Rica's Indian population had dwindled, and the
Spanish population was widely scattered.[35] Roughly two hundred and fifty
people lived spread out over the region between Nicoya and Cartago, and
Miles Wortman cites a contemporary's horror at the fact that in 1719 even

the governor relied on subsistence farming.[36] Despite such indications of poverty, however, Costa Rica was not insignificant economically. The inhabitants of Cartago were not entirely wrong in claiming that given the opportunity, the province could become one of the area's richest. By 1700, the Caribbean coast had become a major cacao-growing region, and its port became notorious for smuggling.[37] Thus Costa Rica's placement beyond Guatemala's administrative reach came to be exploited by many others besides the seventeenth-century *corregidores;* smugglers realized the potential of its trade network connecting it to the Caribbean, Panama, and Cartagena.[38] Costa Rica had no close ties to Omoa and Veracruz, the two main ports for the Guatemalan *audiencia,* and the difficult, lightly trafficked overland route between Costa Rica and points farther north could not draw the weight of the network southward. So despite its mainly Spanish population and its arguable economic importance in the eighteenth century, Costa Rica remained a final stop on the overland route south: beyond administrative control, linked tenuously to the center by a long route, and tied primarily by maritime routes to the Caribbean and Tierra Firme.

Clearly route placement was closely tied to socioeconomic factors, and while certainly in some cases economic demands created routes, in other cases the failure of establishing a route may have stifled potential growth. The perception of Alta and Baja Verapaz (in colonial usage, las Verapazes or la Verapaz) as distant peripheries came about in the colonial period after a failed experiment to establish a route through them to Puerto Caballos, a port on the Caribbean coast west of Trujillo (the first port developed in the sixteenth century). Though the route was meant to benefit the growing city of Santiago, the disadvantages of both the port itself and the route through Verapaz proved insurmountable. The "long, tortuous" road connecting to the capital, the pestilence of the port, and attacks by pirates all served to bring the port disfavor.[39] After the port was abandoned, the route through Verapaz led only to the province itself, and thus the area remained predominantly Indian. In 1682 there were 10,753 Indian tributaries in twenty-seven towns, and only eighteen to twenty Spaniards, mestizos, and mulattoes. The largest non-Indian presence was Dominican: a *hacienda* dating to 1579 produced sugar, relying on some 250 slaves and one thousand Indians in the early eighteenth century.[40] The non-ecclesiastical Spanish presence remained negligible. The Verapazes lay approximately seventy miles from Guatemala City—closer than the cities in what would become El Salvador—but the route was far more difficult. And unlike comparable places with large Indian populations and scarce economic opportunities lying farther west on the route to Mexico, the route led nowhere beyond the Verapazes. From the perspective of an official in the Guatemalan capital, the Verapazes followed a long and difficult route north into towns dominated by Indian and ecclesiastical authorities. Even as late as 1805, an official protested the impossibility of establishing regular communication with the Province of Verapaz because of "la grande distancia que media"—the great distance it measures—from the capital.[41]

Costa Rica and the Verapazes both combine so many potential attributes of peripherality—inaccessibility, cultural remoteness, small population, and periods of relative poverty—that it would be difficult to isolate one or two as the most important in determining their peripheral place. Surely people in the Guatemalan capital considered them in light of their economic and social characteristics as well as in terms of their placement on difficult routes beyond administrative reach. But the recommendations by an official from the province of Tegucigalpa, in present-day Honduras, bring the spatial conception of routes and the importance of administrative reach in determining "centrality" into sharper relief. Lamenting the "distance that separates the district from the provincial capital," the former *alcalde mayor* (district governor) argued that during his tenure it had proved indispensable to have a judge assigned to the district of Cantarranas y Cedros. First, because of "the great number of people of all kinds who arrive, drawn by the mineral wealth of the district," and second to avoid "certain fraudulent behavior that tends to take place on the Northern coast." He recognized that the coast lay at some distance, "but as the mouth of the region, and as a necessary throughway to the other Provinces of this Kingdom, it proves indispensable and essential to have a deputy appointed by this *Real Audiencia*." He warned that "it may be the case that due to the distance of thirty leagues separating Cantarranas y Cedros from the provincial capital, these local transgressions may remain unattended to and their perpetrators unpunished."[42]

Significantly, the district governor describes the area in question as a *garganta*—a throat or funnel—for the region. In describing it as a place, he invokes its use as a route. Furthermore, his description of Cantarranas y Cedros as a place of economic significance and heavy human traffic would seem to contradict its characterization as a "distant" periphery if we consider *distante* to imply primarily socioeconomic marginality.[43] But the district governor's anxieties about the region concern its distance from government authorities. If we consider *distante* in colonial usage to mean, in certain instances, "beyond administrative control," then the district governor's urgent recommendations to appoint a deputy seem to underline the use of *distante* to describe Cantarranas y Cedros. The argument here is not that only routes and administrative reach mattered, but that they complemented and sometimes dominated contemporaries' consideration of other factors.

Projected maps of the region incorporating the notion of routes and administrative reach might look something like what is shown in Maps I.2 and I.3. Consistent with Lauren Benton's elaboration of colonial space

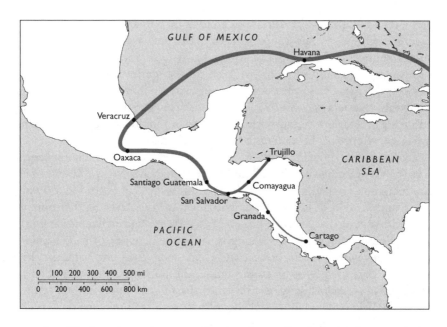

MAP I.2. The late sixteenth-century Guatemalan *audiencia* depicted as a route

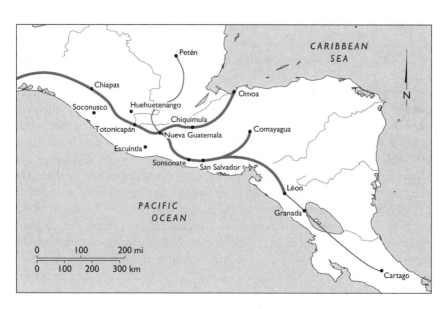

MAP I.3. The late eighteenth-century Guatemalan *audiencia* depicted as a route

as "enclaves" and "corridors," Guatemalan routes connected places of greater and lesser importance.[44] In the late sixteenth century, principal routes connected Guatemala to Mexico and to the ports on the Honduran coast. Just as important as overland routes, maritime routes linked the ports to destinations in the Caribbean, principally Havana, and farther on to Spain. Overland routes to the provinces connected Guatemala to San Salvador and Comayagua, with far more tenuous routes connecting the northern reaches of the *audiencia* to Granada and Cartago.

By the late seventeenth century, the central artery through the *audiencia* was thicker; Chiapas was linked through Huehuetenango and Totonicapán to Guatemala, which in turn reached southeast to San Salvador, Comayagua, and beyond to León. Still oriented toward the Atlantic, the route to Veracruz provided the crucial link to Spain. By the late eighteenth century, the landscape had somewhat changed. A denser network of routes linked destinations within the *audiencia*, and Guatemala—in a new location after the 1773 earthquake—was connected to the port of Omoa (founded in 1752) through towns lying east of it, principally Chiquimula. The central artery connecting Ciudad Real through to Costa Rica branched out, reaching secondary destinations within the *audiencia*.

These maps are derived from an official, bureaucratic experience located in Guatemala City (in its various locations), but as they prioritize communication networks and, indirectly, trade networks, they may well reflect a more broadly held conception of Guatemalan social space.[45] An awareness of social and economic peripheries, as described above, complemented and complicated this conception. To demarcate this space as the territory of official culture is not necessarily to say that others outside of this space did not reflect and reinforce it. As suggested above, people in the internal peripheries such as Costa Rica contributed to this conception; they even actively *delimited* Guatemalan space. And as will be argued in later chapters, people living "off the route" may have contributed as well to both the formation and perception of this space. In his characterization of the early colonial period, Angel Rama describes the Spanish conquest as a "frenetic gallop across continental immensities . . . leaving in its wake a scattering of cities, isolated and practically out of communication from one another, while the territory between the new urban centers continued to be inhabited almost solely by the dismayed Indian populations."[46] While in many ways these maps project a similar vision of "relay stations for the transmission of . . . imperial directives," I would argue that the contours of this network were neither perceived nor determined by the urban centers alone. In other words, officials, Spaniards, Creoles, *ladinos*, and others living in the described space produced these routes of linked places in conjunction with people living outside them.

The view that stands in strong contrast to this particular sketch of Guatemalan space and place is that held by the administrative center in Spain. It seems likely that Spanish officials viewed the ports surrounding the *audiencia* of Guatemala—Veracruz, Havana, Cartagena, and for a time Portobelo—as central, important places, but none of these fall within the *audiencia* itself. Places lying inland within Guatemala were considered more peripheral. Without abandoning the idea that routes and administrative reach informed the conception of distance, the oft-made argument that a "major function of the colonies was to generate a surplus of wealth for export to Spain" should be credited.[47] Ports, as important places along the routes moving this wealth, would have occupied a prominent role in fulfilling this function, while cities such as Santiago would have occupied places of importance proportional to their ability to provide the "underlying structures that made empire possible," to draw on Henry Kamen's elaboration of Spanish imperial power.[48]

But in the larger scheme, Spanish monarchs and administrators were also painfully aware of the Americas as *distante*, if we understand this to mean "beyond administrative control." Even the American centers lay at a great distance. Officials in Spain knew that the long voyage across the Atlantic made necessary some degree of independent governance, but they did not like it. In the words of M. C. Mirow, who acknowledges the "great geographical distance" as a crucial element in Spanish governance, "Spanish institutions effectively bridged this vast space and governed a multitude of aspects of daily life with jealous, watchful specificity."[49] To some degree, it might be argued that Spanish American bureaucracy's primary purpose was to overcome distance. In the early colonial period, the Council of Indies in Seville maintained its "watchful" presence through its American *audiencias* and its related courts and councils. In the eighteenth century, secretaries absorbed the functions previously assigned to the Council of Indies and an intendancy system was created as an additional layer of regional royal power.[50] Nevertheless, sometimes urgent decisions simply had to be made without consultation. Charles III lamented in 1761 the "repeated cases in which emergencies do not permit, due to distance, direct recourse to my Royal Person."[51] One particularly vivid example comes from a Guatemalan mail official who wrote to his superior in Spain immediately after the devastating 1773 earthquake that destroyed the capital. He described the horrors around him, saying, "I bring it to your attention so that in your pity you may relieve us in whatever manner possible of the obvious emergency in which we find ourselves."[52] Needless to say, given the pace of overseas communication—worsened by the catastrophe—the official was forced to make many key decisions alone. To ensure officials in Guatemala and elsewhere remained accountable for their independent decisions, Charles III insisted on precise documentation of their every action.

In other words, documents were used to overcome distance. Yet Charles III and other monarchs, even the *"rey papelero"* (king of paper) Philip II, discovered on a broad scale what the witches in Escuintla discovered—to their benefit—on a smaller scale. Documents did not always overcome distance well. They could get lost, they could be ignored, and they could be interpreted in unpredictable ways. Or, as the earthquake crisis demonstrates, they were simply too slow. Whether they failed or succeeded, documents were a crucial ligature between Escuintla and Mexico City, between Guatemala and Spain, between periphery and center. The workings of empire depended on the flow of paper.

On Documents and Empire

While distance can be approached from many directions, this book arrives at a colonial conception of distance by examining how key ideas were manifested in the treatment of documents. A basic claim here is that documents were an essential tool in the workings of empire, and particularly long-distance empire. The writing, travel, and storage of documents therefore reveal much about how distance was mediated, if not always overcome.

The grouping of distance, documents, and empire draws together several lines of historiography that would not seem, at first glance, to intersect but that nonetheless complement one another well. Studies of communication beginning with Harold Innis's foundational *Empire and Communications* (1950) have established the necessity of documents to empire-building.[53] Communication networks not only underpin the logistics of empire; as more recent publications argue, they also build hubs of information and power at the empire's center. Histories of the Spanish empire have emphasized language, shaded slightly differently than "communication," as an imperializing force. Citing the Bishop of Ávila's comment to Queen Isabella of Spain that "language is the perfect instrument of empire," authors point to the broad sweep of Castilian as a tool of domination.[54] But is it language or writing that works so effectively as a tool of conquest? Scholars focusing on sources of colonial power have pointed to print culture and the power of texts as the crucial instruments of empire building. Angel Rama's vision of *The Lettered City* projects a Spanish America in which the very architecture and space "sprang forth in signs and plans, already complete, in the documents that laid their statutory foundations and in the charts and plans that established their ideal designs." In fulfilling these designs, writes Rama, Spanish "conquerors" relied on the written word as a kind of magical force: "the written word became the only binding one—

in contradistinction to the spoken word, which belonged to the realm of things precarious and uncertain." Its permanence lent the text power, and its power was political.[55] Even authors like Fernando Bouza, who qualify the supposed dominance of text by arguing that images and speech also held power in the early modern period, accept that the written word—and particularly the printed word—gradually gained influence over the course of the colonial period. Bouza reminds us that this ascendancy was not a foregone conclusion.[56] The numerous social and cultural histories of reading, writing, and the rise of print culture that he speaks to (which focus mostly on Europe) nonetheless offer a compelling contextual story for how text was asserting its dominance just as Spain was buildings its empire.[57]

Communication, language, text: these may seem variations on a single theme rather than distinct categories. Yet their differences are sufficient to have guided scholars onto divergent paths. While the rich cultural and social histories of reading, writing, and printing have focused on books and personal correspondence, studies of empire and power, when they speak of texts, largely imply the official paperwork of the Spanish crown. Publications—literary, scientific, and religious—as well as personal writings form part of the story, but the paperwork of the judiciary, of the church, and of the crown are central to its elaboration of a textual imperial power. Yet how much do we know about the production, circulation, and readership of these official documents? How much do we know about the cultural life of the documents that sustained the Spanish empire? The approach I take here, borrowing methods from one body of work and sources from the other, is to examine the social and cultural history of official documents in light of the broader history of empire. Examining official documents as "artifacts of modern knowledge practices" illuminates not only the trajectories of specific documents but also the social and cultural context of these trajectories.[58] The official document becomes an opportunity to observe the cultural life of an institution and, further, a social history of knowledge surrounding it.

In the case of the Guatemalan *audiencia*, the documents considered in this light reveal a particular history about people, processes, and institutions; these histories are many and varied. The social history of knowledge that these documents project is similarly complex, but woven through it is a common theme: distance, and specifically the spatial and temporal distances separating places in the Spanish empire. Here, of course, the argument is not unique to Guatemala. Scholars have connected geography to knowledge building in other regions. As Peter Burke posits in his panoramic social history of knowledge in early modern Europe, an important aspect of the history of knowledge is location, or placement, or geography. Considering centers and peripheries explicitly, Burke addresses "the 'spatial distribution' of knowledge, the places in which knowledge was discovered, stored or elaborated as well as those to which it was diffused."[59] Burke points to how "the Casa de Contratación . . . in Seville was a store of knowledge, especially knowledge of sea routes, the site of a model chart (know as the *padrón real*) which was regularly updated when pilots returned from their voyages with new information."[60] Throughout the early modern period, Spain—more accurately, Seville—was incontestably an immense storehouse of knowledge that arrived in reports, *relaciones*, letters, and petitions from every corner of the empire.

Yet documents were not the only form of knowledge crisscrossing the globe, accumulating in centers across Europe and making possible the expansion of the early modern empires. Rather, as Burke urges, "it should be obvious that there are 'knowledges' in the plural in every culture and that social history, like sociology, must be concerned 'with everything that passes for knowledge in society.'" Oral knowledge, visual knowledge, and diverse others are just as vital. He suggests that one way of focusing on specific forms of knowledge would be to "distinguish between the knowledges produced and transmitted by different social groups. Intellectuals are masters of some kinds of knowledge, but other fields of expertise or 'know-how' are cultivated by such groups as bureaucrats, artisans, peasants, midwives and popular healers." However, this distinction between forms of knowledge—particularly the differentiation of "elite" and "popular" knowledge—quickly breaks down. Can it really be claimed that knowledge found in publications and official documents is entirely the fruit of intellectual and bureaucratic wisdom? Surely not; as Burke himself observes, historians—particularly historians of empire—have begun to document "the contribution made by indigenous inhabitants to the knowledges which European rulers, cartographers, and physicians were claiming as their own."[61] As, for example, Karl Offen has demonstrated for the Mosquito Indians on the Caribbean coast, colonial Spanish knowledge of Guatemala was both enriched and constrained by non-elite, Indian sources. Maps of the region may be signed by Spaniards (or other Europeans), but they represent and reproduce local knowledge.[62] Burke is loathe to overstate his case, but he suggests that what we think of as official, imperial knowledge may even be a kind of enshrining of collected, highly unofficial knowledge. These insights suggest that the documents examined in this book—the paperwork produced in the Guatemalan *audiencia*—cannot be considered purely "elite" productions by officials, bureaucrats, and scribes. As the ensuing chapters will demonstrate, official documents "depended on local informants" to a great degree; not only official knowledge but, just as importantly, the *lack* of official knowledge was determined by unofficial sources.

Therefore, the documents of the Guatemalan *audiencia* should be considered composite productions: informed to a great extent by local knowledge, penned by writers who were of varying degrees culturally Spanish, and composed largely according to guidelines and templates determined by administrators at the empire's center. What can be read in the content of official documents from the Guatemalan *audiencia* is a confluence of practices and knowledges gathered from different parts of the empire onto a single page. The documents of the Guatemalan *audiencia* are also composite in another sense. Their movement and treatment are as much a part of their production as are the knowledges brought to bear. And in this sense, too, documents were literally produced by many hands, from the numerous officials who amended and augmented the content to the mail carriers who transported the pages. As material objects and as knowledge productions, documents were created by many people in diverse times and places.

On Finding the Document's Route

The central claim of this book is that spatial history matters to the social history of knowledge. In the Spanish empire, knowledge was produced over long distances, and this is reflected in how the documents were used to overcome distance. Understanding colonial distance through these documents becomes, then, a way to understand how knowledge was created. So what is there to learn about colonial distance? I have argued in this introduction that in the colonial conception, distance connoted peripherality. The chapters that follow build on this argument, suggesting that space was predominantly organized along routes and that distances were understood as time-space intervals connecting hierarchically organized places. What does this say about how knowledge was created? This Introduction has also argued that documents, as composite creations, were produced across temporal and spatial distances. In the chapters that follow, I argue that these distances resulted in particular contents, forms, and practices. The organization of knowledge within this far-flung empire derived many of its attributes from spatial and temporal distance. Knowledge was created along routes, and it was gathered radially, resulting in a hierarchical structure that favored the accumulation of knowledge at the empire's center.

The book is organized into three parts, which consider distance in relation to the creation, movement, and storage of documents. Chapter 1 focuses on document form, arguing that the formal qualities of Spanish paperwork reflect concerns about distance. Document genres—geographical questionnaires and responding reports—likewise reflect these concerns. Instructions requesting geographical reports were sent to the Americas from Spain from the beginning of the colonial period, and officials in Spanish America complied by writing and illustrating *relaciones geográficas*. Officials in Guatemala created reports that closely mirrored the conceptualizations of space and distance projected by the instructions sent from Spain. Quantifying distance to administrative centers was an important way of "placing" towns and villages. By describing each town as "distant from" an urban center and the capital, officials reinforced the empire's hierarchy of place. Officials also relied heavily on routes to write their reports. In some cases, officials wrote their reports while traveling along a route from town to town, thereby emphasizing, once again, routes and temporal-spatial itineraries.

Taking up the notion of distance as pejorative, Chapter 2 examines the 1769–1771 report written by Archbishop Pedro Cortés y Larraz, a published text whose original is housed at the Archivo General de Indias (AGI). Recently appointed and arrived from Spain, the archbishop traveled throughout his archdiocese in the 1760s and compiled a multi-volume *visita* (visit), a "geographic-moral description" of Guatemalan parishes. The *visita* follows Cortés y Larraz's three-stage journey, during which he wrote a detailed report on each parish accompanied by maps or paintings by an unknown artist. The archbishop's *visita* shares many characteristics with the geographical reports discussed in Chapter 1. It unfolds along a route, and it clearly places an emphasis both on describing the route and on measuring it (an objective the archbishop accomplished by using his watch). Its descriptions also prioritize distances to administrative centers and parish seats as important measures. But the archbishop goes further than do the geographical reports by characterizing long distances in his archdiocese as problematic and even dangerous.

Part II turns from document form and content to document travel. After tracing the early history of the mail system, Chapter 3 concentrates on the changes that occurred in the eighteenth century. For most of the colonial period, few substantial changes were made to the Guatemalan mail system, but in 1764, reforms initiated in Spain resulted in a new mandate. Both in the service of generating revenue and in the interest of improving and centralizing communication, overseas and overland mail services were reformed. Mail traveled more frequently and to more destinations. By the end of the eighteenth century, mail traveled systematically to dozens of places within Guatemala. The mail officials who developed and improved these schedules represented their work to superiors in Spain by means of reports, and these reflect a conception of distance emphasizing hierarchies of place, routes, and temporal-spatial segments along them.

Chapter 4 concentrates on the men who actually traveled along the mail routes, the mail carriers (*correos*). While documents written by mail carriers are scarce, documents about them give us some sense of who they were and what their work consisted of. *Correos* are of particular interest because, unlike most Guatemalans, they traveled long distances on a regular basis. Some covered hundreds of leagues every month, and they therefore viewed those leagues in a somewhat different light. Chapter 4 argues that while *correos* may have shared the same "common skeleton" of distance built around centers, routes, and spatial-temporal intervals, they added to this framework a distinctive musculature geared toward absorbing the substantial potential risks entailed by their work.[63] *Correos* saw the long distances along their mail routes as so many leagues of potential profit or loss. In the nineteenth century, a changing political landscape that made the *correos'* task more dangerous also resulted in altered conceptions of Guatemalan space and its boundaries.

Part III turns to document storage, emphasizing the temporal aspect of distance that underlies its broader conception. Chapter 5 draws together several themes of archival history in colonial Guatemala, pointing out first and foremost the ways in which methods of organizing document storage echoed methods of organizing document travel. Well-run archives, cast as "treasure" houses for documents in the early colonial period, were as essential to document safety as were well-run ships or reliable *correos*. Furthermore, both the mail system and archives were organized around routes. Chapter 5 also examines the role of *escribanos* as officials who were responsible for simultaneously providing access to and ensuring protection for archived documents. Disputes over archives in the late colonial period illustrate the difficulties inherent to balancing these objectives.

Chapter 6 follows the story of inventories as essential organizational tools for document preservation. Three officials from the late eighteenth and nineteenth centuries, Ignacio Guerra y Marchán, Miguel Talavera, and Victoriano Grijalva, organized the Guatemalan archive collections through inventories in revealing ways. The disputes over archival collections that occurred when the Central American states splintered in the mid-nineteenth century and the inventories created to ensure their safe transfer demonstrate that the inventory continued to be a crucial tool for the movement of documents over both spatial and temporal distance. Even as late as 1900, when the task of organizing the archive required a sizeable staff, inventories were relied upon to account for the archive's content. We have no way of knowing how many were lost on the way, but the inventories created by mail officials, *escribanos*, and archivists ensured the safe travel of millions of pages over a distance of several hundred years, making them available for us today.

Part One

1 *Documenting Distance: Form and Content*

This level of discussion is beyond reach for the idiotic men
who sit on the . . . council of the town of San Pedro Carchá,
and however useless their questions, it would be equally
useless to reply. *Vale.*[1]
—Anonymous Guatemalan official, 1792

It may be that in some cases distance presented an opportunity for people
in the Spanish empire. Certainly the "witches" in Escuintla benefited from
their remote placement on Guatemala's Pacific coast, far from the punish-
ing presence of the Mexico City tribunal. But distance was, undeniably,
also an obstacle. From the point of view of officials attempting to maintain
the rule of law or merely gather information, distance created serious problems. One solution, of course, could be found in sending delegates: trusted
individuals who would carry the norms and expectations of the center to
the periphery. At times, however, "idiotic" delegates at the periphery failed
to fulfill expectations. Even when delegates were reliable, those individuals had to find a way to report back, and documents provided an essential
means of overcoming the obstacles posed by distance.

This chapter begins the discussion of this process by examining how
both the form and content of documents reflected the imperatives of distance. Documents were initiated, elaborated, and concluded by many
authors in various places and times: they were produced along a temporal-
spatial route. But the intervals of time and space embedded in a document
do not stand out because authors intentionally reduced them. Indeed, protocols were developed to deliberately flatten the effects of distance and to
ensure that officials everywhere wrote in ways that were universally intelligible. Distance alone did not give rise to these protocols, but the impediments of distance certainly informed them.

Similarly, document content responded to the problems posed by distance. Most obviously, officials in Spain could not "see" the Americas.
They relied continuously on American officials to make it visible and
knowable. Concentrating on questionnaires written in Spain and the official reports—*visitas* and *relaciones*—written from Guatemala in reply, this

chapter examines how documents were intended to "overcome" distance by creating Guatemala as an accessible, proximate place for the king and elite officials in Spain. Studying such content necessarily spills over into considerations of genre and form, as the *relación* and *visita* existed, to a great extent, purely because of long-distance readers.

In overcoming distance, these documents also described distance. Requests for information from the center of empire, initiated in the sixteenth century and repeated into the early nineteenth century, framed distance and space in specific ways. The questionnaires envisioned distance as route-based and organized around central, jurisdictional places. Toward the end of the colonial period and particularly in the early nineteenth century, a new emphasis on boundaries emerged in the questionnaires, but the preoccupation with routes and distances to central places endured.

The responses of writers in the Guatemalan *audiencia* absorbed and echoed this Spanish conception. A clear hierarchy of linked places emerges from the official reports written over the course of a half-century in Guatemala, and it is evident that Guatemalan officials incorporated the Spanish understanding of distance into their geographical descriptions. Yet the reports written in Guatemala were also composite in how they incorporated local (often Indian) geographical information. Thus the reports did not perfectly mimic the ideas projected by the center; rather, they introduced idiosyncrasies—or innovations, or distortions—as they relied on autochthonous sources. Officials created reports and descriptions that presented local, unofficial knowledge in official, Spanish terms.

Distance Protocols

It seems self-evident that in a realm as vast as the Spanish empire, documents traveled a good deal. Less evident is how authors inscribed that travel into their documents' content and form. Official documents for the colonial period that we read today rarely contain one author's writing, composed in a single sitting in a fixed place. Instead, they usually contain a series of compositions in different hands, elaborated in the margins at different points in time. The well-known dialogic quality of such documents does more than produce a conversation among officials; it also produces a chronological route, revealing spatial and temporal distances bridged by the document. The following document, a letter concerning a problematic portion of the King's Highway from Guatemala to Mexico, is typical.

It was signed by an official in Quetzaltenango on December 4, 1797.[2] The *Fiscal* (crown attorney) in Guatemala took up the document, beginning his contribution to the text on the same page and continuing his writing on an appended page (below). By the time of the *Fiscal*'s writing, the

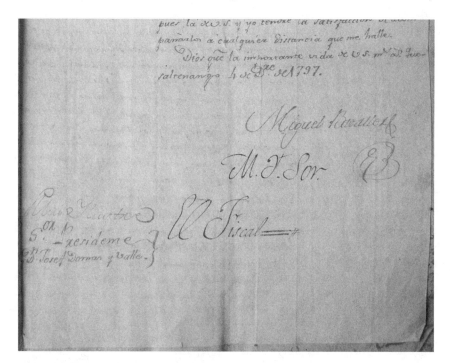

FIGURE 1.1. A document originating in Quetzaltenango in 1797
Source: Archivo General de Centroamérica. Photograph by the author.

document had traveled many leagues to Guatemala and more than a year had passed. Ignacio Guerra y Marchán, the *audiencia*'s *escribano* (secretary and chief clerk), processed the document on the following day, January 12, 1799. The document found itself next in the town of Concepción in Huehuetenango on February 6, 1799. Not evident in the page below but in those that follow, the document was signed in Concepción by three officials. A note in the margin indicates that the document was dispatched on February 8. It next reached officials in Totonicapán in May 1799 and received comment from several officials before continuing on to Guatemala in July of the same year, where Guerra y Marchán passed it on to the *Fiscal*. The document went on from there, processed by the *audiencia* and returning to Totonicapán before finding any conclusion.

This most basic attribute of Spanish documents may seem obvious to the point of insignificance. But I believe examining the obvious here yields some important insights. Most often, historians would read a document like this one to determine what the *Fiscal* opined about the King's Highway and how the officials deliberated and what decision was reached. Reading this document as a statement about distance and knowledge

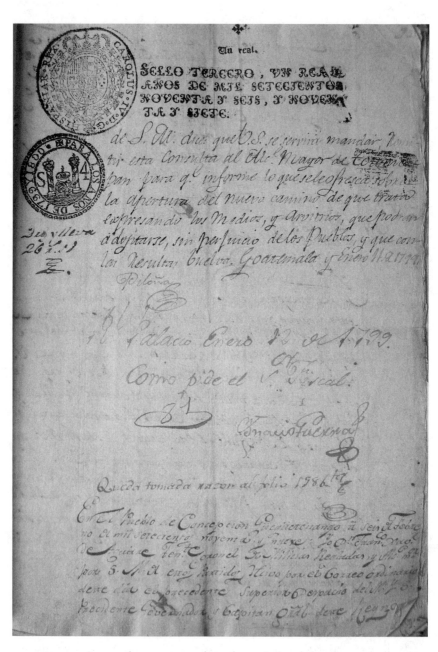

FIGURE 1.2. A 1797 document travels to the capital and elsewhere

Source: Archivo General de Centroamérica. Photograph by the author.

production, however, discloses different content. The document is revealed as a material object, circulating among specific people and places in eighteenth-century Guatemala. It appears as an object produced by the different hands that signed and carried it, the composite creation of many minds. Traveling between the *audiencia* capital and the highland towns near Totonicapán and Huehuetenango, the document was repeatedly read, discussed, augmented, and stored before traveling once again. Eventually, it was archived in Guatemala City.

The document was relied upon by officials to bridge spatial distances between the highlands and the capital and temporal distances between moments of decision-making and deliberation. A temporal chronology and spatial itinerary emerge from it. Here, revealing a first model in use throughout the Spanish empire, knowledge was built along a route. Using what might be termed an "itinerary" mode of knowledge production, a single document accumulated information from each of its stopping points.

While the distances in this case are fairly short, documents of course mediated much greater distances: from Escuintla to Mexico City; from Mexico City to Seville; from the extreme periphery to the center. Temporal

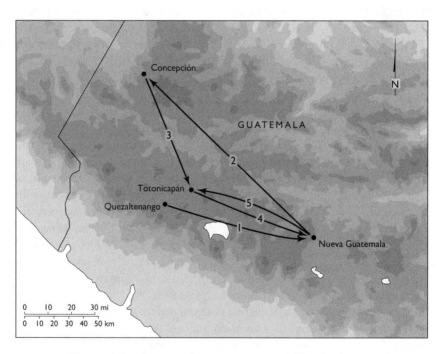

MAP 1.1. The spatial and temporal sequences suggested by the document's itinerary

distances, too, extended far beyond the three years reflected here. Documents not only traveled for longer periods; they remained in *escribano* archives for longer spans of time. In a way, this document and its trajectory reveal in miniature the larger processes examined in this book: the creation of documents in a formal manner informed by long-distance governance; the development of content resulting from spatial movement; and the shaping of both content and form resulting from temporal lapses in archives.

From the point of view of Spanish officials, each of these processes was plagued with possible pitfalls. In archives, documents could be lost or neglected into ruin. In travel, documents could be lost in ships that sank or were seized by pirates. Trunks left unlocked might be rifled through, their correspondence stolen. Every aspect of a document's treatment had to assist in preventing great distances from becoming greater obstacles.[3] Creating multiple copies of original documents lessened the risk, and throughout the colonial period documents were sent in duplicate or even in triplicate.[4] A strict protocol governed the opening and closing of document trunks: documents were to be carefully locked and opened only with the proper authorities present. On the Guatemalan end, where authorities from the mainland could obviously not be present to enforce proper procedures, two high-ranking officials were assigned keys and charged with opening the documents before the *audiencia*. Furthermore, precise inventories of the documents accompanied the trunks and *new* inventories had to be created upon receipt to ensure that each document reached its intended destination. The documents were handled very much like treasure, and the frequent orders specifying protocol for their treatment were intended to ensure their safety both across great distances and at a great distance— within remote peripheries like the Guatemalan highlands.[5]

Even when the documents arrived safely, there might be other impediments. If correspondents in the peripheral corners of the empire did not adhere to a recognizable form, the document could be considered invalid or be rendered unintelligible. The documents' formal attributes were thereby as essential to effective communication across long distance as were the measures taken to ensure their material safety. As such, the guidelines and templates devised by the crown and elaborated by the administrators of the Council of Indies were partly dedicated to achieving consistency. Kathryn Burns discusses the importance of templates and standardization in her study of *escribanos,* and Angel Rama suggests that "the influence of the documentary umbilical cord that carried imperial orders and provided linguistic models for letrados in the far-flung dominions" resulted in unique written forms: "Royal directives elicited lengthy, elaborate replies that advanced counter-arguments point by point, making the official missive—along with official reports and chronicles—into a literary genre in its own right."[6]

This genre (or, more accurately, these genres) was elaborated over several centuries, becoming carefully rule-bound. A major concern for the Council of Indies from the beginning lay in validating the authenticity of documents received from a distance.[7] The "concern with authenticating documents and the desire to leave clear proof of all public documents, letters, and decrees" gave rise to the *Registro General del Sello*. The seal (pictured in Figure 1.2), as well as the signature of a secretary or *escribano,* verified the legitimacy of documents received in Spain.[8] Though the stamp tax, *papel sellado,* introduced in 1639 is cast by historians principally as a fundraising measure, the *papel sellado* shouldered the additional responsibility of ensuring a document's validity.[9]

Other guidelines dictating the proper formal attributes for official documents reveal how document "safety" expanded to mean something more expansive and complex. A Guatemalan official attempted in 1784 to enforce a regulation from the king circulated in 1779 to "all the Viceroys, *audiencias,* Archbishops, Bishops, and judges both ecclesiastical and secular." Sent to the king's administrators at the highest level, the regulation would be repeated and disseminated by his delegates. The Guatemalan president dutifully did so, demanding that "in order to process without confusion or delay . . . the many petitions, reports, and pieces of official correspondence . . . the useful methods and rules expressed in the order should be observed in the preparation and execution of documents." He complained that "the orders have not been followed, and almost universally documents continue to be sent in the same confused way." The orders emphasize a system that both isolates and organizes pieces of information.

The petitions and correspondence sent to this office should address one and only one subject at a time without reference to others; documents should all arrive numbered, with a summary or abstract in the margin that succinctly expressed the relevant topic. They should be accompanied by an index in which the assigned number of each letter corresponds to the numbers in the margins. These letters and their indexes should be identified by a **P** for the originals, a **D** for the duplicates, and a **T** for triplicate copies.[10]

These instructions stated that the numbered index should be continued in subsequent correspondence, so that, in theory, a sequential series of numbered documents would be sent and received in Spain.[11] They specified the procedure for providing cover sheets and for including numbered subdocuments within the main document. And finally, they explained how to pack these fastidiously prepared masterpieces: ordinary documents were to be sealed, but "planos o mapas" (charts or maps) had to be packed carefully in wooden trunks; under no circumstances were they to be packed in "tin cylinders, which always arrive damaged or ruined."[12] These regulations go beyond safeguarding the physical and formal integrity of documents, though this remains a concern; they also reveal something of the documents' use, circulation, and possibly storage upon receipt. Documents were sent to different offices of the larger administration and were archived in different locations, depending on their content. The enumeration of documents suggests a desire to perceive the documents in a chronology, giving them a precise place in a temporal sequence (rather than simply a date). The manner of marking duplicate and triplicate copies points to the frequent necessity of distinguishing identical documents once they had found their way to the same office. A need to prioritize and discriminate, if not stratify, is implied.

The producers—writers, carriers, and handlers—of official documents in the Guatemalan *audiencia* complied with all these regulations to varying degrees. By following regulations, they not only adhered to bureaucratic protocol, they also acquiesced to the political power of the empire's center. But every now and then the weight of administrative and political influence proved insufficient. Documents were stolen or opened on the road, in places along the route, and in the administration's offices. The safety net for the material document, depending on so many people scattered across the empire, sometimes disintegrated.[13] Similarly, writers of official documents also sometimes failed to follow the prescribed forms that provided uniformity and facilitated the production of proper composite documents across temporal and spatial distances. Administrators with daily responsibilities in the *audiencia* or in frequent correspondence with officials in Spain may have had more practice and a greater sense of professional obligation, but this did not necessarily guarantee their adherence to protocol. In the mid-eighteenth century, for example, Guatemalan *escribano* Don Juan Antonio Betancur was accused of having produced no less than eighteen *testimonios*, or certified copies, without having properly verified them against their originals. He was accused not of sloppy copying but of falsifying documents.[14]

A less egregious but rather more revealing example comes from the town of San Pedro Carchá, a town in the province of Verapaz. It will help to keep in mind that Verapaz was decidedly peripheral to Guatemalan officials—a backwater with too many Indians and a handful of friars. The city council's *escribano* wrote a letter of perplexed inquiry to officials in Guatemala City about the proper process for composing a requested document. The *Alcalde Mayor* had forwarded a request from King Charles IV for a "report on the most noteworthy aspects of the town that are worth knowing, such as descriptions of the four-legged animals, birds, trees, plants, and special rocks." Dividing the short, two-page letter into dignified "asuntos" (chapters) headed by roman numerals, the city council wondered "what kind of birds, trees, plants, and rocks should be described?

And if all of the above, which should be given preference?" It further que-
ried what, precisely, made certain birds, trees, plants, and rocks special.
Were the "special" ones those discussed by Spanish and foreign writers
or those mentioned by no one? And supposing the former, were the descriptions to be written based on the accounts of those authors "for the
greater discovery of the truth"? Most tellingly, they asked, "what role are
the *naturales* to play in preparing this report, since it is only from their
statements that the provincial magistrate can form a report without exposing his good name to the censure of wise men and thereby failing in
the tasks set by his sovereign?" The council concluded that since "honor,
love for the King and for country" should be sufficient motivation, the
decision had been made not to offer monetary compensation but to hold a
contest, for which the prize would be the "honorary title of Honorary City
Councilman of San Pedro."[15]

From a certain perspective, the letter seems a mockery of Spanish conventions. Is it really necessary to have "chapters" in a document of only a
few hundred words? Content, too, the letter suggests, can be ridiculous.
"Why would the king possibly want to know about our 'special' rocks?" it
seems to ask. But it is more likely that the document was an earnest attempt
to fulfill the expectations of the center on the periphery. The punctilious
questions reflect a deep concern with observing proper form. The honorary
title indicates a solemn recognition of the symbolic power of the crown in
terribly remote places. Even in Verapaz, the town council *escribano* suggests, we are capable of following protocol, and we are ever cognizant of
the importance of loyalty

There are also, however, clear indications in this letter about the composite nature of document production and how such production could
fall apart over long distances. Here, the physical integrity remained intact
and the formal conventions were observed scrupulously. But the *content*
failed to deliver. Revealingly, the town council admits that its most accurate information would come from *naturales*—from the indigenous people
of Verapaz who were thought, perhaps, less than worthy of participating
in the dignified task of reporting to the king. Ultimately, whether because
of their insolence or because of their perceived incompetence, the members of the town council were unable to complete the report required by
Charles IV. In a bitter postscript, an unidentified official in Guatemala City
deemed the council unworthy of even putting pen to paper, saying, "This
level of discussion is beyond reach for the idiotic men who sit on the . . .
council of the town of San Pedro Carchá, and however useless their questions, it would be equally useless to reply. *Vale*."[16]

Revealing a second model of knowledge production, one that might
be considered "radial" and clearly hierarchical, the reply was intended to

travel back from San Pedro to the *alcalde* of Verapaz, then to the Guatemalan *audiencia,* and on to King Charles IV. Regions, the *audiencia* or viceroyalty, and the center of governance in Spain created nodes at different levels. We can imagine the convergence of replies from town councils all over the Americas, funneled through local administrators as they journeyed and accumulated in the hands of the King. The itinerary model and the radial model are of course not mutually exclusive, but often operated in harmony: documents built around a route would go on to centralize in the Guatemalan *audiencia,* the Council of Indies, or the king's court.

Protocols did not always ensure satisfactory documents, and the norms of the center—however respected—could not always fully acculturate the margins. The failed attempt from San Pedro Carchá to create a successful composite document, providing information to the king about the peripheries of his domain, is only one example in the continuous, often frustrating conversation about producing knowledge that took place over the course of the colonial period. Even when form succeeded in bringing the center to the periphery, content did not always succeed in bringing the periphery to the center.

A Question of Distance: Queries from Spain

As the case of San Pedro Carchá demonstrates, the production of knowledge in the Spanish empire was a conversation in documents. Every institution in the Americas participated in this conversation. While the Council of Indies was the principal overseas interlocutor, particular offices and individuals carried on parallel conversations. Documents on geographic knowledge, as discussed above, offer a particularly clear view on this conversation. Wedding local information to Spanish protocols, such documents comment upon and describe the very distance they are attempting to overcome. This section and the next consider how the documents both mediated and talked about distance.

Official reports in the form of maps, *relaciones, visitas,* and the closely related *descripciones* and *razones* made accessible, known, and proximate places that were impossible for the king and his administrators to view firsthand. María Portuondo's study of Spanish cosmography demonstrates that eyewitness reports and empirical investigations became essential to cosmographers working for the Spanish crown almost as soon as the New World was discovered.[17] But the flow of paper carrying those reports east across the Atlantic ran parallel to a westward current: repeated commands requesting information. As the empire grew dramatically in the sixteenth century, any claim to "know" that empire necessarily rested on the information demanded and then provided by representatives of the crown.

Even as late as the fifteenth century, notes Barbara Mundy in her study of the sixteenth-century *relaciones geográficas*, Ferdinand and Isabella could expect to see much of their kingdom firsthand, as "traveling through their realms by horse or coach, however arduous, was still possible and practical." But as the kingdom expanded, this became impossible, and for Philip II, such travel had to be substituted by other means of covering his territories. "The voyage to the Spanish Netherlands along the Spanish Road took about seven weeks; it took three months to get from Seville to Veracruz . . . Philip ruled over vast areas, even continents, that were out of his reach and far from his gaze." Mundy places an emphasis on Philip's inability to *see* his kingdom, arguing that "knowing was predicated on seeing." Reinforcing Fernando Bouza's argument regarding the importance of images in this period, Mundy stresses the power of images as the means by which Philip sought to bind the pieces of his kingdom, arguing that maps sent from the Americas "filled a void" that "substituted for his own vision."[18]

The notion of "filling a void" created by distance resonates with how historians describe the imperial project in other parts of the world as well. Matthew Edney writes of colonial India that map-reading entailed "an act of spatial denial." Of maps more generally, he argues that "in bringing a distant place to hand, the map reader ignores the realities of geographical space."[19] But cartographic representations are not the only instruments for such spatial denial. Though Mundy stresses Philip's desire to have the New World "made visible for him," she also points to his preoccupation with text as a medium for imperial control, noting that he "insisted on reading and personally signing every significant paper dealing with his realm, [knowing] that such a distance, both physical and psychic, between himself and his subjects hindered his ability to rule."[20]

Without ignoring, then, the importance of images as an essential early means of long-distance visibility, I agree that the desire for information was more all-encompassing, both in Philip II and in later monarchs. After all, the requests were for maps and reports, not just maps. A king so concerned with the textual channels of communication understood the potential for texts to make the distant territories proximate. The "documentary umbilical chord" between Spain and the Americas described by Angel Rama may have first sprung from this awareness, and certainly the *visitas, relaciones,* as well as *descripciones geográficas* and other reports appear to claim that they make the Americas "visible" through text.[21] This is not to say that images were not important, and the repeated push for "visuality," to use Daniela Bleichmar's term, certainly demonstrates that images were valued as means to make the Americas visible.[22] But as the enormous body of documents that crossed the Atlantic also demonstrate, the Americas could additionally be made visible through text.

These documents, along with or apart from images, aimed to make the distant near.

The questionnaires written in Spain provide insights into how officials imagined the replies would achieve this. Sent by the Council of Indies in the form of *reales cédulas* (decrees) or simply as *cuestionarios* (questionnaires) and *instrucciones* (instructions), requests were sent to ecclesiastical authorities and *audiencia* authorities beginning in 1530.[23] Roughly thirty such requests were made throughout the colonial period, ending with questionnaires prepared by the Cortes de Cádiz in 1812. They vary in both emphasis and in the specificity of requested information. The brief 1530 *cédula* directed to the Council of Indies ordered a general but comprehensive account of the Isla Española, demanding information on "all the qualities and things of that island."[24] Only three years later, this request grew more specific, as a *cédula* sent to the *audiencia* in Mexico ordered it to send "geographical reports that describe, in detail, the characteristics of the land, demography, urban centers, waterworks, as well as information on the flora and fauna. . . ."[25] Later *cédulas* sent to the archbishop in Mexico and the *audiencia* in Quito were similarly detailed, listing the subjects to be reported.[26]

The questionnaires sent by Philip II in the 1570s, however, went far beyond these in the specificity of their requests. The decrees approved in 1571 and penned by Juan de Ovando carefully prescribed not only the content of the expected reports but also the method of inquiry, form of presentation, and material treatment of the written product.[27] The section on descriptions of city councils indicated in what manner the reports were to be prepared in books, in what manner the books were to be sent to the Council of Indies, and in what manner officials were to "always observe the prescribed manner of creating and ordering the books containing the investigations, descriptions, and reports, as well as the manner of making copies of them to send to [their] superiors, leaving the original documents in their archives."[28] In other words, every step in the documents' creation, from the research process to the storage process, was carefully delineated. The intention was to create a comprehensive volume in Spain, radially incorporating New World knowledge. Had the project succeeded, the geographic knowledge would have been accumulated and synthesized for the benefit of Philip II and his governance.

While all of the previous questionnaires had requested information on the land and terrain, the instructions of the 1570s were more pointed. Among other things, they aimed to establish the basic proportions and distances of the New World, an objective that posed significant problems for the cosmographers in Spain: "as was emblematic of its stand outside the known order of things, the New World had yet to be reined in by cosmographers with lines of latitude and longitude, lines that would make rationally visible its global position in relation to Europe."[29] Calculating longitude and latitude were essential, the decrees argued, not only to place the locations in the New World but also to make their subsequent geographical descriptions more accurate and intelligible. "It is necessary," the decrees stated, "that a Cosmography be created . . . that states the site and position that the Indies and every part of them occupies in the universe, because in this manner the particular descriptions that are afterwards made will be more true and will be better understood."[30] Explaining the method of calculation, the decrees recommended that "the descriptions be made using degrees of longitude and latitude written out in full and not in sum, because of the facility with which errors with numbers occur."[31] Ovando expected the reports on geography, chorography, and topography to build upon the foundation of longitude and latitude, stating that knowledge of these was "very necessary for those who govern, in order to make the subject closer to the things he must govern."[32]

As is the way with leading questions, the manner of the questionnaires prompted a certain kind of content. A more general questionnaire sent in 1577, with its slightly different emphasis, probed further than had previous requests for information. Also designed by Ovando, the questionnaire first drafted in 1569 with thirty-seven questions ballooned to two hundred questions before its final draft with fifty.[33] The extensive questions not only asked for more detailed information; the thoroughness of the instructions themselves necessarily communicated a particular vision of how the New World would be made known, visible, and proximate. As well as inquiring into each region's history and political organization, the questions investigated "the leagues separating each city or town of *españoles* (Spaniards) from the city where its governing *audiencia* lies," and "the leagues separating every city or town of *españoles* from the others with which they share borders." The instructions were careful to qualify that the respondent should indicate "if the leagues are large or small, over flat land or hilly land, and along roads that are straight or crooked, good or bad to walk along."[34] Prioritizing distance to an administrative center as a crucial variable, the questionnaire also emphasized distances—and their qualities—along routes connecting places within a jurisdiction. The instructions on Indian towns isolated the importance of distance just as starkly, stating, "for the Indian towns report only how distant they are from the principal town of their jurisdiction . . . as well as how distant they are from the other Indian or Spanish towns."[35] And the questions pertaining to ecclesiastical institutions similarly inquired "which town it lies in and which jurisdiction it lies in; and how many leagues there are to where the cathedral and administrative authorities are, and if the leagues are large or small, along straight roads or crooked roads. . . ." The instructions seemed to imply that quantifying distances between places was tantamount to describing them. They went on, of course, to request information on the terrain, the weather, and nature of the people, but not without leaving a strong impression that *place* was determined by distance from a jurisdictional center.

The instructions for visual renderings were far less leading, asking only for "the location and setting where the towns are, and if they lie in highlands or lowlands, or flat lands," alongside an accompanying "plan" of the towns.[36] For guidance as to how this "location and setting" were to be figured, respondents would have to look elsewhere. If the respondents considered the questionnaire as a whole, the dominant organization of space projected by the instructions would be one of the places located at specific distances from jurisdictional centers, connected to the center and to each other by measured routes.

The responses to these questions were varied and partial. From the point of view of the Spanish cosmographers, the instructions had been followed poorly, if at all. The information provided to establish longitude and latitude was almost nonexistent, and the *relaciones* were too diverse in their substance and form. As a result, the initial plan "to take the written responses and distill them into a descriptive chronicle of the New World" was never completed.[37] But the failure of the project did not deter future investigators from attempting to collect information that would make the distant Americas knowable to readers in Spain, and the steady dispatch of questions was more successful than they knew.[38] Though the 1570s survey was a "fiasco" from the perspective of Philip's cosmographers, it did succeed in establishing a language about distance, space, and place.[39] The great diversity of pictorial responses tends to conceal how two crucial conceptions communicated in the questionnaires—routes and distances to key administrative centers—were absorbed by the respondents.[40] Over time, the ongoing conversation between questioners and respondents further reinforced these two conceptions.

The Replies: Overcoming Distance, Producing Distance

Responses to the questionnaires trickled in from the New World, including from Guatemala. Replies were sent from Guatemala beginning in the sixteenth century, and several of the *relaciones geográficas* in response to the Philip II questionnaire feature places from the Guatemalan *audiencia*. In the eighteenth century, officials in Guatemala responded once again; in 1740, more than a dozen *relaciones* were prepared in response to a questionnaire sent from Spain. These replies reveal a few key tendencies. First, they demonstrate an obedient mirroring of the questionnaires' emphasis on distance. Second, they use routes not only to explain distance but also as a mode of understanding space. Third, they showcase local knowledge as both a source and a constraint of official information.

Though the complete text of the questionnaire has been lost, Jorge Luján Muñoz has reconstructed the essential material of the *real cédula* based on the internal orders of Guatemalan officials. The questionnaire seems to have been brief, as the *audiencia* president states that in a *real orden* dated 28 July 1739, the king had requested "that there be sent . . . reports with the most precision possible of the cities, towns and villages contained in each province of this kingdom." He asked for "their names and the names of their respective jurisdictions, listing numerically the residents in each" and he wished to be informed of "which fruits, crops, mines of gold and silver" there were in each region. Lastly, the president reported that the king wished to be apprised of "the distances to the capital of their jurisdiction; the characteristics of the land, their healthfulness and temperament, and anything else that might provide the most exact geographical description."[41] Distances, requested here along with only a handful of other variables, are clearly prioritized.

The questionnaire may have been a precursor to one circulated more widely in New Spain after 1743; Luján Muñoz points out that while it was not sent to Guatemala, it stresses similar topics. Two of these pertain to distance: it inquires first into "the distance from the center of the jurisdiction to the capital, and in which direction it lies, and the same information for all the towns, villages, and places within the jurisdiction, with their temperament, leagues, and orientation"; and after inquiring about the people, the state of the agriculture, the possibilities for mining, the ecclesiastical organization and "miraculous images," it ends by asking about "the distance that separates each place from the administrative center . . . and if there is any need, due to difficulties posed by long distances, to create any new settlements."[42] Similar in both their scope and emphasis, these two questionnaires prioritize the question of distance to administrative centers and even state an explicit concern about the difficulties of distance.

The responses written in 1740 clearly bear the imprint of the Guatemalan president's general line of questioning. Without exception, they list the distances between the towns of the province and its administrative center, and in most cases there is also mention of the distance to the Guatemalan capital. This distance is invariably measured in leagues and formulated in terms of distance *away from* the center. The *relación* for Chiquimula and Zacapa states that "to the capital city which is Santiago, Guatemala, there are fifty leagues."[43] But in other cases the towns are said to "be distant from" Guatemala by use of the verb "distar." The author of the *relación* for Escuintla and Guzacapán, for example, stated that the town of San Pedro Aguacatepeque in Escuintla "lies distant (*dista*) from Guatemala three leagues in a south-easterly direction."[44] Similarly, the town of Huehuetenango "lies fifty miles distant from the capital of Guatemala."[45] In some cases the *relaciones* provide only limited information on climate, demographics, and commerce, but they unfailingly quantify distances to central places.

Though the questionnaire reconstructed by Luján Muñoz does not ask specifically about routes, the *relaciones* also frequently discuss distance in terms of routes. Precedent, here, influenced the manner of reply. As established early on by the 1570 questionnaire and repeated in later instructions, routes were crucial to describing space. In some cases, the authors actually traveled the routes in order to compose their *relaciónes*. In other cases the authors describe the routes based on prior travel, simply using the route as an organizational tool in the text for the description of the towns. In both instances, the mode of travel directed the form of geographical description. As Paul Carter has written with regard to the travel narratives of a very different time and place, "travelling was not primarily a physical activity: it was an epistemological strategy, a mode of knowing."[46] For the writers of *relaciones* in Guatemala, knowing beyond the route was impossible; their manner of both experiencing and describing Guatemalan space was therefore entirely contained by how they traveled.

Don Alonso Crespo, for example, a high-ranking official in Escuintla and Guazacapán, envisioned the towns placed along an itinerary, listing the "first town of the province of Escuintla" and then going into detailed description for the route to the town that "followed."

The Town of San Andrés Echanosuna follows. Following a southeasterly direction for six leagues, the first league is a sharp and rocky decline, where there are many gorges and two very long and deep ravines. After one league there follows a savanna two leagues long which they call 'the great savanna' and which has a few shallow ravines and in the savanna there is a small *hacienda* called Mirandilla and some variation in the vegetation caused by the rather warmer climate. There follow another three leagues with a few ravines and two large arroyos and a great deal of rocky outgrowth where one encounters a very large hill covered with trees produced by the warm climate, with a substantial banana grove that in the rainy season becomes impassable due to the mud and undergrowth.[47]

The detailed description is worth considering closely as it demonstrates not only the official's familiarity with the changeable conditions of travel but also how completely, in the author's mind, the quantifiable measure of distance—the *legua*—is linked to particularities of a route and its surrounding terrain. His repeated use of "seguir," to follow, clearly brings the process of travel into the text and partly recreates it for readers. This is typical of how, as Paul Carter has pointed out, travel writing constitutes "space as a track." In Carter's conception, "the life of this space resides in succession, in the demonstration that its parts link up, looking forward and backwards along the orientation of the journey."[48] Naming the landscape around the route, the Guatemalan official described the leagues of the route as steps in a journey that would be made vivid to distant readers in Spain who were unfamiliar with the region, let alone the route.

This conception of routes is corroborated by the account of Don José Antonio de Aldama, the district governor of Verapaz, who explicitly described the region's space in terms of route-based travel. "The province of Verapaz begins," he writes, "as one leaves Guatemala, eighteen leagues to the north at a river called the Rio Grande, from which one follows the same direction for ten leagues until reaching the town of Salamá." Aldama saw this as the "first" town of the region, calling it "the first in the jurisdiction, which is followed by others along the King's highway until reaching Cajabón, the last in this province."[49] Arranged from "first" to "last" along a route, the towns created an itinerary. The path continued fourteen leagues beyond the "last" town of Cajabón, leading through to the entirely uninhabited wilderness of El Petén. Aldama further relied on this route for a calculation of the area's total size.

In this manner . . . it measures eighty leagues longitude from its stated starting point, the river, to the stated mountain were it ends. It is not possible to make a formal estimate of the latitude since the most impenetrable wilderness serves as walls on either side. This wilderness is largely unknown, and it has only been partly explored by some Indians who with considerable effort and with the intention of sowing their crops have made inroads into the formidable undergrowth. For this reason one can only describe the latitude of the areas that are populated and therefore transitable in this province; in these terms I would say it measures in some parts fifteen leagues, in others eight, and it goes on in this way until it ends.[50]

Aldama's account of Verapaz is especially telling, because while it demonstrates a clear conception of the region as a two-dimensional space (rather than a one-dimensional itinerary), Aldama nonetheless relied on the itinerary of the route to construct and measure the broader area. Using "longitud" and "latitud" to mean length and width rather than to indicate coordinates, he described the route from Salamá to Petén as the region's principal—and only feasibly quantifiable—dimension. Aldama's accompanying explanation is also revealing because it points to the source of knowledge for the region's routes and its dimensions. Only "some Indians" he says, had delved into the deep undergrowth to plant crops. This uneven knowledge of the terrain was evident in many parts of the *audiencia*.

Aldama provides a valuable glimpse into the landscape of Verapaz as perceived by colonial officials. While the region may today be cartographically represented as a two-dimensional space dotted with place-names, the region for Aldama was essentially a long, north-east leaning route.

Known places were scattered on the route and at short distances from it. Beyond the route spread a vast uncharted territory that was not entirely unknown but was unknown *to him*. Placing knowledge of that region squarely in the hands of "some Indians," he revealed an invisible boundary between the areas that were knowable to people like Andama and the areas that were not. He further emphasized this invisible boundary by effectively drawing the dimensions of Verapaz along the lines of the areas that were "populated and therefore transitable." The region Aldama drew was an inhabited swath of land on either side of a long, arching route from Salamá to Cajabón. Beyond this strip lay "asperísimo monte"—dense jungle, impenetrable wilderness—that was known only to others and was therefore, effectively, another territory.[51]

While Crespo and Aldama wrote their texts in ways that recalled and then re-created the process of travel, other officials actually created the *relación* while traveling. Don Antonio Castellanos of Soconusco, the province on Guatemala and Mexico's Pacific coast, traveled from place to place in order to gather the necessary information for his *relación*. Castellanos followed his initial statement, written in Escuintla, with a declaration of his departure in which he stated that in order to complete the relación "it was necessary, for greater clarity, to begin in the town of Tonalá as it is the first in this province and to return from there going town by town."[52] Castellanos visited Tonalá on 13 May 1740 and collected the necessary information for his account, certifying it by the hand of several witnesses since no *escribano* was present. He continued on to Pijiapa, a town twenty leagues distant, and on the nineteenth of May he "used the horn and drum to call together all the neighbors of the town," and with all of the residents gathered before him he collected names and occupations from the roughly thirty mulattos—"people who were very poor," he noted. Castellanos proceeded in this manner to compose the document from stop to stop, counting on locals to witness his account. The very composition of the *relación* incorporated the distances traveled by its principal author.

The 1740 *relaciones*, then, provide repeated and vivid illustrations of how two crucial elements informed conceptions of distance, space, and place in Guatemala. The importance of central administrative places was prompted by the questionnaires and duly acknowledged by the accounts. All of the *relaciones* are careful to note the distances, in leagues, to the capital and to provincial capitals. But while the guiding hand of the questionnaire might largely account for the emphasis on central places, the absence of any specific questions about routes in the *cédula* suggests that officials necessarily brought prior conceptions of space and distance into their writings. These conceptions, informed by previous official questioning, clearly cast Guatemalan space as oriented through and within routes. The route-based conception of space elaborated by the officials in Escuintla, Verapaz, and Soconusco is evident at several levels: in the creation of the text, as it is experienced by the traveling officials (whether the travel occurs in the moment or is remembered); in the organization of the *relación*, as it orders the places along a textual itinerary; and, by extrapolation, in the reader's experience of the text, as the *relación* recreates the process of travel. Local informants were essential to the production of these documents, but they also delimited the boundaries of official knowledge. As Aldama reveals, there were other territories and other knowledges beyond the ones he offered.

The consistency of the officials' replies in 1740 suggests a certain universality of spatial perception—or at least a certain agreement as to how space and distance should be explained on paper. But to what extent were these two elements, routes and hierarchies of place, dominant in later *relaciones?* My argument here is that routes and hierarchies of place were important and sometimes dominant modes of conceiving space, but this does not mean that they wholly excluded other conceptions. On the contrary: these modes complemented other ideas, becoming foreground or background, depending on the circumstances. Other *informes, razones,* and *relaciones* composed after 1740 provide some sense of how characterizations of space and distance differed depending on the particular requests of the questionnaires and the explicit purposes of the replies.

At least one example from the early 1740s suggests that *relaciones* for other purposes in this period may have also relied on different methods of description. The military engineer Don Luis Diez de Navarro was commissioned in 1742 to produce a series of reports on the ports of Guatemala, and the *relaciones* he prepared in the years that followed depended on a range of explanatory methods.[53] Describing Nicaragua, he situated the *alcaldía mayor* by naming the regions that bordered it to the north, south, east, and west, a method that the authors of the 1740 *relaciones* did not utilize. He additionally surveyed the rivers that had access to the principal ports and indicated the distances traveled along them. Diez de Navarro relied on routes to both measure and describe regions as well, apparently perceiving route information as supplemental and qualitatively different to descriptions of coterminous territories. He described arriving in the city of Cartago in Costa Rica, for example, by recounting the day of his departure and by stating that he had traveled seventy-eight leagues along a route that was "in some parts flat and in others hilly."[54] Only after describing his entry to the city did he set out Costa Rica's jurisdictional boundaries. From that point on, Diez de Navarro wrote a report that followed the familiar formula of *relaciones geográficas,* unfolding his narration along a route. "Leaving the aforementioned city for the Valleys of Barbilla," he reached an Indian town after traveling for two leagues and a high ridge called "la Cordillera" after traveling for four leagues. He observed that the ridge followed the entire coast from the Gulf of Honduras to Tierra Firme, and he estimated that it was about ten leagues wide in some places and up to thirty leagues wide in others. The valleys formed by the ridges could be reached by two routes, he noted: one was the King's highway and the other was called "de tierra adentro" (the inland route).[55] Similarly, he followed the route from Cartago to the sea for thirty leagues, noting that this was a winding route through high hills and that parts of the route were so swampy that the horses sank in the mud up to their bellies. The remainder of Diez de Navarro's account goes into great detail as to the populations and fortifications of the southern provinces, thereby demonstrating an appropriate focus in response to his original mandate. But while he relied on several methods to describe distance and space, accounting for borders and rivers, he never abandoned his perspective on routes and road conditions.

Other documents from the late eighteenth century demonstrate less of a preoccupation with roads and hierarchies of place. A set of *relaciones* written around 1763, for example, includes very little discussion of routes and terrain, emphasizing instead the demographics and agricultural products of each jurisdiction. However, the brief mandate sent by the king makes the reason for this emphasis immediately evident. Having consulted with the Council of Indies, he requested for each jurisdiction a brief and succinct *relación* that described its governance and its "value" or commercial potential.[56] Demonstrating once again the composite nature of document creation, the officials in Guatemala determined that "the safest and most advisable method of acquiring the information is to request reports from Christian people who are intelligent and impartial," and they thereby wrote to each jurisdiction requesting detailed *relaciones* which they would use to write the summarizing *relación*. The instructions sent from Guatemala to each jurisdiction requested information on the "value and utility" of each region, inquiring "what it produced and what it is capable of producing." More specifically, it asked after "the extension of the territory, the number of settlements, the crops it produces and their quality" along with information about the jurisdiction's administration. Details were requested as to the treatment of the local population and the presence or absence of governmental abuses.[57] The resulting *relaciones* contained very little geographical information, as they intended to speak directly to the inquiries from the capital. What began as a laconic request from the king for information regarding the commercial potential and administrative function of each jurisdiction was interpreted more fully by the Guatemalan officials and thereby oriented away from a geographical description. By ignoring routes and distances in their reports, officials responding to the questionnaire were demonstrating an ability to follow instructions, not a diminished appreciation for these geographical elements.

Similarly, a report written by Joseph Gregorio Rivera after the 1773 earthquake relied on a different formulation of space necessary for the fulfillment of his prescribed task. Asked to survey the communities lying outside of Guatemala City for their possible resettlement to the new capital, Rivera created what he alternately called a "mapa" or "plano": a table listing the towns, their dimensions, and the number of houses in each community. (His description of this text-based "map" is significant, as discussed further in Chapter 3.)

Rivera described the towns in terms of "varas cuadradas" and then re-calculated the dimensions in terms of "cuerdas."[58] It is worth noting that Rivera distinguished these dimensions as "areas" and not distances.[59] The report prepared by Rivera formed one part of a long discussion on how and whether to transplant the communities, and one of the most important considerations proved to be the total area they occupied rather than their respective distances. In other words, when necessary to the task at hand,

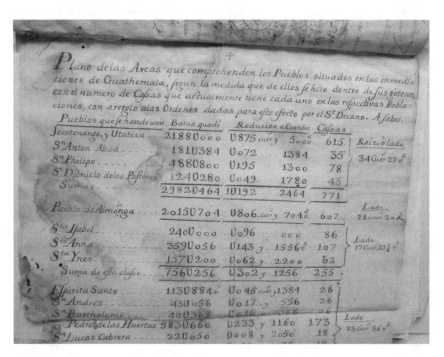

FIGURE 1.3. *Mapa* of places resettled after the 1773 earthquake
Source: Archivo General de Centroamérica. Photograph by the author.

other measures beyond distance to central places and route descriptions were readily utilized.

Rivera's plan also addressed the need to "unir" or unite groups of communities as part of the effort to resettle them. As discussed further in Chapter 2, the process of reorganizing and resettling communities had a long history in Guatemala, and the efforts to do so after the Guatemalan earthquake were by no means unique. The reorganization of communities was consistently motivated by concerns about effective governance—both spiritual and secular. Most frequently, the solution was seen to lie in either gathering the population or dividing jurisdictions. While Rivera's plan addressed the need to "unite" communities, another report prepared a couple of years earlier on the *Alcaldía* of San Salvador recommended subdividing the region. Don Francisco Antonio de Aldama y Guevara wrote of the "need to divide the *Alcaldía Mayor* due to the reports of its large dimensions." Echoing the concerns of the officials quoted in the Introduction, Aldama y Guevara observed that the existing distribution of officials permitted far too many abuses. Among the forty-two Indian villages and the twelve communities of mulattoes, there were some places that he lamented were "dens of evil which no pitiable district governor from San Salvador can do anything about."[60] Relying on considerations similar to Rivera's for the resettlement of the Guatemalan communities, Aldama y Guevera took into account the sizes of the populations and the rough dimensions ("length" or "extension") of their territories. He recommended at the very least dividing the *alcaldía* into two *partidos*: San Salvador and San Miguel. But he believed the better solution would be to divide the *alcaldía* into five smaller regions in order to make it possible to better govern so "great an area."[61] In describing the area, Aldama y Guevara did not rely on route measurements, counting instead on the size of the populations and the general league-measurement of the regions' "extensión." However, the entire purpose of his report necessarily emphasized the placement and reach of administrative centers. Without using the word "distant," he was nonetheless arguing that the sizeable population lay at too great a distance from the local authorities.

As these few examples written between 1740 and 1780 demonstrate, *relaciones* did not uniformly rely on routes and central places to describe the Guatemalan landscape. Rather, *relaciones* were written in response to different inquiries and with various objectives. Officials throughout the *audiencia* relied on other descriptive methods and other important measures to describe ports, boundaries, and jurisdictional areas. However, the specific nature of these *relaciones* makes it unwise to assume that routes and the hierarchical organization of place were unimportant to the authors. Rather, these examples should be taken as evidence that *relaciones* were flexible documents in terms of scope and perspective, and, further, that an official preoccupation with routes and distances to central places did not preclude other methods of spatial description and explanation.

Indeed, while *relaciones* were flexible, allowing varied descriptive tools, the recurrence of routes and hierarchies of place in other document genres demonstrates the prevalence of these conceptions. Later chapters discuss the emphasis on itineraries and hierarchies in the documents penned by ecclesiastical authorities, mail officials, and *escribanos*; I'll mention here two other common document forms used throughout the *audiencia* that emphasized these elements. The longer *relaciones* were, in some sense, elaborations of the more cursory reports prepared for calculating tribute. Listing distances from place to place, tribute reports abbreviated and summarized the findings of the *relaciones*. Two such itineraries for Quetzaltenango make apparent how vital such information proved for both exacting tribute and for communicating a sense of the region's space. A 1747 itinerary for Quetzaltenango (Table 1.1) lists about ten places.[62]

In a method similar to that employed for the *relaciones*, the author notes in the last paragraph that he traveled from town to town, leaving no doubt that the measured distances were created by intervals along the route. The document "produces" the region as an itinerary of sixty-nine leagues connecting ten places. A tribute document prepared almost fifty years later, in 1796, relies upon a similar formulation to describe travel, stating that it provides the distances "from one town to another, as they

TABLE 1.1.

1747 *Itinerary of towns near Quetzaltenango*

Account of the distances measured pertaining to the towns that are newly numbered	
From Quesaltenango to San Antonio there are nine leagues	9 leagues
From San Antonio to San Xristobal Cucho there are six leagues	6 leagues
From Sacatepeques to Santa Cruz Comitan there are seven leagues	7 leagues
From Comitan to Santiago Tejutla there are four leagues	4 leagues
From Tejutla to San Miguel Ystaguacan there are eight leagues	8 leagues
From Ystaguacan to San Bartholome Sepacapa there are eight leagues	8 leagues
From Sepacapa to San Xristobal Cabrica there are ten leagues	10 leagues
From Cabricana to San Matheo there are nine leagues	9 leagues
From San Matheo to Quesaltenango there are three leagues	3 leagues
As evidenced here after traveling from town to town there are sixty-nine leagues which will be made known in each town.	69 leagues

Source: Derived from AGCA documents

were visited."[63] (See Figure 1.4.) The route is incorporated into the creation of the text much in the same manner as the *relaciones*. Here, the document produces a region with twenty-four towns and two hundred and three leagues.[64]

Similarly, a 1780 "account of distances or leagues" between Guatemala and Omoa, organizationally identical to the 1796 itinerary prepared for tribute purposes, was prepared for discussions on improving the road to the port (Figure 1.5).[65]

Distance was thereby produced in a variety of document forms, not just in *relaciones*, as segmented intervals along a route. Complementing this conception was the notion of hierarchically organized places, which might be visualized along a route—as in the itineraries above—or at specified distances from an administrative center. The questionnaires requesting geographic information and the responding *relaciones* reinforced and built upon this foundational conception. The repeated usage in various document forms made this conception exceedingly durable, as the documents considered above demonstrate.

Further Questions

The fact that routes and hierarchies of place continued to influence the geographical understanding of administrators in Spain as well is evident in the kinds of questions sent to the Americas in the late eighteenth and early nineteenth centuries. A 1776 *cuestionario* sent to New Spain spent considerable space on the question of how to measure the terrain. After a brief and pessimistic request for calculations of longitude and latitude accompanied by topographical maps, the questionnaire stated that "in the absence of both, the following method will be employed: 2. The Kingdom of Mexico will be considered the principal location and center, from which point the distance for every place described by the report will be measured." Distances were to be described according to the cardinal points and expressed as "such-and-such a distance from that capital." Beyond the capital, a further hierarchy was delineated. "Where there are *Audiencias* these will be used as central points to determine the subordinate places, these being wherever there are Bishops." Similarly, these bishop seats were to be used as centers for determining distances to the subordinate municipal governments. And beyond these, parish towns were to be considered regional centers. Recognizing that distances would be measured by travel along routes, the questionnaire instructed that "these distances should be measured according to the common league, as measured by the distance traveled while riding over the course of an hour, this being the

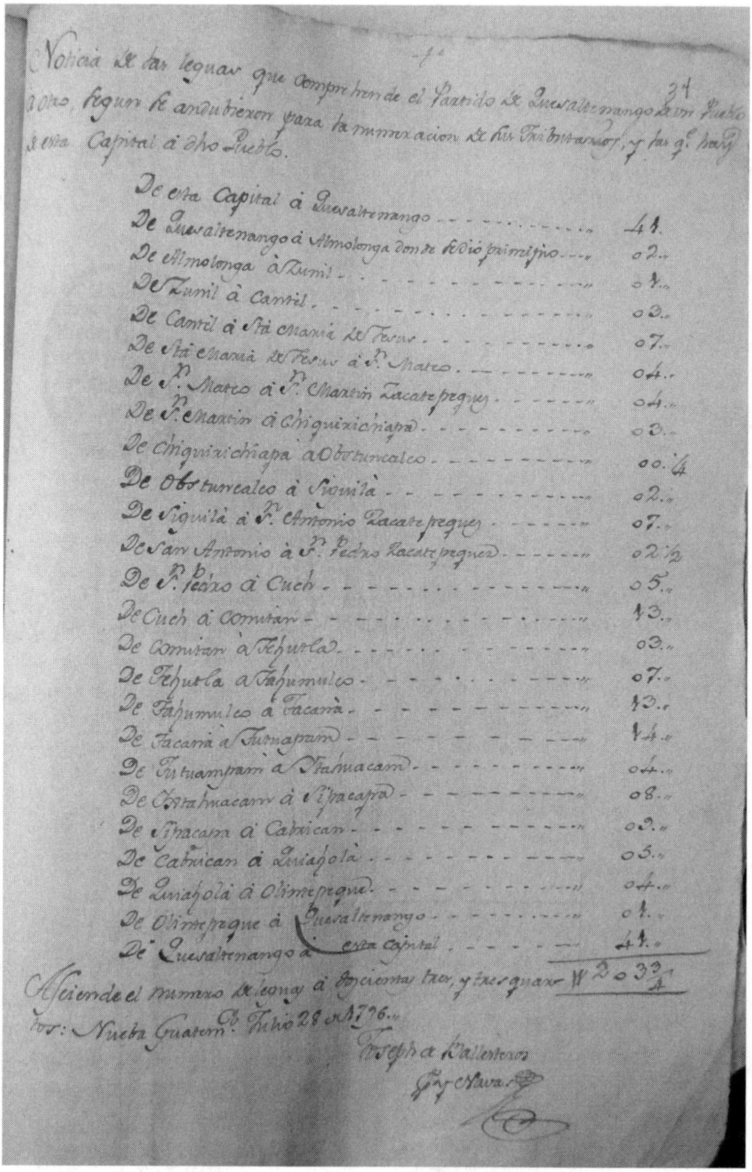

Noticia de las leguas que comprehende el Partido de Quesaltenango de un Pueblo a otro, según se anduvieron para la numeración de sus Tributarios, y las q.e hay de esta Capital á otro Pueblo.

De esta Capital á Quesaltenango	41
De Quesaltenango á Almolonga donde tubo principio	02
De Almolonga á Zunil	02
De Zunil á Cantel	02
De Cantel á Sta. Maria de Jesus	07
De Sta. Maria de Jesus á S.n Mateo	04
De S.n Mateo á S.n Martin Zacatepeques	04
De S.n Martin á Chiquixichiapa	03
De Chiquixichiapa á Ostuncalco	00 ½
De Ostuncalco á Siguila	02
De Siguila á S.n Antonio Zacatepeques	07
De San Antonio á S.n Pedro Zacatepeques	02 ½
De S.n Pedro á Cuch	05
De Cuch á Comitan	13
De Comitan á Tejutla	03
De Tejutla á Tajumulco	07
De Tajumulco á Tacaná	13
De Tacaná á Tuituapam	14
De Tuituapam á Ostuacam	04
De Ostuacam á Ysacapa	08
De Ysacapa á Catuican	03
De Catuican á Zinajola	05
De Zinajola á Olintepeque	04
De Olintepeque á Quesaltenango	04
De Quesaltenango á esta Capital	41

Allende el numero de leguas á fracciones tres, y tres quartas .... 033 ¾

Nueba Guatem.a Julio 28 de 1796.

Joseph de Allentean

FIGURE 1.4. 1796 Itinerary of places near Quetzaltenango
Source: Archivo General de Centroamérica. Photograph by the author.

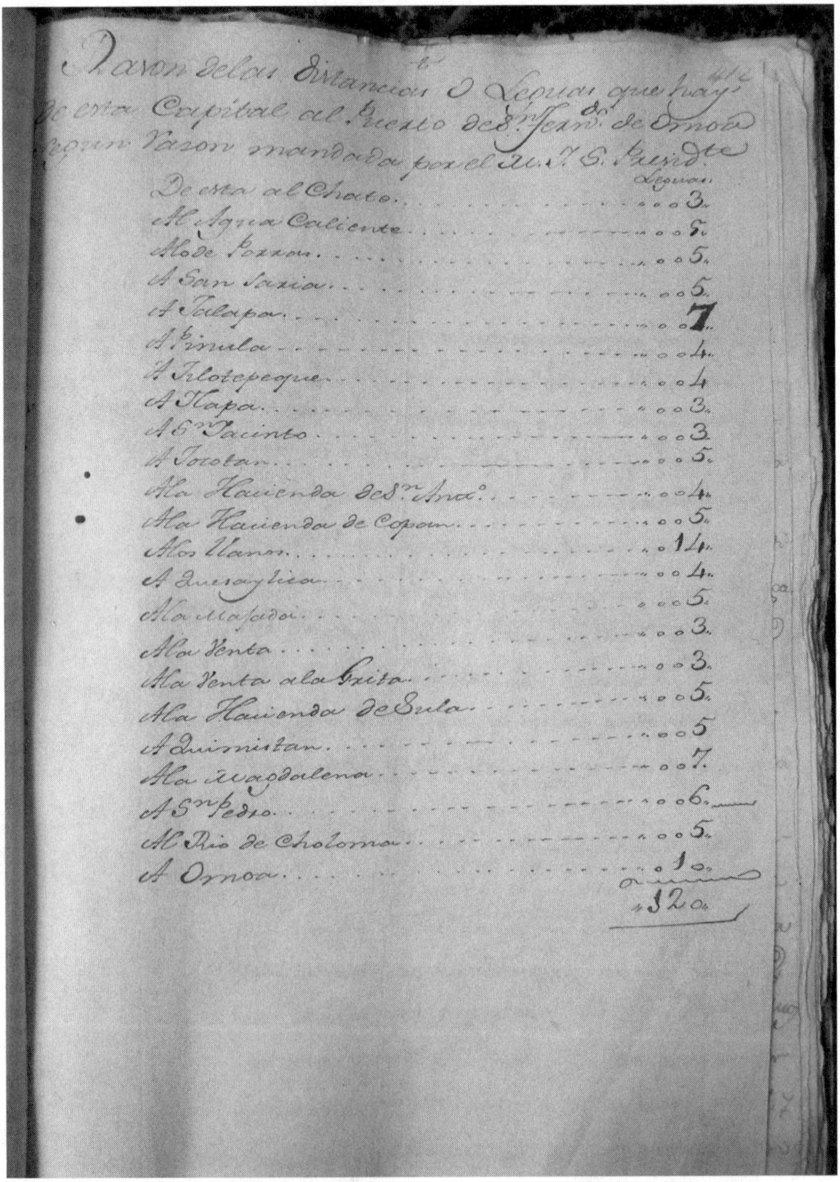
Razon de las distancias ó Leguas que hay de esta Capital al Puerto de Sn. Fernd.o de Omoa segun razon mandada por el M. I. S. Presid.te

Leguas

De esta al Chato ... 3.
Al Agua Caliente ... 5.
Al de Pozas ... 5.
A San Saria ... 5.
A Jalapa ... 7.
A S. Pinula ... 4.
A Jilotepeque ... 4
A Itapa ... 3.
A Sn. Jacinto ... 3
A Jocotan ... 5.
A la Hacienda de Sn. Anto. ... 4.
A la Hacienda de Copan ... 5.
A los Llanos ... 14.
A Quesaylica ... 4.
A la Masadas ... 5.
A la Venta ... 3.
A la Venta ala Grita ... 3.
A la Hacienda de Sula ... 5.
A Quimistan ... 5
A la Magdalena ... 7.
A Sn. Pedro ... 6.
Al Rio de Choloma ... 5.
A Omoa ... 10.
132.

FIGURE 1.5. 1780 Itinerary of destinations between Guatemala and Omoa
Source: Archivo General de Centroamérica. Photograph by the author.

easiest method."[66] Thus, abandoning the possibility of a consistent spatial measure, the instructions relied on a temporal measure based on travel. However, to compensate for the irregularities of travel and to produce a measurement "in a straight line, or as the crow flies," the questionnaire instructed the following:

10. On flat terrain that is not interrupted by ravines or noticeable crests, the travel time is reduced by one-fourth, and the remaining three-fourths are calculated as leagues, and this is to account for the twists and turns that the road always takes. 11. On terrain that has ravines or hills that cause the road to rise and fall, the travel time is reduced by one-third. 12. On terrain that follows a circuitous route, such as those routes taken to find a crossing point across or a river or avoid passage through a mountain, it is advisable to reduce the travel time by half; and if the road is very circuitous, by three-fifths, and even on occasion by two-thirds, decisions which are judged subjectively and aided by the observations made at the time of travel.[67]

The instructions required the traveler to make highly subjective judgments based on the terrain and the amount of time spent traveling. At best, such a method would have resulted in a rough estimate. Putting aside the questionable accuracy of calculating distance in such a fashion, it becomes evident that the questionnaire strove for objective measures but relied necessarily on subjective ones. The process of travel, and the calculations that resulted from travel along specified routes, remained the unavoidable basis upon which to both measure and understand distance. Prompted by the replies they had received over the course of the colonial period, officials had come around to the idea of travel as the most realistic "mode of knowing."

Though it seems likely that this questionnaire did not reach Guatemala, as it did not elicit immediate replies, its formulation provides undeniable confirmation that a hierarchy of places and intervals of distances along routes remained crucial to the administrators who continually requested information from the Americas, even as they compromised on the manner of measurement. In fact, as late as 1812, instructions requesting "reports and descriptions" of the jurisdictions of Spanish America emphasized these elements. The Cortes de Cádiz inquired exhaustively into the topography and political geography of the region in three sub-points. They first asked for a plan or map ("plano o carta") of the indicated province.[68] The second sub-point emphasized surface area, terrain, and political boundaries, looking ahead to the nineteenth century's dominant modes of spatial representation. It demanded the lines of latitude and longitude for each region and placed a particular emphasis on the borders, requesting that any boundaries with "foreign powers" be marked with particular precision. If there were territories to be reclaimed or if there were parcels of land whose purchase might improve the jurisdiction's security, these facts were to be noted. Any barbarian Indian tribes had also to be clearly indicated. And the instructions requested a calculation of area—in leagues squared—as well as an exact description of the topography.[69] Reflecting the heightened awareness of hostile territories occasioned by the wars in Europe, the instructions placed a new emphasis on borders, and above all boundaries with foreign powers—be they European or Indian. In this emphasis, it is possible to see the faint outlines of national boundaries that would come to dominate the maps and geographical descriptions of the nineteenth century.

But the shifting perception of the political and social landscape did not entirely exclude preexisting conceptions. The third sub-point of the instructions returned to the traditional method of describing space and distance, providing a table for the calculation of distances to central places. The seven columns of the table asked first for a list of the "names of the political jurisdictions, their municipal centers, towns, estates, farms, and settlements." The remainder focused on distances and directions to and among these places (Table 1.2).[70]

TABLE 1.2.

Portion of the 1812 questionnaire

Names of the jurisdictions, their municipal centers, towns, estates, farms, and settlements	Distances from the municipal centers to the capital	Direction from the municipal center to the capital	Distances from the towns, estates, and farms to the capital	Direction from the towns, estates, and farms, etc. to the capital	Distances from the towns, estates, and farms, etc. to the municipal centers	Direction from the towns, estates, and farms, etc. to the municipal centers
Province of ...						
Its municipal center ...						
Town of ...						
Town of ...						
a list of towns to follow						
Estate of ...						
Estate of ...						
etc., etc.						
Farm of ...						
Farm of ...						
Settlement of ...						
Settlement of ...						

Source: Derived by the author from documents at the Archivo General de Indias

While the Cortes de Cádiz had begun to envision the Americas in a different manner, placing a heightened emphasis on borders and hostile territories, they had not yet discarded the traditional understanding of space and place that linked hierarchically organized population centers along routes. To make the Americas visible to readers in Spain, routes and hierarchies of place were still necessary. Officials over the course of the colonial period had incorporated these conceptions into their replies, but they had also shaped Spain's conception of what was possible. Travel as a mode of knowing dominated. And local informants, often Indians, both supplied that knowledge and, as the keepers of the "wilderness" beyond the track, constrained it.

2 Dangerous Distance:
A Visita by Archbishop Cortés y Larraz

> The true solution would be to congregate the towns in more well-appointed locations; in this manner the four annexed towns could become one and they would be placed on favorable land and not at such great distances, among hidden nooks and high peaks, where they gain only freedom from good conscience and freedom to disobey the law.
>
> —Archbishop Pedro Cortés y Larraz, describing the parish of Opico

Archbishop Pedro Cortés y Larraz distinguished himself from other writers of geographical descriptions of Guatemala in many ways: among these, by his willingness to propose a solution to distance. But the archbishop also went further than other officials in identifying and articulating distance as a problem. Not content to merely observe the great obstacles posed by poor roads and impenetrable jungle, the archbishop argued that such obstacles created sizeable dangers in the form of "freedom." Though Cortés y Larraz may have written of these dangers more explicitly than other authors, the assumptions about distance underlying his arguments are not unique to him. At the Spanish peripheries, distance from ecclesiastical and secular authorities was a problem that imperiled the spiritual and moral health of the empire.

Focusing on the *visita* written by Archbishop Pedro Cortés y Larraz in the late 1760s, this chapter examines how the conception of routes and key administrative centers, established in Chapter 1 as fundamental to many *cuestionarios* and *relaciones,* likewise influenced the archbishop's understanding of distance and space. Archbishop Cortés y Larraz, who visited more than one hundred parishes in Guatemala and wrote a multivolume illustrated *visita*, placed a great deal of descriptive emphasis on the route that he traveled. He thought carefully about how to measure the route, and his text places importance on rendering the length and conditions of each route for his prospective readers. Similarly, Cortés y Larraz emphasized central places, and distances to them, in his study of each parish. Placing the parish seat conceptually at the center, other towns, *haciendas*, and settlements were understood in terms of their distance from it.

This chapter also continues the consideration of "distant" as a pejorative term, in certain usage, for contemporaries in colonial Guatemala.

Cortés y Larraz voiced a strong opinion throughout his text about the dangers of distance. The *visita* produced distance as a condition to be overcome and a problem to be solved. His text can be read as a strenuous argument for extending the reach of individual parishes and bringing the Guatemalan population closer to ecclesiastical centers. He despaired of succeeding in this, and when he returned to Guatemala City, he attempted to resign his post. On August 31, 1769, he wrote to King Charles III, saying that "with no other motive than to serve the glory of God and to serve you, I return to your hand this diocese with which you have honored me." But the king replied on July 5, 1770 with a refusal, and Cortés y Larraz was forced to remain.[1] Though the arhbishop's concerns were widely shared, they were not universal. Certainly people in the parishes he visited viewed their "dangerous" freedoms differently. Two contrasting perspectives complicate Cortés y Larraz's conception of dangerous distance. The paintings that accompany the text, which were painted by an unknown artist, provide subtle challenges to the argument of the archbishop's text. And the account of a non-ecclesiastical traveler, an eighteenth-century writer and statesman who traveled the same routes and enjoyed many similar privileges, offers a very different view of Guatemalan distance.

Producing Dangerous Distance

Born in Zaragoza in 1712, Pedro Cortés y Larraz remained in Spain into adulthood, studying at the Universidad de Zaragoza and obtaining his doctorate in theology in 1741. He was appointed archbishop of Guatemala by Charles III in 1766 and arrived in Veracruz soon afterwards, in July of 1767. The archbishop embarked on the three-stage *visita* of his diocese the following year, traveling extensively and with only brief rests in Guatemala City: first from 3 November 1768 to 1 July 1769; then from 22 November 1769 to 9 February 1770; and lastly from 6 July 1770 to 29 August 1770.[2] The reports that he prepared during and after these journeys were sent to King Charles III in 1771.

Though the document he created belongs to the tradition of parish *visitas* conducted in Guatemala and elsewhere, the *descripción geográfico-moral*—geographical and moral description—is in many important ways a *relación geográfica* as well.[3] Cortés y Larraz was necessarily concerned with the state of his parishes, the work of his *curas* (parish priests), the practices of each congregation, and the consequent moral health of the Guatemalan population. But he was equally concerned with the demography of the region, the terrain across which the parishes were scattered, and the means of travel from one place to another. In fact, he found that the two concerns were inextricably bound together. From its inception, the document was conceived as a broad and comprehensive investigation into the social and geographical features of the region. Sending each parish in Guatemala a brief, ten-point questionnaire in the manner of the *cuestionarios* sent from Spain, Cortés y Larraz gathered preliminary information and ensured that every parish would be prepared for his arrival. Just as questioners in Spain had found replies from Guatemala varied in scope and quality, so the archbishop found the reports supplied to him sometimes thorough, sometimes remarkable, and sometimes entirely inadequate.

The contributions from local parishes reinforce two of the *visita's* most striking characteristics: the *visita* is a composite document, informed by people all over the archdiocese; and the document is route-based, or produced around a route in the manner of the eighteenth-century *relaciones*. The document thereby incorporates both the radial and itinerary models of knowledge production proposed in Chapter 1. Like other European men who explored the New World, Cortés y Larraz depended heavily—both for his journey and for his text—on the assistance of people around him. The composite nature of the *visita* is evident in how the reports sent from parishes form an important appendix to the main text. Cortés y Larraz referred to the reports within his own writing, creating an internal dialogue that openly complimented or contested the portions written by individual clergy. In this sense, Cortés y Larraz was perhaps more explicit than other eighteenth-century authors—travelers, explorers, scientists—about the assistance he received. Neil Safier writes that Frenchman Charles-Marie de la Condamine, in his exploration of South America in the eighteenth century, relied on "Creoles, Jesuits, Amerindian informants, and enslaved peoples of African descent. But in order to impress his superiors at the Academy of Sciences, he suppressed the sources of much of this information and hid much of the assistance he received." This allowed La Condamine to "fuse exceptionally diverse materials together and provide the illusion that they were collected and compiled using unified and recognizable standards."[4] Cortés y Larraz's *visita*, like La Condamine's text, is composite in less visible ways as well: the substantive material presented in both the reports and the main text was gathered knowledge which required the participation of parishioners in every town. To provide data on a town's population and descriptions of its customs, parish priests relied not only on their own knowledge but on the information provided by their congregations. Similarly, Cortés y Larraz drew his information about the unfamiliar territory from his guides and assistants. One of these invaluable assistants was the unknown artist who accompanied him and created the landscape-maps that complemented the text. The images painted in an unknown hand for each parish, which were no doubt crucial to making the places accessible to Charles III, are at once one of the *visita's* most expressive and most impenetrable elements.[5]

The reports contributed by the individual parishes also bring to light the underlying organization of the *visita* as a text. From its inception, the *visita* (meaning both the journey and the document) was conceived and executed around a route. The archbishop's instructions to his parishes reflect the projected itinerary structure for his travels and the creation of the reports. As Julio Martín Blasco and Jesús María García Añoveros note in their introduction to their published version of the *visita,* the archbishop "introduced the novelty of sending ahead to each parish a letter with precise instructions regarding his visit as well as a ten-point questionnaire concerning the parish." The archbishop ordered, "make a copy of this letter and the instructions, sending on the original to the closest parish, so that in this manner it will pass from one to another sequentially, and so that I may collect it at my last parish visit, for which purpose you will see in the margin the administrative centers of the parishes in order." As the editors point out in reference to these instructions, Cortés y Larraz "expected to receive accounts of the parishes in the order in which he was to visit them."[6] The archbishop's use of the word "order" both identifies explicitly a chronological "order" dictating travel (for him and the documents) and implies indirectly a hierarchical order. In the archbishop's mind, travel and text would coincide to create a document that would unfold along the routes of the archdiocese.

This organizing structure, so clearly essential to Cortés y Larraz's initial conception of the *visita,* was closely followed in the subsequent production of the text. Throughout the archbishop's three journeys, the route became not only a foundation for the archbishop's mode of knowing but also an essential narrative device. As rendered by Martín Blasco and García Añoveros, the archbishop's itineraries crisscross central Guatemala and the Pacific coast.[7] He traveled north into Chiapas, visiting the parishes around Jacaltenango, northwest into Verapaz, and south as far as Conchagua. Without reaching the coast of the Pacific or the westerly reaches of the Petén, he nonetheless crisscrossed the more densely populated corridor running north to south along the curve of the isthmus.

Cortés y Larraz introduced each of the towns he visited by noting its distance in leagues from either the *cabecera* or the town "prior" to it on the route. In each he also described the conditions of the route and the circumstances of his travel along it. The archbishop learned from experience what the authors of the 1776 questionnaire suspected: leagues were a slippery measure in Guatemala and they varied from one journey to the next. He warned in his opening prologue that "in calculating the distances from one town to another, or from the mountains to the sea, there can be several and even many errors made; because in this Kingdom the leagues are not measured, nor does anyone know how many leagues it contains." Cortés y Larraz found that for all his careful questioning, these measures were elusive, "because even though I asked, it always happened that one person would say there were four leagues while another would stretch them to six or eight." There were as many measured distances as there were travelers: "each person counted the leagues according the speed at which he traveled; on every occasion I made certain to use my watch, knowing well the deceptive effect of traveling on good roads or bad, traveling quickly or slowly."[8]

The archbishop consequently made careful note of route conditions and timed his journey to measure the routes.[9] The resulting descriptions are vivid snapshots of travel. Leaving Guatemala City, accompanied by servants and guides, Cortés y Larraz made the following representative observations:

From the city of Guatemala to the town of Petapa there are six leagues, traveling from west to east. The road is mostly good but it has its bad aspects as well; when one emerges from Guatemala the road follows a violent climb on a very bad road for about a league; after traveling two leagues one comes across some ranches called Las Ventillas, which belong to the parish of Santiago Sacatepequez. After traveling three leagues one comes across an *hacienda* called the Embaulada. At the four-league mark the Bárcena *hacienda* lies to the right and the García *hacienda* lies to the left; both are situated near the road and belong to this parish. At the five-league mark one passes through a town called Villa, an annex to the main parish, and at the six-league mark one reaches Petapa. From the *hacienda* called the Embaulada, the whole route is downhill, without any notably steep parts.[10]

Checking his timepiece as he traveled along the route, Cortés y Larraz surveyed the landscape around him and gathered information from his traveling companions. In his resulting description of Petapa, and many other parishes, he also included a "tabla" or table of distances for the town and its dependent *haciendas*, an itinerary that echoes the tribute tables pictured in Chapter 1. (See Table 2.1.)

Cortés y Larraz thereby laid out clearly for Charles III two views of Petapa: a timed and measured entry along an unfolding route, with named landmarks and travel conditions; and a hierarchical schema of the parish center, Petapa, and its dependent settlements and farms. With these two perspectives fully revealed, the archbishop proceeded to add detail to his portrait of Petapa, listing population data, describing the landscape, and recounting the recent history of the town. In Petapa the town counted primarily on "maize and beans," as well as plantains which were taken daily to market in Guatemala. The majority of the population spoke Pokomam. Cortés y Larraz mentioned the *cura*, one "middle-aged" Don Antonio Laparte, and his income before reporting briefly on the content of the *cura's* report and then drifting into one of his typically lengthy "reflections."[11] Cortés y Larraz is best known to historians for his detailed

TABLE 2.1.

Distances by Cortés y Larraz

	Leagues
1. Town of Petapa, parish center	
2. Town of la Villa to	1½
3. Town of Santa Inés to	1
4. Town of Viejo to	½
5. *Hacienda* of Arrevillaga to	1½
6. *Hacienda* of Villalobos to	2
7. *Hacienda* of Bárcena to	2
8. *Hacienda* of los Aracenas to	2
9. *Hacienda* of Orantes to	2¼
10. *Hacienda* of Arece to	2½
11. Pastures of Granadillas to	2¾
12. Pastures of la Horca to	2¾
13. Pastures of la Bautista to	3
14. Farm of García to	2
15. *Hacienda* of García to	2
16. *Hacienda* of San Joseph to	1

Source: Derived by the author from documents at the Archivo General de Indias

descriptions of Guatemalan parishes' social and cultural characteristics, but to the archbishop, placing these parishes—measuring, describing, and rendering them visually—was just as important. In fact, locating the places he visited along a route and in relation to the *cabeceras*, the parish centers, appears to have been a prerequisite for understanding their other qualities.

As Cortés y Larraz continued his travels, he had occasion to observe more closely the "good and bad aspects" of the routes. Some of the unfavorable conditions the text describes are readily recognizable to modern readers. "A terrible, violent climb" leading to Los Esclavos was understandably challenging, and fording dangerous rivers would prove difficult today for even expert travelers.[12] Cortés y Larraz repeatedly stated his preference for flat or moderate terrain, open pasture, and (to a lesser extent) straight roads. Dense forest and steep, winding paths created the quintessential "bad road." To a great extent, his assessment of roads corresponded to contemporary European aesthetics and notions of transportation improvement. Bourbon policy emphasized the improvement of roads and transportation across New Spain and Guatemala with mixed results.[13] "Good" roads both pleased the eye and served the crown by being broad, smooth, and easily traveled on horseback or coach.[14] But considered more fully, the archbishop's assessments of "bad roads" and "good roads" reveal themselves to be deceptively transparent. His judgments went beyond considerations of efficiency and ease. The "descripción geográfica-moral" of his title takes on new meaning as the text argues that, in fact, the landscape could be morally "good" or "bad": conducive to moral behavior or not.[15]

In a manner likely surprising to most modern travelers, Cortés y Larraz on occasion signaled a vehement dislike for foliage and trees—particularly those growing densely and close to the road. As he traveled toward the parish of Guanagazapam, the archbishop noted that "everything is forested by trees and bushes, which even in the level parts of the road are extremely troublesome, as the mules get entangled or collide with the branches; the ground is a web of tree roots and one continually tears at the branches above with one's head."[16] In this case the trees were an obstruction to travel; but Cortés y Larraz also objected to forested areas that obstructed his view. "From the moment one arrives in Parrasquín," he wrote of the area near Quetzaltenango, "everything is boxed in by immense mountains, with no meadows or pastures and entirely enclosed by trees."[17] When the trees did not obstruct the road or his view, they struck him as more picturesque. The archbishop noted the attractive qualities of trees along the route to the parish of Guaymoco, commenting that "the road is a good one with many mountains and hills on every side and with abundant trees and foliage."[18] Confirming this view, he observed of the very different route to San Vicente that "all the land is very barren, like that near Titiguapa, and without any trees."[19] Evidently, the archbishop made a subtle distinction between types of trees—or, rather, types of tree growths. With a preference for "llanos" (meadows) and "valles" (valleys) that were both more attractive and easier to navigate, Cortés y Larraz objected to dense tree growth that was "frondoso" (leafy)—growth he frequently described as "monte," meaning wilderness—when it obstructed the road or the view.[20] However, individual trees in sparser formation indicated a healthy soil and could assist the appearance of the landscape. Vegetation had its proper place: far from the road.

Cortés y Larraz commented on the relative flatness or steepness of the route with far less ambivalence. The ideal route was flat and straight, as was the road to San Sebastián del Texar. "The road is quite good and very agreeable," Cortés y Larraz wrote, "it is flat along an avenue of trees and there are many fields for the growing of maize and beans; the road can be traveled by coach."[21] There were precious few roads that could be traveled by coach; but even narrower paths through plains or between hills met with the archbishop's favor. Seen from a distance and on either side of the route, hills complemented the route. However, once the route wandered into the hills the archbishop complained bitterly of the steep and "violent" climb. Among the *pueblos* and *haciendas* of San Pedro Matzahuat, he wrote, "there are terrible roads, because the whole area around the parish is a labyrinth of hills and ravines that are high and deep; in the towns of San Juan and San Miguel they are called *tepezontes,* which in their language means twenty score hills."[22] No route was worse, however, than the route to San Pedro Zulumá, which the archbishop traveled as he left Huehuetenango. The "incredibly bad road" stretched for nineteen leagues, and he wrote that "even though the first two [leagues] appear to be flat, they have their bad parts; the two that follow have violent ascents and descents along very poor, rocky paths." Deeply affected by the route, he stated, "this road is so sad that it seems to make the sadness palpable. After leaving the ranches behind, the six remaining leagues are the worst kind of road imaginable. It is impossible to even explain what it is like: the route winds its way through rocky crags, and everything is rocky—steep cliffs and peaks and chasms of stone." He saw the palpable dangers of the landscape in the "caves underground" where "many people and horses have fallen into the abyss." He concluded, "it causes one horror to even contemplate having to penetrate such a great gathering of mountains."[23]

The archbishop's complaints—and horror, in this case—were less the protestations of a weary traveler and more the concerns of a spiritual leader.[24] In the poor roads he traveled, Cortés y Larraz saw obstacles to the effective congregation of the parishes and obstructions to the diligent ministrations of the *curas*. In the landscape perceived by the archbishop, poor roads were, quite literally, spiritual hindrances. That this view was not shared by all of his travel companions is evident in the discussion he had with the Indians of Guaymoco. Both his estimation of the roads' navigability and his conception of their spiritual necessity were hardly universal.

I stated above that the main town is located in a meadow, but the area around the parish is full of steep mountains and ravines, for which reason all the paths leading to the town's adjoining settlements are extremely rugged. They are full of such precipices and dangerous turns, that even the Indians consider them as such, and it seemed only appropriate to put the question to them directly. It happened to me on one occasion as we commenced a particularly violent climb, that I said to them: Why didn't they repair the roads that were in such a poor state? They answered me: That roads that are good enough for the deer are not poor roads; and that there are other roads in the region that are considered so bad that they do not always dare to walk along them, and if they have to travel along them by night some do it with the aid of a light and on hands and knees. For three years now the *cura* here has had the problem of sending his deacon to administer the sacraments to some sick person only to have him turn back on the road, not daring to go any farther.[25]

As Cortés y Larraz learned throughout his travels, there could be even less agreement between Indians and non-Indians as to the difficulty of roads. In some cases, such radically different views actually resulted in the existence of two different routes. The route from Jocotán to Chiquimula, for example, wound two leagues south, then two leagues west, and then two leagues north again. But, the archbishop noted, "the Indians can walk this road straight through, without the detour, climbing over the mountain that divides the two parishes; and they do it in two or three hours, walking east to west; I think perhaps not even deer could walk along that route that the Indians use."[26] Cortés y Larraz signals the wildness of the routes by claiming they are unsuitable even for animals; yet the Indians traveled these roads that were impassable and off-limits to him.

What emerge from such passages are different landscapes—not all of them visible to a single viewer. To some, certain routes were closed. Whether because Cortés y Larraz and his guides considered them impassable or because knowledge of them was not made available to him, many routes remained "off the map," much like the territories described by Aldama in Verapaz. Alongside the network of principal routes traveled by the archbishop, other routes remained unseen. And Cortés y Larraz viewed the routes he did travel in a qualitatively different manner. Roads that were difficult, "sad," "violent," not to mention "bad" in his perception were not so to locals. Traveling with greater knowledge, familiarity, and possibly physical strength, other people in Guatemala experienced the roads differently. Finally, not everyone could see what the archbishop perceived in the difficult routes of the archdiocese: a labyrinth of spiritual obstacles, the undergrowth and precipices impeding the vital movement of *curas* and parishioners and thereby imperiling their salvation.

What began as a repeated observation in the early stages of the archbishop's three-stage journey became a clamorous cry by its conclusion: the people of Guatemala were separated by impossible distances. In the parish of Atheos, which Cortés y Larraz visited fairly early in his travels, he made his argument as clearly as possible, claiming that "it is simply not possible but rather morally impossible for all the parishioners to attend mass on the days of celebration." One problem was, of course, that "the Indian officials disdain the mass and the Christian doctrine as much as the rest do." However, even had the Indian officials been more cooperative in bringing people together, the *cura* faced an additional obstacle:

What is more, this measure would perhaps be successful in the towns where mass is celebrated, but by no means would it be of use in the other towns that lie at such a distance and along such rugged roads, because even if the officials put the greatest care and effort into gathering people (which they certainly do not) it would be necessary for the officials to spend their whole lives on the roads. After going to mass and returning home, they would scarcely have arrived before they would have to leave again to attend another mass. Once one considers the distances between the towns, what I am stating here is made quite evident.[27]

Nor was it a solution for the *cura* to travel continually to his parishioners. Requiring guides and mules "because he must carry with him his bedroll, his water, his chair, a table, and in sum everything he might have need of because these things are not available in the villages," the *cura* would have to be shuttled back and forth. A distance of eight leagues, Cortés y Larraz argued, would be quadrupled: "the Indians who travel to one town to find the *cura* to celebrate mass must leave town A and go to town B, which lies for a example eight leagues away; they then return with the *cura* from town B to town A, which totals sixteen leagues." Then, they would have to repeat the journey "to return the *cura* to his home, and then head back to their own, which totals thirty two leagues." A journey of eight leagues would become an unmanageable thirty-two. The archbishop concluded that, either way, such travel was too much to expect: "how can they be expected to suffer distances of 13, 16, 22 and 20 leagues, which are the distances between the main town and the smaller towns in this parish?"[28]

The archbishop recognized that this formidable obstacle, distance, was worsened by the population's willingness and even eagerness to live out of reach. In the town of Guaymoco, near Atheos, people intentionally chose to live in remote places, even taking advantage of areas where routes did not connect. Remarking the great distances he had traveled in this region to get from one place to another, he acknowledged that his complaints might seem overstated: "with what I have said my narrative might grow irritating and might even appear to exaggerate the ruggedness of this mountain and the difficulty of the routes leading to the smaller towns." But he was not belaboring the point, he insisted: "it seems necessary to repeat for the sake of clarity that between one town and another there are no routes nor can any be built." There could be no doubt in his mind that people intentionally exploited this fact, for the places where they chose to live were "barren cliffs without any particular crops . . . which makes it clear that what they seek in such places is purely freedom from the officials and the *cura*, to wallow in ignorance and every manner of vice."[29] Such intentional isolation proved manifestly hazardous to the moral health of the population. As Robert Patch points out in reference to parallel circumstances in Yucatán, "libertad," or freedom in this context, was incontestably bad—and dangerous.[30] The *cura* of Guaymoco reported many "scandals" in this remote area, including "sensuality, drunkenness, theft, adultery, rape, incest, and couples living out of wedlock."[31] Clearly there were consequences to living in total freedom beyond the reach of the *cura*.

As Cortés y Larraz continued his *visita*, he returned again and again to the great obstacle posed by distance. And as he repeated this conclusion in one town after another, his recommendations for how to overcome distance grew more strident. Cortés y Larraz had determined at the start of his journey, after his measured analysis concerning the town of Atheos, that there was no possible solution other than "the division of the parish so that the *cura* has neither more territory nor more parishioners than those that he can teach and govern himself."[32] His reflections on the parish of Suchitoto were even more explicit. "This parish cannot by any means be well governed," he concluded, "because it is evident that there are more than 136 families or 2794 people in the three towns, and there are an additional 185 families or 1355 people living beyond the towns." He noted that those thirteen hundred people living in remote areas "lie at a significant distance in a tangle of highland wilderness, hills, and forests that make it impossible for the *curas* to minister to them and makes it equally impossible for them to travel to the parish."[33] In his sharp observations of how and why people lived so remotely, Cortés y Larraz invoked the need for "reducción," the centuries-old policy of "reducing" the native population into congregated towns.

What they call *haciendas*, fields, and pasture should be considered nothing more than mere pretext to shake free every manner of spiritual and secular law, because these places are not in the least productive agriculturally. Consequently the only remedy is to reduce the people into a single settlement. Even the towns of Tenancingo and Jucuapa should be relocated, because they lie among rugged mountains, they produce no crops and their land serves for nothing else because travel through them leads nowhere. All of this arises from a single problem, and that is the stubborn tendency of Indians to live hidden away in isolation and the tendency of Ladinos (who comprise about half of the parish) to form settlements wherever they wish to, in order to avoid observing the law and to live in complete freedom.[34]

The parishioners not only avoided the parish priest, they also avoided the local *corregidor* or *alcalde,* in the archbishop's view. He believed that seeking agriculturally productive land was the only valid reason for living remotely. No other justifiable motive was conceivable to him. His assessment that the mountains near Tenancingo and Jucuapa "serve for nothing" rested on the conclusion that they led "nowhere." Naturally, in the archbishop's estimation, a remote settlement was not itself a worthwhile destination. His characterization of Indian and Ladino motives is illuminating as well. While Indians sought to live hidden and in isolation, Ladinos sought to live wherever they pleased, far from the reach of authorities and in absolute freedom. Both strategies resulted in an equally damaging distance, but the archbishop shaded their intentions differently.

Cortés y Larraz recommended for the population at large a policy that had historically targeted the native population of Mesoamerica, beginning in the sixteenth century. The Laws of Burgos (1512) and the *Leyes Nuevas* (1542) both emphasized resettlement of the population through "congregación" or "reducción." The *Recopilación de leyes de las Indias* (1680) made explicit the spiritual necessity of *congregación*, resolving that "the Indians should be reduced to villages and not be allowed to live divided and separated in the mountains and wildernesses, where they are deprived of all spiritual and temporal comforts, [and] the aid of our ministers."[35] In Guatemala, the process of *congregación* was initiated in the 1540s. Relocated both willingly and forcibly, Indian families gathered at new town sites where church, plaza, and other elements of Spanish architectural order were gradually assembled. "Designed with the goals of Christianization and economic exploitation foremost in mind," George Lovell writes of the process in Guatemala, "the order inherent in *congregación* stood in sharp contrast, in Spanish eyes, to the morphological anarchy of the dispersed pattern of settlement characteristic of pre-conquest times."[36] However effective *reducción* may have been initially in Guatemala, its results were not uniform or permanent. In many places, settlement patterns either resumed their pre-conquest form or took on new, equally "scattered" formations. Lovell writes of the Cuchumatanes region that "recurrent fugitivism, triggered and sustained by a complex interplay of cultural preference and existential circumstance . . . constantly eroded Spanish notions of orderly, town-focused living."[37] Similarly, in Yucatán, "the Maya ever so gradually reversed the reducción policy imposed by their colonial masters." Robert Patch observes that "the Maya of colonial Yucatan seem to have moved all over the place, in order to use their resources more conveniently, to seek opportunity elsewhere, or to escape from the colonial regime altogether."[38] Whatever the motivation, it seems clear that many sites of *congregación* failed to preserve the nucleated order envisioned by the Spanish.

That Archbishop Cortés y Larraz echoed the call for *reducción* more than two hundred years after the initial *congregaciones* in Guatemala speaks both to the durability of the concept among Spanish reformers and to the ineffectiveness of its implementation. Had the original *congregaciones* succeeded in concentrating the population, the archbishop would not have found so much of the Guatemalan population living "among hidden nooks and high peaks." And while Cortés y Larraz updated the idea by applying it to both Indian and Ladino, in its essentials the concept remained unchanged. The archbishop identified scattered settlement as the single greatest obstacle to spiritual access; his solution was to physically relocate the population in order to facilitate the work of his *curas*. As his three-stage journey progressed, Cortés y Larraz heightened his language, calling for *reducción* in terms that recalled sixteenth-century practices. After visiting Chalchuapa, he offered the following stark prognosis: "based on the conditions of this parish and of nearly all of the parishes, it is evident that they cannot be competently instructed or governed, and that the true remedy can only be to burn pastures, ranches, and huts, reducing everything into the towns."[39] His recommendations for Metapa, which he visited shortly afterward, were similarly uncompromising:

The flat lands of this parish, which I have described as measuring roughly one league, would fit all of the parishioners in this parish, which measures fourteen leagues in longitude and nine in latitude. Reduced to the stated one league of flat land, it would be well served and governed; but spread out as it is, the parish necessarily will remain utterly abandoned, a condition made worse by its terrible roads. As a result, the only remedy is to burn pastures and farmland and for the people to live in the town.[40]

In his proposed remedy to burn and congregate, Cortés y Larraz appears aggrieved by what he perceived as literally *too much* space. If only, he lamented, burning could reduce a space of fourteen by nine leagues to one. The violent solution he proposed was one he emphasized more firmly later in his journey. Though in Atheos he recommended a more judicious re-parceling of communities and the deployment of additional *curas,* in Metapa he could see no alternative other than a drastic reduction of space through fire.

Archbishop Cortés y Larraz came away from his journey profoundly unsettled by the damaging effects of distance throughout the archdiocese. The dangers were several and occurred at many levels. Families—at times entire communities—frequently lived beyond reach of a parish's *cura.* Whether they lived in isolation intentionally or not, their spiritual health was greatly imperiled by the lack of access to the *cura* and the sacred space at the parish's center. But he also observed, on other occasions, that the *curas* themselves lapsed in their practices when they lived far from the influence of the archbishopric. After concluding that the parish of Ozicala could not be governed by a single *cura* and would have to be reduced, he considered the issues. "The impossibility of finding a solution may contribute to the carelessness of the *curas* and priests, to the point where they seem indistinguishable from the secular clergy, but the distance from the capital is also in this case a contributing factor." Added to this, their involvement in "dye manufacturing" jeopardized their work, such that "several priests have entirely forgotten their true nature."[41] Distance from the capital was one factor among many that degraded the integrity of the *curas.* Finally, the archbishop observed a parallel phenomenon among secular officials. Toward the end of his journey, in Santiago Sacatepéquez, he hypothesized explicitly that greater distance from the capital led to greater dereliction of duty. "I comment once again here on the utter carelessness of the district governors," he wrote, echoing the concerns of secular officials. Santiago lay only three leagues from the Guatemalan capital, and this led him to wonder: if at such a short distance from the capital, in the very presence of the President and the judges, they demonstrate such carelessness, what must occur in the more distant towns?[42] In fact, he had seen what occurred in the more distant towns; it worried and aggrieved him. At the conclusion of his *visita* the archbishop appears to have believed some of the difficulties posed by distance were simply insurmountable.

Producing Proximity

The paintings that accompanied Cortés y Larraz's text were intended to make the Guatemalan parishes visible for the Spanish monarch. They were, more specifically, intended to render visually the descriptions provided in the *visita*, particularly the hierarchical schema that Cortés y Larraz presented in tables. The towns and *haciendas*, numbered in tables in the text, were also numbered in the paintings. As such, the paintings were meant to reproduce and explain the spatial configuration described in the text. However, the paintings by the anonymous artist in many cases went beyond reproducing and explaining, at times subtly challenging Cortés y Larraz's descriptions. They emerge from a different mode of knowing, clearly, than the archbishop's. Though in some aspects they remain faithful to the literal descriptions of the text, they frequently deviate from the intended effect of the text, exposing a tension that pulls at the seams of the *visita*'s argument about distance.

The more than one hundred paintings are evidently created by the same hand, but their manner of composition varies. The paintings are neither purely cartographic representations nor purely landscape paintings. Their varied use of perspective is one attribute that places them between the two genres. Few paintings rely fully on a "profile view" or "prospect," using terms discussed by Richard Kagan in his study of urban images. Such a view would show the landscape "as seen from the vantage point of a viewer standing directly on the ground." Rather, the artist relied most heavily on views taken at different angles from above. The painting of the parish of Apaneca (Figure 2.1), for example, relies on an "oblique view," which surveys the landscape from a higher vantage point.[43]

Other paintings, such as the one for the parish of Garcia (Figure 2.2), combine perspectives from various angles: an oblique view merging with a cartographic view.[44] The coastline near Garcia and the rivers leading to the sea are depicted as they would appear viewed from high above, but the towns are seen in high profile.

FIGURE 2.1. The Parish of Apaneca
Source: Archivo General de Indias

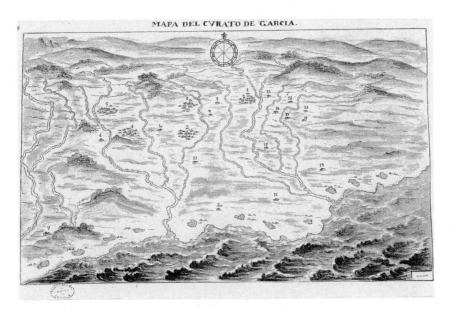

FIGURE 2.2. The Parish of Garcia
Source: Archivo General de Indias

In other aspects beyond the use of perspective the paintings combine elements of cartography and elements of landscape painting, creating mixed images that I consider "landscape-maps." Richard Kagan describes such images as "map-views," but in this case it seems appropriate to use a term that emphasizes the cartographic aspect less.[45] It is impossible to know for certain whether the artist traveling with Cortés y Larraz relied on surveying or measurements, but the cartographic element was clearly valued. Some of the paintings contain elements that lean more toward cartography in images that otherwise stylistically resemble landscape paintings. The use of numbers to identify towns and *haciendas* is the most visible cartographic element. A discreetly placed and unmarked scale at the corner of each painting and the compass marking north are two others. Towns are frequently symbolized by a single building rather than reproduced in their architectural detail. Finally, some of the paintings use dotted lines, rather than more realistic ribbons of road, to mark routes.

The paintings reveal fundamental tensions between the archbishop's narrative and the unknown artist's perspective. Cortés y Larraz placed greatest descriptive emphasis on the route between parishes. Though concerned with how parishes were connected internally, when he spoke of the landscape he devoted most space and effort to how parishes were reached from without. The paintings, in contrast, focus deliberately on the parish, often placing it at the center of the image and leaving the connecting route to the edges. In fact, routes sometimes do not make it into the landscape-maps at all. The parish of Apaneca (Figure 2.1) is depicted as a remote series of towns arranged on a steep descent. Dense forest at the bottom of the painting suggests that the mountain is inaccessible, and no route appears in the painting. Cortés y Larraz, in contrast, describes the route in detail:

The first league follows a good and very flat road, which crosses the above-mentioned valley; then it climbs a mountain and there is a league and half's ascent that is violent in the extreme, but that is not considered a poor road because there are no rocks or cliffs; it is true that on either side there are ravines, but these are agreeable—fertile and in full flower—as is the entire mountain, planted with maize, beans, and sugar cane. Then one reaches the mountain peak, and the path begins an extremely steep decline of about two leagues. Along this part of the route it is neither fertile nor agreeable; one does not see crops, although there are dense outgrowths of trees and bushes. One then arrives at a small clearing surrounded by hills where the town of Apaneca is located.[46]

The artist has represented, in the faint rectangles on the mountain's side, the crops described by the archbishop, and the towns appear in the suitably forested eastern slope. However, the route traveled, though invisible in the painting, clearly runs from left to right across the mountain's peak.

As a result, the painting and the text provide the reader with two different points of access. Grounded in the route, Cortés y Larraz described the rise and fall of the road and the changing view. The artist depicted Apaneca from a perspective entirely off the route, allowing the reader to see the parish from a distant, aerial view. In this case and in others, it appears that the artist placed a far greater emphasis on rendering the parish landscape, while distance and routes were of secondary importance.

Further, the artist often represents "good" roads and "bad" roads as essentially the same. Access to Mexicanos, of which Cortés y Larraz said "the road is a good one," is presented to the viewer in the landscape-map as accessible by a subtle depression between low hills (Figure 2.3). Access to Texistepeque appears much the same (Figure 2.4).

Just to the right of center, a clear point of entry seems to lead directly into the open valley where the parish center lies. And yet Cortés y Larraz complained of the route to Texistepeque, "there are many hills and patches of forest everywhere; in sum it is a bad road."[47] The artist has faithfully represented the numerous mounds in the vicinity of Texistepeque, and a striking *barranco* lines the river, but in this landscape-map there are no obstacles to access. The routes, invisible for both Mexicanos and Texistepeque, are unimportant when the viewer enjoys a wide, aerial view. A consistent, if marginal, acknowledgment of distance remains in the unmarked scale at the corner of each painting. But as the paintings do not include routes, these scales seem designed not to quantify distance along routes but to give the viewer a sense of perspective.

The paintings that accompany Archbishop Cortés y Larraz's *visita* demonstrate that not everyone who traveled through Guatemala placed routes at the center of their perspective on distance. Even someone traveling alongside the archbishop apparently experienced the route differently. At the very least, the artist and the writer had different opinions regarding which aspects of the human and natural landscape merited emphasis. Part of this difference doubtlessly lies in the descriptive potential of text versus image. But as much, if not more, of this difference is due to the perspective of the traveler. Cortés y Larraz perceived a spiritual landscape in which routes were vital conduits and distance was a hazardous obstacle. People, and particularly people as parishioners, were central to the landscape he perceived. The artist accessed an aerial perspective that in some sense made the routes inconsequential. Seen from above and with the human presence reduced to small buildings, the terrain unfolded effortlessly before the artist's eye. It must have struck King Charles III that the text described such torturous means of access to the parishes of Guatemala while the paintings described broad, airy vistas that seemed just within reach.

FIGURE 2.3. The Parish of Mexicanos
Source: Archivo General de Indias

FIGURE 2.4. The Parish of Texistepeque
Source: Archivo General de Indias

Toward a Different View

Travel conditions in the Guatemalan *audiencia* did not change dramatically in the decades following Cortés y Larraz's *visita*. Most roads continued to be impassable for coaches, and travelers journeyed them on foot or on horseback and with hired mules, when they could be afforded. This does not mean, however, that perceptions of travel—and correspondingly of distance and space—were uniform. As the anonymous artist traveling with Cortés y Larraz demonstrates, even two travelers in the same party might perceive the journey—or at least the landscape—differently.

Another example from the early nineteenth century notes that while the roads themselves remained very much the same, the mode of and motive for travel captured different views. Antonio José de Irisarri (1786-1868), a Guatemalan statesman and journalist who traveled extensively in his lifetime through South America, North America, and Europe, experienced the rigors of overland travel in Guatemala during a journey to Mexico when he was twenty years old. As someone who would later be involved in the struggles for independence in South America, he was in some sense at the heart of the political transformations taking place in the landscape in the early nineteenth century. His autobiographical account, published for a general audience, describes the difficulties of the routes in Guatemala with rather more humor than Cortés y Larraz, though the conditions he describes are much the same.[48] In the manner of a *relación* that guides the text along the route, Irisarri addresses his reader, saying "let us follow the route from Quetzaltenango to Soconusco along the eternal San Pablo ridge," a route, he notes, "that could easily be mistaken for the road to hell."[49]

For the space of several lines, Irisarri describes the route as Cortés y Larraz would have, informing the reader that "the journey across the aforementioned San Pablo mountain is four leagues downhill from San Marcos to San Pablo and four leagues uphill from San Pablo to San Marcos."[50] He qualifies the difficulty of the peak by claiming that "whether one is traveling up or down along that Jacob's ladder, it is essential to travel with mules that have learned the art of gymnastics necessary to transform ordinary humans into squirrels."[51] Not only the horses, but also the riders had to become expert gymnasts in order to survive the route. "In some parts of the road it is necessary to take perilous leaps more fitting to a fish or an acrobat," he protested, "in others it is necessary to swim in deep pits of mud; in others one is forced to slide downhill as if on a roller coaster, and, in conclusion, along that route one travels in every manner imaginable other than in a comfortable manner."[52] No horse or mule in the world, he exclaimed, other than those native to San Marcos and San Pablo, would be able to navigate the route without breaking all their bones. Writing many years later, Irisarri was able to laugh at his inexperience, observing that he was continually "falling and getting up again, slipping, jumping, plunging into pits of mud, and learning to swim on horseback"—a skill he had not learned since it was not taught in Europe, he noted wryly. But it was a talent very necessary in the Americas, he observed, "because without this skill it is impossible to travel along the routes that were then called 'royal highways' and are now called 'national highways,' despite the fact that neither then nor now are they highways worthy of any name whatsoever."[53]

Surely Cortés y Larraz would have sympathized with the slipping and sliding Irisarri laughingly complained of. But despite their concurring accounts of the route, the archbishop and the young adventurer observed different human landscapes. For one thing, while Cortés y Larraz was received as an eminent ecclesiastical authority, Irisarri was received as a companion of the traveling *correo,* or mail carrier. Irisarri had hit upon this solution because he knew that along the routes of Spanish America "there are no inns, or post houses, nor any of the other establishments one finds in England, France, and other European countries." He had to travel with a bedroll and a cot, enough clothing for a five hundred league stretch, and a pair of mules to avoid hiring the "abysmal mules for hire" available in the towns along the way. It was also necessary to take measures to avoid being robbed, and Irisarri solved all his difficulties by hiring "as cook and butler, guide and bodyguard, one of the official mail carriers." His name was Melchor Martínez, a "practical man" who readily agreed to be his personal traveling companion.[54]

It was easy to persuade the general administrator of the mail service to lend me the services of Melchor Martínez, for this was his name. He traveled as if on royal business, with the royal coat of arms emblazoned in silver on his chest like a military badge and the horn with which he announced his arrival at every point along the route, indicating to all within earshot that they were to allow free passage to the bearer of the King's arms and announcing his presence to the Indian towns from a half-league's distance. The Indians were thereby alerted that they had to prepare fresh mules, light a fire and fetch water for the *cabildo*, which was at that time the resting place for all travelers. The idea to travel like a portmanteau, under the care and protection of the mail carrier, was truly an inspiration . . . because while it was far more expensive than any other method of travel, it made ordinarily insurmountable difficulties disappear effortlessly.[55]

The Indians, upon hearing the horn, would go in search of fresh horses, and everywhere he went they assumed that the mail carrier was a special courier, traveling in the company of an official, because Irisarri "traveled in his uniform and carried a sword longer than he was." Then all the town officials would emerge to ask him for news gathered along the route and to invite him to eat, sleep, and share conversation. Irisarri enjoyed this mode of travel immensely, concluding that "with the novel idea of being carried around by a *correo* like a letter, the journey succeeded in being as comfortable and entertaining as is possible along a route that is so long and that some have considered difficult and bothersome because they have not known how to make it pleasant and informative."[56]

As Irisarri's final comments suggest, he not only traveled with different company but also with different objectives. Cortés y Larraz traveled with the great burden of his concerns for the archdiocese's spiritual and moral health continually hanging over him. Where he saw perilous distance at the end of the difficult routes, Irisarri saw "in all those places a liveliness, activity, and progress" that he had not expected to find. Where the archbishop saw entire villages at risk due to frequent "scandals," Irisarri saw "Indians who were industrious, intelligent, capable, awake to their circumstances, well-built, robust, and earnestly dedicated to agriculture, commerce, and the arts." In fact, he concluded, "everything could be found there, other than any sign of scarcity or misery."[57]

The two men traveled with vastly different perspectives and purposes, and consequently perceived markedly different human landscapes. While the happy outcome of his observations may have been due as much to his background, education, and personality, Irisarri credits the success of his journey to his opportunity to travel with the mail carrier, "as if I were a letter." Was his journey representative for a letter—or a mail carrier, for that matter? The following chapters turn their attention to the institution and travel mode of which Irisarri caught only a glimpse.

Part Two

3 The Mail in Time

MOVING DOCUMENTS

My Dear Sirs—My pen is incapable of expressing the tragic
consequences visited upon this city (that was once Guatemala) by the many and forceful earthquakes, the heavy and
copious torrents of rain that fell at the same time. . . . And I
must tell you that all the goods, letters, notices, and papers
sent on June 1 to these kingdoms and all of the monthly
mail to and from the provinces lie entombed—buried in the
fragments and ruins of the roof and walls of the old office,
such that to send you this letter, we have been forced to take
refuge under a straw roof in the little plaza of San Pedro.[1]
—Don Simón de Larrazábal,
Administrator of the Guatemalan mail, August 1, 1773

To travel like a letter in colonial Guatemala entailed something very different in 1700 than it did in 1800. By the time Antonio José de Irisarri traveled
with a *correo* in the early nineteenth century, the Guatemalan mail system
was a fairly efficient and reliable means of moving documents across the isthmus and farther, to Mexico and Spain. But the development of such a system
occurred only in Irisarri's time. For much of the colonial period, the mail
system was an unreliable and above all sluggish means of communication.

Concentrating primarily on the operation of the mail system in the
Bourbon period, this chapter argues that the regular and frequent exchange of documents did not become possible in Guatemala until the last
quarter of the eighteenth century. In this period, the pace of communication grew systematic and more places were incorporated into regional mail
routes. This change in pace would greatly influence the type and genre of
document sent through the mail. It would also influence the conception of
space and distance, as communication from previously "distant" places
became more readily accessible.

An earlier version of this chapter appeared in Sylvia Sellers-Garcia, "The Mail in Time:
Postal Routes and Conceptions of Distance in Colonial Guatemala," *Colonial Latin America
Review*, Vol. 21, Issue 1, pp. 77–99. Reprinted by permission of the publisher (Taylor &
Francis Ltd, http://www.tandf.co.uk/journals).

The conception of distance projected and utilized by administrators of the mail system in Guatemala shares the "common skeleton" elaborated in the previous chapters. But the mail administrators in Guatemala were men who traveled infrequently outside of the capital. Their conception of space and distance encompassed a broad swath of territory anchored in the Guatemalan capital, and it thereby offers insights into how regional peripheries were perceived from the region's administrative center. The accounts and "topographic plans" that they created did not rely on state-of-the-art cartographic techniques, and the absence of detailed cartographic information in Guatemala only partly explains this choice. Examining documents created by mail administrators in the context of contemporary definitions of space and distance, this chapter argues that textual representations rendered Guatemalan distances more effectively. The term "league" described temporal—as well as spatial—intervals, and text-based itineraries therefore expressed distance best.

The Workings of the Mail System

The early colonial mail system in Spanish America patched an essentially Spanish system onto an Indian labor force.[2] It is certain that, especially in the early colonial period, Spanish officials relied on indigenous roads, indigenous knowledge of routes, and indigenous guides. The scarcity of sources on early communication, however, makes it impossible to determine whether the Spanish and Indian systems merged or whether a parallel Indian system existed in the sixteenth and seventeenth centuries. What can be determined is that many continental Spanish conventions expanded with the empire. Legislation prohibiting the opening of mail packets, distinguishing urgent mail from "ordinary" or private mail, and instituting the practice of paying prior to delivery gives some sense of the state of the peninsular service in the mid-fifteenth century. Under Ferdinand and Isabel delivery grew more frequent, and, importantly, more uniform. What had been the royal and public postal services of Aragon, Castile, Mallorca, and Catalonia fell for the first time under the jurisdiction of a *correo mayor*, or principal mail administrator.[3]

However, a functional network of continental communication by no means expanded easily into a transatlantic mail system, however earnest the efforts by monarchs in Spain. Charles V established the position for *Correo Mayor de Indias*, principal mail administrator of the Indies, in 1514, long before anyone was available to take the post.[4] Philip II followed Charles V in drafting legislation that attempted to address the problem of mislaid correspondence, protesting that "many people and even entire towns and cities have failed to inform us of many things we would wish to know." Declaring that the remedy of this was "vital to the crown," he ordered his subjects to "take care that all letters and packets written . . . by any cities, towns, places, and people of every quality and station be sent to us with utmost care so that we may receive it."[5] Yet fluid and reliable communication proved almost impossible to achieve. Weather, piracy, and the difficulties of establishing safe ports all presented formidable challenges.[6]

In the sixteenth and seventeenth centuries, two large fleets left Spain each year: one bound for New Spain, the other bound for Tierra Firme. The mail directed to Guatemala and its provinces traveled with the fleet bound for New Spain, leaving between April and June, and the return mail leaving New Spain departed in March.[7] As a consequence, while the maritime route between the American and Spanish ports could take as little as two to three months, an exchange of correspondence might take much longer. A letter written in Guatemala in February might be in time to depart with the March fleet out of New Spain and might then reach Seville as soon as May or June. But a reply from Seville could not be expected until, at the very earliest, May or June of the following year. Between 1559 and 1573, when it was still common practice for the king to acknowledge receipt of every piece of official correspondence received from the Indies, the dates of his notices indicate that letters sent to him by the *audiencia* in Guatemala took anywhere from five to seventeen months.[8] In 1599, a typical letter sent by the *audiencia* took about a year to reach Spain.[9]

The maritime route was certainly erratic, at best, and unreliable, at worst, and as a consequence much of the *correo mayor*'s early energy was directed toward safeguarding and systematizing the Atlantic routes. But the emphasis placed upon improving communication between the Americas and Spain indirectly influenced the pace of development within the Americas. While internal communication was doubtlessly important to colonizing Spaniards, the weight of continental Spain as administrative center drew the early networks' emphasis outward rather than inward. In other words, the need to formalize communication with Spain in no small part determined the use—or, rather, neglect—of local routes within the Americas.

Placing the weight of its direct supervision on the transatlantic route, the Spanish *correo mayor* left overland administration to individuals in the Americas, who largely fended for themselves throughout the sixteenth century. Their solution was to develop messenger systems that relied on semi-official couriers. A historian of the postal service in Mexico describes an informal system in New Spain that relied on "the goodwill of travelers" in the early to mid-sixteenth century.[10] In Guatemala, Spanish administrators counted on a large body of Indians from Mixco Nuevo, an Indian town outside of the capital, and about two hundred mules for transportation of the mail by 1590.[11] But as the Spanish and *criollo* population grew to inhabit places farther and farther afield of the colonial centers and administrative units were established from Chiapas to Cartago, the need for internal communication grew greater. Gradually, the crown attempted to systematize the internal network. The office of *correo mayor* was created by the *audiencia* in Guatemala in 1619. Spain had promoted the sale of office for *correos mayores* on the peninsula since the early sixteenth century; in the seventeenth century the crown continued this practice in the Americas, selling the office of *correo mayor* in Mexico, Guatemala, and Cuba.[12] Three men held the office in Guatemala before Don Pedro Ortiz de Letona, who oversaw the mail system in Guatemala from 1730 until its incorporation by the crown in the 1760s.[13]

In the eighteenth century the Spanish crown, assisted by Bourbon administrators, finally—albeit only partially—achieved a greater systematization of the mail service, both in Spain and in the Americas.[14] In 1706, Philip V placed all of the public offices, including the *correos mayores,* under the jurisdiction of the crown. In the mid-eighteenth century the postal service was reorganized and the *Real Renta de Correos* (Royal Post Office) began naming officials with fixed salaries.[15] Several attempts were made throughout the century to regulate payment and carriage of the mail. A notable piece of legislation from 1720 set strict guidelines for how mail was to be carried on foot and by horse, both within Spain and to European cities outside of the kingdom.[16] These reforms were eventually extended to the Americas, where offices were gradually incorporated into the crown. The second half and particularly the last quarter of the eighteenth century brought considerable and constant modifications to the mail system. In the eyes of Bourbon reformers, the movement of documents across New Spain had for too long been unreliable and slow.

The shape of these reforms can be appreciated most readily by taking a brief step back to consider the efforts of Don Pedro Ortiz de Letona, the last Guatemalan administrator to own the post before its incorporation by the crown. Shortly after acquiring his post in 1730, Ortiz made a first attempt to establish monthly mail service between Mexico and Guatemala. Until then, the mail to Mexico had traveled by courier, dispatched as the need arose by the order of the president.[17] The Mexican administrator in the 1730s established a weekly service between Mexico and Veracruz, and he urged Ortiz to take advantage of this improvement by establishing a regular service as well. Opposition from Guatemala's *audiencia* president, however, stalled the project for several years, and only with the appointment of a new president in 1746 did the project become possible.[18] In 1748 the monthly mail service between Oaxaca and Guatemala was established, at a cost of 2,040 *pesos* per year, marking a significant improvement over the 32,000 *pesos* spent previously in *correos extraordinarios* over a six-year period. The *correos* would travel five hundred leagues in twenty-six days, leaving the remaining days to rest and collect mail.[19]

In the early 1750s, Ortiz made a similar attempt to improve the mail service heading south to the provinces. The Guatemalan *audiencia* president approved a set of measures in 1753 that would carry mail on a monthly basis to San Miguel, Tegucigalpa, and Granada; Costa Rica, lying further south, would send a *correo* north to meet the Guatemalan *correo* in Granada. (See Map 3.1.) Correspondents in all the provinces other than Costa Rica, where the turnaround would be bimonthly, would have at least a few days before the *correo's* departure and could thereby expect to both receive and reply within a single month.[20] The *correos* sent to the provinces would travel on horseback, in the manner of *correos extraordinarios*. Though transporting the mail on horseback added greatly to the cost of the journey, it was the only way to cover such significant distances: two hundred and sixteen leagues to Granada and two hundred and thirty leagues to Nicaragua.[21]

A proposal developed in the same year to carry mail to Omoa gives some sense of how efforts to improve the mail to remote locations con-

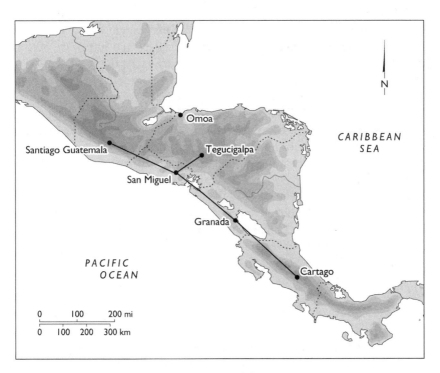

MAP 3.1. Mail destinations to the southeast of Guatemala City in the 1750s

tinued to depend largely on extra-official carriers. The proposed route required that a soldier carry the mail from Guatemala to the nearby town of Petapa. From Petapa, another soldier would carry the mail to Cuiginiquilapa, where it would be passed on to *correos* who would travel in turn to Jutiapa, Santa Catarina, Ipala, Chiquimula, and Zacapa. From there one carrier would make the long journey to Omoa. The *correos* would be compensated at a rate of one *real* per league. The return trip, however, proved far more tenuous. From the fort in Omoa, the mail would be carried by a soldier to the ranking officer in the nearby outpost of *los Vigenes*, where he would request that a traveler on his way to Gualan carry the mail to a local Indian offical. From there, an Indian would carry the mail to Zacapa, where the return route would resume. In the orders establishing this route, the official concluded by requesting that the officer at the fortifications in Omoa express his profound gratitude to the travelers who assisted in carrying the mail.[22] Attempting to balance the necessity of communication with the dangers of entrusting correspondence to extra-official carriers, he could only hope that reliable travelers would be on hand.

Efforts to systematize such routes proved difficult to sustain. In 1768, Don Joseph de Garayalde, appointed as the first administrator of the newly created *Administración General de Correos* in Guatemala, surveyed the past operations of the mail system with evident disappointment.[23] While the mail to Mexico had managed to maintain itself, the mail service to Omoa apparently had never become a permanent fixture. The monthly service to the provinces had survived only from 1755 to 1763, during which time it was partly subsidized by a sales tax.[24] In 1766 the mail to the provinces was resumed, this time financed directly by *portes*, the fees charged for mail delivery, but this had only proved sustainable by allowing the *correos* to carry *encomiendas*, or goods entrusted for private delivery. As discussed further in Chapter 4, this measure was less than desirable, as the weight of the goods tended to slow the *correos*' journeys significantly. The route had, at least, expanded beyond the handful of towns on the proposed route in 1753. Leaving the capital mid-month, it returned on the ninth or tenth of the following month "with all the replies from Sonsonate, San Salvador, San Vicente, San Miguel, Choluteca, Tegucigalpa, Comayagua, Puerto de Realejo, Leon in Nicaragua, and Granada." The only exception was Cartago, in Costa Rica, "which only delivers mail until three or four months later as a result of the scant correspondence and the great distance to Granada."[25]

Nevertheless, it was evident to Garayalde and to his superior in Spain, the Marques de Grimaldi and General Superintendent of the Post and Mail, that the Guatemalan system would need to be reformed. In regulations sent to Guatemala and dated September 24, 1764, the Marques de Grimaldi had already overhauled the maritime mail route. The "Provisional Regulations, which his Majesty orders be observed for the establishment of the new monthly mail that is to leave Spain for the Indies" set out exhaustive instructions for the passage of monthly mail between *La Coruña*, in Spain, and Veracruz. The guidelines discussed in Chapter 1 concerning the treatment of paper were here articulated explicitly, specifying the routes to be followed in the Caribbean (through Havana), setting strict measures for compliance to avoid delays, and indicating how the packets of mail were to be packed, in labeled trunks, so that each would reach its appointed destination in New Spain. The regulations also established the official rates for mail delivery.[26]

For Guatemala, as for most of New Spain, one of the greatest obstacles to creating a workable system lay in the fee schedule. Until the incorporation of the mail system, each piece of mail was paid for twice: by the sender, who paid the *porte*, and by the receiver, who paid a *sobre-porte*. A select group of officials were excused from payment, but private individuals and merchants were not. As a consequence, these often preferred to send their correspondence privately by personal messenger or trusted traveler.[27] For the crown's new mail system to be sustainable, it was necessary to capture these unofficial currents of correspondence and incorporate them into the official mail service. The fees, routes, and schedules had consequently to create an official alternative that would render the unofficial conduits of communication either redundant or too costly. The new guidelines for the mail service established by *audiencia* president Don Pedro de Salazar Herrera on February 22, 1768, attempted to do both. As an inducement, the crown authorized the Guatemalan president to abolish the fee (*sobre-porte*) charged to people in Guatemala for mail received from Spain.[28] Guatemalans would pay nothing for the overland transportation of any mail sent to them overseas. But, at the same time, sending what was now termed "clandestine" mail—mail sent by any means other than through the official system—would be punished with a stiff fine.[29] Any mail sent by private messenger to a destination on the route would be considered "clandestine." Documents sent privately to locations off of the routes would be allowed, but only on the condition that they were stamped at the central office before being dispatched.[30] This measure, which the administrator Garayalde described as "lenient," was intended to acclimate the residents of Guatemala to the presence of the post offices while more routes were introduced.[31] It allowed him to report some initial success after the first month under the new guidelines. While the majority of mail was still traveling clandestinely, the office stamped a fair number of packets.

TABLE 3.1.

Pieces of outgoing mail from Santiago, Guatemala in 1768

Pieces of outgoing mail: March 1768			
8 to El Salvador	2 to Ciudad Real	1 to Sapotitan	1 to Sololá
6 to Masatenango	2 to Atitan	1 to Jutiapa	1 to Samayá
5 to Quesaltenango	2 to San Miguel	1 to Cuiotenango	1 to Gracias a Dios
4 to Petén	2 to Esquipulas	1 to Guajinicuilapa	1 to Amatitán
4 to Sonzonate	2 to Santo Domingo	1 to Comayagua	1 to Quesailaica
3 to Oaxaca	1 to Chiquimula	1 to Los Llanos	1 to Gualán
3 to San Vicente	1 to Sacatecoluca	1 to Panajachel	1 to Patalul
		1 to Esquinta	1 to Zacapa

Source: Derived by the author from documents at the Archivo General de Centroamérica

However, as Garayalde's list of successfully dispatched letters made clear, it would be impossible to curtail the volume of clandestine mail unless more postal offices were added to the system. Of the outgoing letters that Garayalde inventoried in March of 1768, only those traveling to Mexico were headed to an *estafeta* (post office); all of those heading south to the provinces had to be sent to the care of other officials, most often the local *alcalde* or *corregidor*. Furthermore, the routes created by Don Pedro Ortiz de Letona simply did not reach all the destinations in Guatemala where people—private individuals and officials alike—wanted to send their mail. Neither the route to the provinces nor the route to Mexico, for example, would carry correspondence to Omoa or to the Pacific coast.

The other significant challenge lay in trying to provide mail service to remote places in less time than a private messenger would have required. The first important step in this direction would be to establish regional post offices throughout the *audiencia*. Garayalde recommended the creation of at least three post offices in an initial attempt to redirect clandestine mail through the official channels: in the Golfo de Honduras, Castillo de San Felipe, Omoa; in Cobán, the Presidio del Petén; and in the Provincia de San Antonio, Soconusco.[32] Don Joseph Melchor de Ugalde, Garayalde's successor in the post of administrator in Guatemala, continued the effort to expand the mail routes and add *estafetas*. In a January 1, 1769 letter to his superiors in Spain, Melchor discussed the route to the gulf, which Garayalde had apparently not yet established, as well as additional routes to Soconusco and Verapaz, provinces to the west and north of Guatemala. Melchor recommended replacing the occasional service to the gulf with a regular *correo*, and for Soconusco he suggested that the governor of that province send a *correo* north to meet the Guatemalan carrier at a convenient *hacienda* on the route. But Verapaz, Melchor claimed, did not need mail service, and his argument makes evident the logic behind the establishment of new post offices.

To the Province of Verapaz it is not necessary to establish mail service because there would be no way to finance it, considering that there is only one Spaniard in the town—the district governor. All the other people are Indians, *mestizos* [mixed Spanish and Indian], mulattoes, and *zambos* [mixed Indian and Black], and they neither write nor have use for writing. The correspondence by the Dominican friars in the area would defray the expenses very little, because all of them including those at the monastery in Cobán add up to barely twenty, and the rest of them have no correspondence.[33]

In establishing post offices, then, administrators made assessments as to the literacy of the population and its demands for correspondence. These factors doubtlessly influenced Melchor's decision to give priority to the routes heading east. In April 1770, he wrote to announce the first official departure to Chiquimula, Zacapa, and Omoa in the gulf.[34] The other principal factor that influenced Melchor's decisions to expand provincial routes was commerce. He recommended improving the service to Gracias a Dios as a benefit to the tobacco industry, and he suggested adding an additional carrier to the Quetzaltenango route "because of its commercial ties and its abundance of Spaniards and Ladinos."[35]

By 1772, these efforts had created a far more cohesive communication network across Guatemala than had existed ten years earlier. A list of place names created by Don Simón de Larrazábal, Melchor's successor, offers an exhaustive account of all the "Cities, Valleys, Provinces, Towns, Settlements, Farms, and other Places" attached to the Guatemalan *renta*: about six hundred places of varied size and importance could expect to send and deliver mail.[36] While not all of the places Larrazábal listed had *estafetas*, they were at least serviced by the route. Reaching all the way from Ciudad Real in Mexico to Cartago in Costa Rica, the mail system had managed to solidify the routes set out in the mid-eighteenth century, creating an expansive network of linked places.

Larrazábal details, at the end of his document, a few areas that were not serviced by the mail system, due to their "scant or non-existent correspondence." The Partido de Verapaz, the Presidio del Petén, the Provincia de San Antonio, the Provincia de Soconusco, the Alcaldía Mayor de Esquintla, the Partido de Guazacapán, and the dozens of smaller villages near them were not connected to the Guatemalan mail system. These remained, for a time, off the map. With the fundamental network established, all that remained for Larrazábal in 1772 was to formalize *estafetas* in many of the places on his route and extend the routes to the few un-serviced areas.

But Larrazábal's plans were interrupted and the foundations of the growing mail system were violently shaken with the earthquake of 1773. The city was destroyed, and after several desperate days Larrazábal made his way with the majority of Guatemala's inhabitants to *la Hermita*, a valley several leagues distant that had once been used to pasture cattle and would soon become the new capital. In Cortés y Larraz's landscape-map of the valley, *la Hermita* appears as a barely habited expanse of yellow hills. By September 1773, a month and a half after the earthquake, the valley was being transformed; Larrazábal had begun to reestablish the postal system in *la Nueva Guatemala* (New Guatemala), and the old capital, now *Antigua*, had only a farmhouse to receive and dispatch occasional correspondence.[37] He must have worked incessantly in the years following the establishment of the new capital, because by 1778 his reports to administrators in Spain reflected a highly functional regional mail system.[38]

Before his retirement to a post in Mexico in 1779, Larrazábal sent a requested report on the Guatemalan *renta's* revenues. Overall, the *renta* was doing well, and it promised to do better soon thanks to the new fee schedule. In August 1778, the payment of *sobre-portes* in New Spain was reinstated, and the original fees set out in 1764 were raised.[39] But certain basic challenges remained in place, such as ensuring a reliable and profitable communication link with Spain. Larrazábal sent his superiors a balance sheet of the *renta's* expenditures for each trip to Oaxaca. At a total cost of 1,398 *reales,* the trip to Mexico generally proved worthwhile, from the *renta's* point of view, only when the *correo* was able to collect correspondence from Spain. The returns without it could be as low as 300 *reales;* with the arrival of correspondence from Spain, this figure could jump to 2,500 *reales* or more.[40]

Larrazábal further detailed the cost of the round-trip journeys to the principal destinations in Guatemala in his October 1778 report (Table 3.2).[41] Larrazábal's table demonstrates starkly the cost of maintaining peripheries. While journeys to Oaxaca were among the costliest, these were amply justified by the link to Spain, when it occurred. But places like Petén, León, and Verapaz looked quite different. Sustaining contact with these lightly trafficked peripheries had quite a price.

With the *correo* on horseback costing nearly ten times as much as the *correo* on foot, and the bulk of the *portes* coming from overseas correspondence, Larrazábal made it his priority in the last year of his administration to coordinate the schedule of the monthly mail with the arrival of correspondence from Spain in Veracruz. The date of the mail's departure for Oaxaca (where it would go on to Veracruz) had since the 1760s been a point of debate among *audiencia* members and mail administrators in Guatemala. The ships' uncertain arrival dates inevitably made the Guatemalan mail's timing in Oaxaca hit-or-miss. In 1778, Larrazábal attempted to correct for the

TABLE 3.2.

Distances and costs of mail routes from Nueva Guatemala in 1778

From Nueva Guatemala	Leagues	Round-trip	Reales for correo on foot	Reales for correo on horseback
to Antigua	8½	17	13	109½
to Zacapa	31½	63	48	403
to the gulf road juncture	35¼	70½	53	451
to the gulf	51½	103	77 ½	659
to Santa Ana	45	90	72½	576
to Sonsonete	51	102	76½	653
to San Salvador	60	120	90	768
to Gracias a Dios	81	162	121	1037½
to San Vicente	74	148	111	947
to San Miguel	97	194	145½	1241½
to León	183	366	174½	2342½
to Granada	216	432	324	2765
to Nicaragua	230	460	345	2944
to Comayagua	117	234	175½	1497½
to Totonicapán	38	76	75	486½
to Quetzaltenango	43	86	64½	566½
to Tuxtla	140	280	210	1792
to Ciudad Real	129	258	193	1651
to Oaxaca via Tuxtla	271	542	406½	3469½
to Oaxaca via Ciudad Real	276	552	414	3534
to Verapaz	147	294	220½	1881
to Petén	297	594	445½	3801½
to Esquintla	13	26	19½	166½
to San Antonio	38	76	57	486½

Source: Derived by the author from documents at the Archivo General de Centroamérica

uncertainty inherent in the schedule by creating a second monthly mail to Oaxaca. If the first mail failed to coincide with the arrival of overseas mail in Oaxaca, the second mail would ensure that the entire month did not pass without receiving the packets from Spain. Don Juan Miguel de Yzaguirre, Larrazábal's successor, adhered to this schedule until 1781, when he suggested doing away with the second monthly mail to Oaxaca and creating instead a regular link to Spain through Omoa.[42] He canceled the second mail, which departed Guatemala on the twentieth of the month, but as a consequence coordination with the maritime mail once again became dif-

ficult. In the late 1780s and early 1790s, the mail administrators in Guatemala continued to debate with the *audiencia* the most favorable date for
the Oaxaca mail's departure.[43] Despite the significant improvements in mail
service overall, Guatemala still lay at a great distance from Spain.

In contrast, local distances seemed to be shrinking. While coordination
with the arrival and departure of overseas mail remained profitable but
problematic into the late eighteenth century, the regional system that gathered and distributed mail overland grew progressively more expansive and
efficient. Don Miguel de Ateaga y Olozaga, the Guatemalan administrator
in the 1790s and early 1800s, steadily added nearly a dozen post offices
each year in the 1790s. The result was a wide-reaching communications
network that, while not immediately profitable, laid the groundwork for
substantial future earnings in the form of local traffic. In 1795, Ateaga sent
a "plan topográfico" (topographic plan) to his superior in Spain that listed
exhaustively the places serviced by the mail system and the distances, in
leagues, between them.[44] The fold-out "plan topográfico," housed today at
the Archivo General de Indias in Seville, is almost identical to a 1793 plan

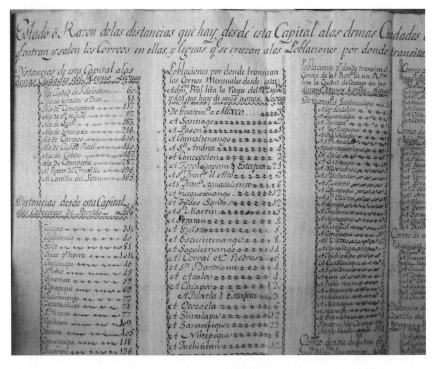

FIGURE 3.1. Portion of the 1793 "Estado o Razón" showing Guatemalan distances
Source: Archivo General de Centroamérica. Photograph by the author.

created by Ateaga and housed at the Archivo General de Centroamérica in Guatemala (Figure 3.1).[45]

Both plans intended to provide a comprehensive picture of the distances covered by the mail system. The 1793 plan, titled "Account or report of the distances that exist between this Capital and the other Cities or Provincial Centers: days in which the mail arrives and departs from them and leagues covered on the way to places transited by the mail on foot and on horseback," like its 1795 counterpart, lists the place-names of locations along the *correo* routes, traveled both by horseback and on foot, and it further includes a monthly schedule of the arrival and departure dates to principal locations. As such, it provided administrators in Spain with the most complete reckoning of mail travel in Guatemala they had seen.

The Conception of Distance among Guatemalan Mail Officials

The lists and tables prepared by late eighteenth-century mail officials in Guatemala reinforce the route-based, hierarchical conceptions of distance and space discussed in previous chapters. In one important regard, however, the *correo* documents are different: the supplemental documents surrounding the *correo* charts and itineraries provide much greater context than that available for other itineraries and route-based documents. These documents go beyond illustrating the widely held conception of route-based, hierarchical space to provide some explanations for why officials may have relied on these concepts to make Guatemala visible, knowable, and quantifiable.

It bears notice that the Guatemalan administrators' tables and lists were not the only format utilized by *correo* officials. Other representations of mail routes were sent to Spanish administrators from across the Americas in the late colonial period. A 1772 mail chart created in Chile, titled "Table of the distances that exist between the cities and other principal places in the Kingdom of Chile, based on the most exact calculation possible according to estimates," places the quantification of distance at the axis of two places (Table 3.3).

TABLE 3.3.

Portion of 1772 Chilean distances chart

Angeles Pza			
32	Arauco Pza		
192	198	Aconcagua Villa	
152	158	48	Algue Villa

Source: Derived by the author from documents at the Archivo General de Indias

Similar to a modern chart calculating driving distances, the Chilean chart maximizes the use of space on the page to quantify the distances between more than forty places.[46] While the distances are likely calculated along routes, the format of the table does not emphasize routes, ignoring intermediate destinations in favor of total distance. The table furthermore places no emphasis on the relative importance of places, locating place-names along the steps of the table in alphabetical order. Only prior knowledge of the region would permit a reader to identify the most administratively significant places.[47]

An 1804 document sent to Spain from Buenos Aires takes a different approach, approximating most closely what a modern reader would expect. A detailed cartographic representation, the "mail and postal offices" map from Buenos Aires, quantifies the distances along the mail routes from place to place. The viewer is able to contrast the aerial, spatial representation with the quantification of distance.[48] However, while it identifies places and distances along routes, the map places as much if not more emphasis on topographical features, namely the network of rivers and tributaries. Spreading across the surface of the map like veins, the detailed waterways dominate the landscape, covering all but the top two-thirds of the left side and filling the map with their prominent titles.

At the other extreme of visual and textual representations, an 1806 document from Peru, titled "Itinerary of the mail and post offices and other stopping points among the communities of *naturales* that live along the four routes of this Kingdom, these being the Cuzco, Arequipa, Valles, and Pasco routes," traces a narrative journey from place to place along the routes, quantifying distance for each leg of the journey but also describing the state of the road, the availability of supplies, and the nearby settlements.[49] Resembling some of the *relaciones* discussed in Chapter 1, the Peruvian itinerary places a heavy emphasis on routes in their context. Road conditions, supply sources, and climate are as integral to the description of distance as is the measurement of leagues. As these few varied examples demonstrate, American postal administrators in the late eighteenth and early nineteenth centuries relied on a variety of visual and textual forms to quantify distance and represent the extent of their mail systems.

The itinerary-table prevalent in Guatemala was, nevertheless, a widely used form. The *relaciones*, tribute reports, and other genres discussed in previous chapters all demonstrate its prevalence. Prevalence and precedent alone, however, do not account for why itineraries remained a favored form of representing the mail system into the late colonial period.[50] After all, the requests for information from Spain in this period specifically requested maps. Ateaga wrote in April 1795 regarding the administrators' request, in what is probably an exact quote of their language, that he will work on the "comprehensive Topographic Map of the post offices in this administration, the distances between them, their local situation, their stopping points and subdivisions."[51] Why, then, send itineraries instead?

Part of the explanation lies in examining what cartographic tools Ateaga had on hand. By the late eighteenth century, mapping technology was sufficiently well developed in Spain, and by extension in Spanish America, to have made an accurate cartographic representation of the mail routes possible—at least in theory.[52] The 1804 map from Buenos Aires created only a decade later testifies not only to the technological capacity of American administrators but also to their willingness to see distance along postal routes quantified visually. It is almost certain, however, that such mapping technology was unavailable in Guatemala.[53] The existing printed maps of Central America, while reasonably accurate, were insufficiently detailed for the postal officials' purposes.[54] And while Spanish archives are full of maps sent from Central America to Spain in the colonial period, there is no evidence to suggest that these maps (or their duplicates) were considered useful cartographic guides within the region itself. In other words, the maps by Cortés y Larraz's anonymous painter, the maps accompanying the *relaciones geográficas*, and the numerous other maps created in Guatemala did not serve any demonstrable purpose for officials living within Guatemala. These maps were clearly intended to make Guatemala visible to distant readers, and it may be that this was the only goal they accomplished.

The replies by mail officials suggest that what they required and lacked was a spatial representation that would address their understanding of the region and, presumably, contain the requisite amount of detail. Simón de Larrazábal complained in 1778 that "in this Kingdom there is no general map of its territory, as I have already made known to my superiors."[55] And Ateaga, when pressed by Madrid to create a map, protested, "the local placement of post offices cannot be represented due to the absence of formal Maps of the Kingdom, and the information provided by the Administrators is an inadequate substitute."[56] The information provided by subordinates for his composite document was of a different nature.

The other part of the explanation regarding why administrators sent itineraries lies in examining how they defined *mapa* and its related spatial concepts. Ateaga's protests and disclaimers indicate that the tables he sent to Spain were *not*, in his estimation, "mapas formales." What, then, did he understand a *mapa* to be? Ricardo Padrón's study of early modern Spanish cartography in the new world traces the development of the term *mapa*, shedding light on how the Guatemalan officials may have understood it. Comparing entries from Sebastian Covarrubias Horozco's 1611 *Tesoro de la lengua castellana o española* with others from the Real Academia Española's *Diccionario de autoridades* (1726–1739), Padrón observes that *mapa* shifted markedly in meaning. By the eighteenth century, *mapa* reflected centuries of scientific and technological innovations: what Padrón calls "the cosmographer's hegemony."[57] The *Diccionario de autoridades* defined *mapa* as follows:

The geographical description of the earth, usually done on paper or canvas, and upon which one puts the places, seas, rivers, mountains, other notable things, with proportionate distances, according to the scale one chooses, marking the degrees of latitude and longitude of the country one describes, so that the location or place of these things on earth can be known.[58]

As Padrón argues, by the eighteenth century *mapa* suggested an abstract, almost scientific conception of space, represented on a flat surface in relation to topographical features. In contrast, Covarrubias' definition of *mapa* is both vaguer and more inclusive: "MAPA. Is what we call the table, canvas or paper on which one describes the earth, in whole or in part, and might be derived from MAPPA, which means canvas or cloth."[59] Padrón's insightful comparison suggests that by the eighteenth century, cartographic innovations had narrowed the term so that the tables prepared by the administrators could no longer legitimately be called maps. Innovations in cartography beginning in the Renaissance and furthered by technological innovations during the Enlightenment had served to transform the category.[60]

In some sense, however, the administrators' use of the word *mapa* is misleading. While their usage of *mapa* suggests a break with pre-Enlightenment and pre-Renaissance cartographic tradition, their treatment of distance, space, and place points to certain continuities. Specifically, they appear to have preserved a traditional conception of distance incorporating a temporal component. In his analysis of sixteenth-century narrative accounts of the new world, Padrón argues that early Spanish colonists understood space in terms inherited from the middle ages: "they perceive 'place' and 'nonplace,' and they understand 'space' as the route one takes to get from one place to another." They relied, in other words, on the idea of "*space* as interval rather than area."[61] Padrón goes on to argue that by the eighteenth century and in formal Spanish usage, this conception had changed. He describes a change concurrent to the evolution of *mapa* in the meaning of the term *espacio,* or space: a change that eliminates the temporal dimension. Covarrubias describes space, he indicates, as a synonym of place: "From the Latin word SPATIUM, *capedo, intervallum*; meaning place." But, significantly, he also uses *espacio* temporally: "It also abbreviates the interval of time," Covarrubias writes, "and so we say for *space* of time of so many hours, etc."[62] In contrast, the eighteenth-century *Diccionario de autoridades* defines *espacio* as "capacity, breadth, longitude or latitude of a terrain, a place, or a field. It is taken from the Latin *spatium*, which signifies the same."[63] The definition appears to have incorporated many of the scientific principles informing the definition of *mapa*.

It is tempting to see in this contrast a sharp break in the conception of space; but these definitions from the respective dictionaries do not tell the whole story. The second definition of *espacio* in the *Diccionario de autoridades* echoes Covarrubias: "it also means interval of time: and it is said as follows, for the space of an hour, of a day, of a month, of a year, etc. *Intervallum. Temporis Spatium.* Santa Teresa, Biography, Chapter 29: She can well envision it with her imagination, and look at it for some space [of time]."[64] Essentially, the *Diccionario* and the *Tesoro* both foreground the spatial description, but the *Diccionario,* with its enumeration of primary and secondary definitions, only appears to do so more starkly. (Covarrubias does not enumerate meanings.) The split of time and space seems even more doubtful if definitions of place and time are considered in comparison. For Covarrubias, "place is said of all that which contains in it other things. . . . Place often signifies city or town or village, and we say: in my place, in the town where I was born. . . . To make a place for something, to make way. To not have a place, to not have time."[65] And of *tiempo* he says, "to have time, to have a place. . . . To make time for something, to make a place."[66] The Real Academia definition follows Covarrubias closely: "place: a space that contains other things. It derives from the Latin *locus,* which signifies the same; place2: also signifies site or point; place3: also means City, town or village; . . . place6: also signifies time, space, opportunity or occasion."[67] *Tiempo* it defines with only indirect reference to place as "the successive duration of things," but considering the scope of Covarrubias's laconic musings, most of which are in Latin, not much is lost.[68] The definitive entry in *Diccionario de autoridades,* however, concerns *distancia:* "The space or interval of place or time, by which things or events are separated from each other."[69] As the various entries make clear, far from being divorced of the temporal element, space itself and even more so its related forms, distance and place, remained closely tied to time in the eighteenth century according to formal Spanish definitions.

It is unlikely, therefore, that by the eighteenth century space and place had completely shed their temporal components in Spain and Spanish America. Cartography and the related term *mapa* evolved while conceptions of distance, space, and place preserved a more traditional temporal emphasis. A similar coexistence of competing conceptions is evident in the use and definition of the league, which geographer Roland Chardon has exhaustively studied in the North American context. The league emerged from two distinct metric bases.

The first was a time-distance concept by which the league was defined in terms of distance walked in an hour (or other temporal unit), and became linearly manifested in standards of human movement, such as the foot, step, and pace; from these were created states, miles, and leagues. The second basis was geodetic, wherein itinerary measures were defined in terms of a certain number to the degree of the terraqueous great circle.[70]

Despite efforts to unite and standardize these measures, the league eluded a stable definition. Chardon points out that in the European context, he has come across more than one hundred "specific and different definitions of the league." To some extent this variety proliferated also in the colonial Americas, where the diversity of leagues—for example, in South America—could be "bewildering."[71]

Covarrubias defines "legua" rather inflexibly as "the space along a route that contains three miles."[72] The *Diccionario de autoridades*, however, defines "legua" as "a land measurement whose magnitude varies greatly among Nations; seventeen Spanish leagues correspond to one degree, and each league is what one regularly travels in an hour."[73] Definitions in modern sources that consider colonial usage also vary, despite the fact that "the standard of 5,000 varas or somewhat over 2½ miles was adopted by Viceroy Antonio de Mendoza in 1536 in Nueva España."[74] Even after the attempted standardization in 1536, no single definition prevailed across Spanish America.

Fortunately, according to Chardon, only a few different leagues were employed in Central America and the Caribbean, and those rather uniformly. The Spanish league may have varied across North America as a whole (as Chardon's table of more than a dozen Spanish American leagues confirms), but it varied less within specific regions.[75] Of the two most common measures, the *legua común* (common league) and the *legua legal* (legal league), the *legua común* was used most in the *Reino de Guatemala*: "It is listed as the *legua* in Guatemala, Nicaragua, and Costa Rica, but in general the *legua común* appears to have been used primarily to describe itinerary distances rather than precise land measurements. As such, it tended to represent an hour's travel on foot." Even in Europe, Chardon argues, the "league's original purpose . . . to delineate an hour's travel on foot . . . seems never to have been fully discarded."[76] So while the Spanish league may have officially—and in most of the empire—been an exclusively spatial measure of roughly 2.6 miles, in Guatemala it was very likely different.

Leagues were temporal not only in theory. Further scrutiny of the *correo* tables from Guatemala confirms that distance and leagues were clearly temporal in practice, too. Three marked tendencies emerge when the charts are considered together: an emphasis on hierarchy of place; a conception of space organized through routes; and the quantification of distance as space-time intervals along those routes. These tendencies echo the representational choices in the document genres considered previously. They also, significantly, mirror the two models of composite documents discussed in Chapter One: documents built cumulatively over time-space intervals along routes and documents produced radially by peripheries informing the center.

The hierarchical organization of place is evident in every aspect of the charts, most clearly in how they place the Guatemalan capital clearly at the "center." The first two sections of Ateaga's 1793 table, as well as Larrazábal's 1778 table, quantify distances from the capital to other cities and *cabeceras*. Recalling Henri Lefebvre's description of Spanish-American space as a "gradual progression outwards from the town's center, beginning with the *ciudades* and reaching out to the surrounding *pueblos*," this approach for cities and *cabeceras* can be rendered visually as lines radiating outward.[77] Lefebvre's description, which hinges on a spatial/temporal

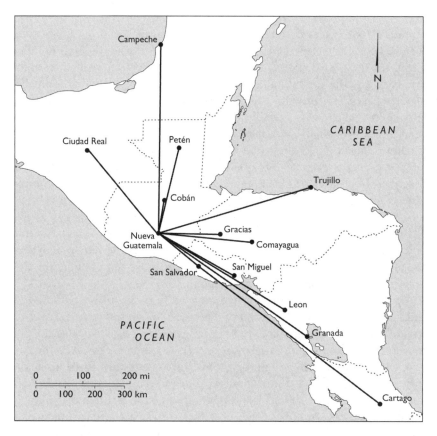

MAP 3.2. Representation of 1793 table, showing destinations of the Guatemalan mail

descriptor, "progression," suggests a hierarchical, radial organization: a central place connected to subordinate locations by paced intervals.

The itinerary sections in Ateaga's chart further establish relative importance by designating certain places as destinations and others as merely transit points. A picture emerges of one central place—Guatemala City—surrounded (or rather followed) by a constellation of second-tier places. This hierarchy of place is reflected even more explicitly in Larrazábal's 1772 list of places. The document heads each sublist of towns and villages with a principal place, which can be a "valle," "provincia," "partida," or "villa."[78] Every place is subsumed by the hierarchy and defined by its place in it.

The more interesting aspect of hierarchically organized place reflected in the tables is the manner of rendering unnamed space invisible. Terrain surrounding these listed places is suggested only indirectly by the league-measures; specific places beyond those listed are negated. The itinerary-as-list does not even allow for "blank spots," as would appear on an aerial map.[79] It simply makes them impossible to see. Instead, the itinerary draws attention to the places themselves and, indirectly, the route connecting them. The route appears not as a line or a ribbon of road but as a number.

Space, then, is depicted as a network of measured segments, some originating in the capital and others originating in important cities farther afield. These segments, the crucial ligatures linking places along the Guatemalan postal routes, are leagues, listed in Ateaga's charts as numbers. As the leagues are not defined, it is at first glance impossible to know what version of *legua* the Guatemalan official utilized. By visualizing the itineraries, however, it becomes clear that the mail officials surely used the *legua* described by Chardon as comprehending the distance covered in an hour. Indeed, without such a definition, many portions of the 1793 itineraries seem preposterous. The route from Guatemala to Petén (Figure 3.2), for example, lists an interval of 18 *leguas* for Guatemala to San Raimundo and 10 *leguas* from San Raimundo to Salamá. On a modern map, however, the distance from San Raimundo to Salamá is more than double the distance from Guatemala to San Raimundo.

Without knowing the precise road traveled from one place to another, it is difficult to discount the possibility that a very circuitous road for the first part of the journey—measured only in terms of spatial distance—accounts for its exaggerated length in relation to the second part. However, the two segments of the journey lying between San Agustín and San Luis make this possibility unlikely. (See Map 3.3.) The interval between San Agustín and Cahabón (then Cahbon) is 8 leagues, despite the fact that it is roughly three-quarters the length (as the crow flies) of the 62-league interval between Cahabón and San Luis. When we consider the additional fact that the previous interval between Cobán and San Agustín is also 8 leagues but

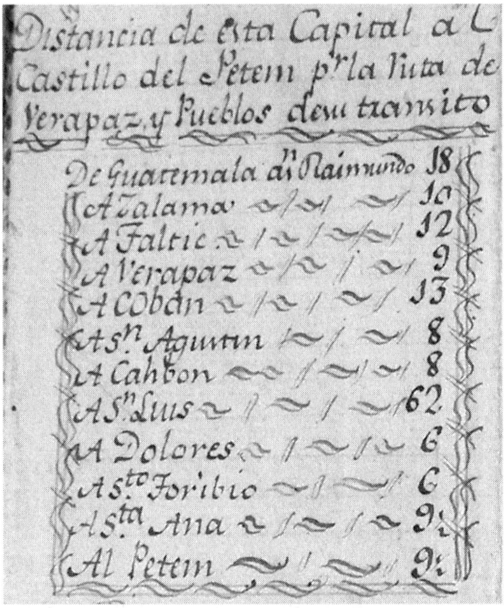

Distancia de esta Capital al
Castillo del Petén por la ruta de
Verapaz y Pueblos de su tránsito

De Guatemala a Raimundo — 18
a Zalamá — 10
A Taltic — 12
A Verapaz — 9
A Cobán — 13
a Sn Agustín — 8
a Cahbon — 8
A Sn Luis — 62
a Dolores — 6
a Sto Toribio — 6
a Sta Ana — 9½
Al Petén — 9½

FIGURE 3.2. Portion of 1793 chart showing the route to Petén
Source: Archivo General de Centroamérica. Photograph by the author.

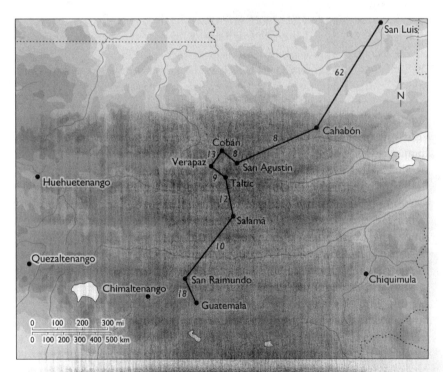

MAP 3.3. The 1793 route from Guatemala to Petén

spatially less than a quarter of the San Agustín-Cahabón interval, the solution becomes clear.

The route from San Agustín to Cahabón plummets downhill dramatically, as the highlands of the Verapazes (between 1,500 and 2,100 meters above sea level) descend into the lowlands (Cahabón sits at less than 300 meters above sea level). In contrast, the journey from Cobán to San Agustín follows a less dramatic but still noticeable rise (between 900–1,500, rising to 1,500 to 2,100), and the terrain between Cahabón and San Luis is mostly flat. If *leguas* were only a measure of spatial distance and apparent inconsistencies were due only to windy roads, the doubtlessly circuitous descent from San Agustín to Cahabón would register as relatively long, not dramatically short. The only way to account for the reckoning of *leguas* is to consider them as expressions of spatial distance over time: "the distance covered by a mule in an hour," or some like definition.[80] Distance, in this conception, clearly signifies places along routes divided by space-time intervals.

If *leguas* are thought of as quantifying both space and time in this context, the tables take on a different aspect. Visual representations of the routes such as the maps presented here *distort* distance, since "distance," in the mail administrator's terms, encapsulates the temporal as well as the spatial. Visual depictions serve only to artificially constrain the itineraries to one dimension and thereby, paradoxically, flatten them. The more accurate depiction renders both variables at once without privileging one or the other. An official who consulted a visual map of the *reino* would determine very little about when correspondence might reach its destination. By perusing the 1793 and 1795 tables, however, he would be able to glance at the first line and know at once that if the *correo* rode for ten hours a day, he would get the trunk of mail from Guatemala to San Salvador in less than a week.

This conclusion suggests that the temporal-spatial measure was more than a mere matter of convenience or an imperfect alternative in the absence of formal maps. Archbishop Cortés y Larraz used his watch, as he implied, out of necessity. Similarly, the instructions sent for geographical reports recommended relying on temporal measures when reliable spatial measures were impossible. But the mail documents suggest that for the particular conditions in Guatemala, the temporal-spatial measure was more than a measure of last resort. Leagues that accounted for time as well as space actually quantified Guatemalan distances more accurately, and tables and lists thereby represented Guatemalan distances best.

Such a conclusion also helps to more fully render the conception of peripheries—those places lying at a great distance—in the Spanish empire. To be distant entailed being temporally, as well as spatially, remote. The table prepared by Larrazábal reveals starkly the cost of overcoming such temporal-spatial obstacles. Governing a periphery from the center, that is communicating with its officials and staying appraised of its happenings, was costly and time-consuming. And it was fraught with physical inconveniences and dangers; communication with places like Verapaz, Petén, and Costa Rica was only as reliable as the men who carried correspondence there and back.

4 Taking It to the Periphery

OVERLAND MAIL CARRIERS

> I, Blas Cabrera, his majesty's mail carrier, with all due re-
> spect . . . state: That the receipt here enclosed . . . by the
> Administrator of the mail in this kingdom, proves that I
> delivered to the office in his care the closed mail trunk con-
> taining the correspondence from land and sea pertaining to
> the roundtrip journey that I undertook to Oaxaca.[1]
> —Blas Cabrera, official mail carrier, 1773

The *correos*, or mail carriers, of late eighteenth and early nineteenth century Guatemala covered hundreds of leagues on foot and on horseback. Traveling as far north as Oaxaca and as far south as Costa Rica, they passed through cities, Indian towns, and long stretches of uninhabited terrain. Some *correos* served the postal system for fifteen or twenty years, journeying across Guatemala almost monthly. But even those who worked as *correos* for less time engaged in far more long-distance travel than the average person in colonial Guatemala. They experienced the journey to distant peripheries more often than others. Sources about *correos* therefore not only document how the peripheries were reached; they also offer a far more textured impression of what reaching the peripheries actually entailed.

The first three sections of this chapter focus on these *correos* in the colonial period, considering who they were, what their work required, and how their extensive travels informed a particular conception of distance. These shed light on the economic motivations, social violence, and interethnic relationships that marked the *correo* experience. The last section of the chapter considers *correo* travel in the context of the early nineteenth century, when a changing conception of distance redefined space, place, and political boundaries for Guatemalan society as a whole.

Carrying the mail in late colonial Guatemala demanded of *correos* a continual balancing act. The dangers of the road—insufficient supplies, injury, banditry, inclement weather—could result in illness, assault, or even death. *Correo* travel consequently required a certain mettle, and as it tipped toward bravado, this necessary willingness to confront danger frequently brought its own, equally dangerous kind of peril. Officially, *correos* worked for the Spanish crown, but they often intentionally or unintentionally worked against it. They were on occasion arrested in late colonial Guatemala for insulting officials, for attacking people on the road, or for unduly harassing the residents of Indian towns. These arrests could end a correo's career and take him off the road for good. Working as a *correo* also required a certain willingness to engage in financial risk, as payment barely covered the cost of travel and was, in any case, often difficult to extract from the central office. *Correos* found themselves attempting to supplement their income in ways that could also put them on the wrong side of the law.

The experience of long-distance travel under these conditions necessarily contrasted sharply with that of people like Archbishop Cortés y Larraz, who traveled rarely and with an entourage. But the overall conception of the Guatemalan landscape remained the same. Central, urban places were more tightly governed and more predictably disciplined. The routes or corridors leading away from them to some degree preserved these characteristics. But the greater the distance traveled into remote peripheries, the weaker the governing presence of the law. Dangerous and profitable in varying proportions, distance for *correos* was on every occasion a high-stakes gamble. While they may have measured distance in ordinary leagues, *correos* understood those leagues in terms of undeniable, often unpredictable, costs.

The Guía: Documentation on Correo Travel

Who were these men, the overland mail carriers of the Americas? For the period prior to the formation of the official mail system, little documentation exists on the travel of *correos* and almost none exists on *correos* themselves, and documenting their identity is challenging. It is certain that Indians were pressed into service as early as 1681 and likely earlier.[2] They continued to form the backbone of the mail system, especially in the highlands and southern Mexico, well into the early nineteenth century. As discussed in Chapter 3, a motley crew of travelers, soldiers, and Indians serviced some routes. Joseph Melchor de Ugalde, the Guatemalan mail administrator in 1770, provides a more specific appraisal of such characters:

If the need arises to send mail during the interval between the monthly mail deliveries, it should be sent by special courier, because while using couriers is more expensive than using militia to carry the mail, the following fact deserves consideration: from here to Zacapa there are daily twenty men who wait with no other motive than to await the chance of carrying a piece of mail, and if there is a regular mail on this route, it might happen that these men will wait a year or more before having occasion to carry a single letter. And while it is true that these are mulattoes, who do not pay tribute and in no other way recognize our sovereign king, it is also the case that almost all of them are miserable, naked wretches.[3]

The picture Melchor de Ugalde conjures up of men waiting along the main roads is suggestive. While we have no way of knowing how widespread this may have been, the description indicates a more than occasional expectation on the part of unofficial carriers. Despite Melchor de Ugalde's recommendations, such "miserable, naked wretches" were gradually supplanted by official mail carriers after 1770. The practice of passing the mail from one person to another along segments of certain routes was replaced by the practice of sending a single carrier along the length of the route.[4]

Even before the incorporation of the mail, an informal distinction was always made between *correos de a pie*—those who traveled on foot—and *correos de a caballo*—those who traveled on horseback. By the late eighteenth century, a clear categorical separation is apparent in the documentation between the *indios correos*, Indian mail carriers who travel on foot, and the *mestizo* or Spanish *correos* who travel on horseback. The few cases that identify *correos'* background in the eighteenth century showcase carriers who were mostly in their twenties or thirties (though one remarkable correo carried mail into his seventies) and were tradesmen—tailors, weavers, and carpenters—for whom carrying the mail became a second profession.[5]

While documentation on the identity of *correos* is scant, there is relatively more information on *correo* travel. Whether they traveled on foot or on horseback, early *correos* traveled as *correos extraordinarios*, or special-delivery couriers, and they traveled with a document called a *guía*, or register, that served the functions of permit, travel log, and delivery confirmation sheet. The official at the point of origin wrote the *correo's* name, his date and time of departure, and the packages of correspondence he carried. As the *correo* progressed along his route, officials at each point signed the register with the date and time, acknowledging receipt of the mail. Thus in its ideal form, the *guía* is a composite document that reflects accurately each detail of the *correo's* journey.

This document form continued in use after the formation of the official mail system, though few examples of it survive. Unless the *correo's* journey became the focus of a legal dispute, the *guía* was discarded. However, after the formation of the official mail system, other documents came into use, allowing a broader view into *correo* travel. Logbooks recorded the departure and arrival times of *correos* to Mexico and the provinces. As the employees of the postal system came under the protection of a special *fuero* (exemption from prosecution in ordinary civil or criminal courts), their activities produced a growing body of correspondence and legal cases. And, increasingly, *correos* themselves found voice in official documentation by demanding pay, testifying as to the conditions of their travel, and weighing in on disputes about the administration of the system.

The *correo guía* continued to offer the most reliable, if not the most detailed, description of how a *correo* traveled. The case of Blas Cabrera, a *correo* who traveled the Oaxaca route, is illustrative. The opening page of the register provides information about the author of the document and the *correo*'s departure:

Don Simón de Larrazábal, appointed by his Majesty Principal Administrator of the Royal Mail in this Kingdom: I send Blas Cabrera, his Majesty's mail carrier on horseback, to travel roundtrip from this Capital to the City of Oaxaca, with the trunk that contains the Document Packets of the Crown and the General correspondence of the Public, which he will deliver successively to the Administrators at each postal office he passes until reaching the city of Oaxaca. The Administrator in Oaxaca, as well as those along the route, will note the date and time at which they receive and dispatch the mail carrier, and on his return they will do the same until he returns to this Administration in my charge. And on behalf of his Majesty I order and require, and for my part I beg and charge the Magistrates, Officials, District Governors, or their officers of whichever towns he passes through to provide the said Blas Cabrera with all the supplies and pack animals necessary, as well as all the assistance he may ask for or require, so that there is not the smallest delay in the execution of this service so important to the Crown and the Public.[6]

Larrazábal goes on to list the packages of correspondence, which on this occasion—the first of December of 1772—were destined for Totonicapan, Quetzaltenango, Chiapas, Ciudad Real, Teguantepeque, Oaxaca, Puebla, Mexico, Jalapa, and Veracruz, this last including a package for Havana. Blas Cabrera arrived in Tuxtla on the seventh of December; the official there signed him in at nine in the evening and signed him out at nine-thirty. He arrived the following day at five in the afternoon in Teguantepeque and left half an hour later. Arriving in Oaxaca on the thirteenth at eleven in the morning, he deposited the remaining packages and waited three days to collect the return mail. He departed for Guatemala at midnight on the night of the sixteenth. After stopping at his destinations on the route back, Cabrera arrived in Guatemala on the twenty-seventh of December at eleven in the evening. The *guía* gives a clear sense of the journey's duration, and it makes evident that *correos* frequently traveled at night. It further indicates that stopovers in the towns along the route were brief—as short as half an hour. Like the geographical descriptions discussed in Chapters 1 and 2, the *guía* was built along a route. While providing an overall arc for the *correo*'s journey, however, the *guía* has little to say about the conditions of travel and the misadventures that occurred along the way.

The Profits of Distance

The *guía* for Blas Cabrera's journey to Mexico became one crucial document among many in a drawn-out administrative dispute, and the case as a whole offers some insights into the dilemmas of distance often confronted by Guatemalan *correos*. A resident of Guatemala City, Cabrera presumably planned to rest when he returned to the capital on December 27, 1772. As it happened, he did not have the opportunity to rest for long; the moment he arrived in Guatemala, city officials pounced on him. They had heard rumors before his arrival that Cabrera was illegally carrying two packages of clothing imported from China and destined for none other than Simón de Larrazábal, the administrator of the postal system.[7]

The debate over whether *correos* were permitted to carry *encomiendas*—parcels with items other than documents—raged throughout the late colonial period, and the central issue at stake was profit. Categorically different from *arrieros*, the muleteers who carried goods along Spanish American overland routes, *correos* were never intended to carry bulky or voluminous items. Muleteers traveled many of the same routes, but as the backbone of the overland trade system they journeyed with mule-trains and worked closely with merchants in Spanish American cities and ports. *Correos*, in contrast, were assigned to carry documents as their first and principal priority.[8] But everyone recognized the potential afforded by the *correos'* long-distance travel. Officials in urban centers, individual *correos*, and villages along the routes all stood to profit from the passage of the mail, but a continual and conflictive negotiation persisted over who would profit more. The carrying of *encomiendas* raised the prospect of additional gains or losses. On the one hand, *encomiendas* provided *correos* with extra income and individuals who could afford them with much-coveted goods. And it simply made good sense to send a vital packet of medicine to an ailing relative or a yard of lace to a friend with the only person reliably traveling to a given destination. On the other hand, *correos* were not always moderate; *encomiendas* sometimes ballooned from a handful of precious packets to a mule-load of heavy crates. They threatened to delay the mail by slowing the *correo's* pace; as discussed below, they purportedly placed an excessive burden on Indian towns along the route; and in certain cases they defrauded the government by circumventing customs. For these reasons, the carrying of *encomiendas* was formally prohibited with the incorporation of the mail. In practice, however, *correos* continued to carry them with the tacit approval of administrators.

In the 1770s, the dispute grew particularly acrimonious as it became evident that many of the parcels carried by *correos* were destined for high-ranking officials in the city and the provinces. One illustrative and much

belabored case concerned a crate of grapes carried all the way from León
in Nicaragua to the homes of Lieutenant Colonel Domingo Cavello and
Audiencia President Martín de Mayorga in Guatemala City. Though he
should not have been carrying the grapes in the first place, *correo* José
Rivera had difficulty exonerating himself with these august personages
for his decision to abandon the grapes—rotted well before his arrival in
Guatemala—along the route.[9] Officials such as these had much to gain
from sending and receiving the occasional *encomienda,* which almost always consisted of luxury or specialty goods unavailable in Guatemala. The
Bourbon administration's fiscal reforms beginning in 1763 (and nearly co-
inciding with the reform of the mail system) had the effect of significantly
raising sales taxes in Guatemala on all imported goods. The *alcabala,* or
sales tax, rose and fell during the 1760s, as the powerful merchants of
Guatemala City battled the tax hike, and application of the tax was gradual and uneven across the region. Nonetheless, the unavoidable result was
that goods carried by *arrieros* could no longer be received legally in Guatemala City without paying the *alcabala,* and receiving parcels through the
correo thereby became one simple, if unreliable, way of dodging the tax.[10]

The others who stood to gain from carrying parcels were *correos* themselves. *Correo* Mateo Lopez, apprehended in 1805 for carrying *encomiendas,*
might have made a substantial profit from the fifty items he carried to Guatemala, which included numerous rolls of fine lace, four pounds of chocolate,
a barometer, packets of cigars, half a pound of cinnamon, four nutmegs, a
pound of medicinal herbs, two packets of arsenic, copper sulfate, and two
lumps of opium.[11] *Correos* had insisted from the inception of the mail system that their pay was insufficient; accepting *encomienda* commissions was
a much-needed way of supplementing their income. In one of the documents
added to the Blas Cabrera dispute, Cabrera himself demanded the 170 *pesos*
he was owed for his round-trip journey to Oaxaca. Yet a payment schedule
from 1778 indicates that the payment to a *correo* traveling to Oaxaca on
horseback should have been more—about 289 *pesos.*[12] The continual complaints and demands made by *correos* throughout the colonial period suggest that they were often short-changed.[13] A detailed estimate of travel costs
prepared by three *correos* in 1784 puts the total cost of transportation for a
round trip to Oaxaca at more than 146 *pesos.*[14] The *correos* maintained that
without even accounting for food, these expenses exceeded their payment.
Complaints from other places in Guatemala tend to bear out the *correos'*
argument. A plaintive letter from the *correos* of Costa Rica written in 1787
suggests that if anything, the longer and more marginal routes were even less
adequately compensated. "Until today," they wrote, "we and our predeces-
sors have been paid fifteen *pesos* for our work along each monthly mail
route it being our responsibility to supply the Mule for the long passage of

more than one hundred and fifty leagues." However, travel along this route took a significant toll on the cargo animals. The *correos* pointed out that "if the Beast is incapacitated on the route, as often occurs, the cost of leasing a mule grows even greater." Worse still, "if it should occur as is sometimes the case that the Beast should die while we are walking—this occurs mainly during the winter because of the poor roads—then the owners ask us for thirty or even thirty-five *pesos* and on top of this the four *pesos* for the lease." The *correos* concluded that even when the mules did not die, the fifteen *peso* salary was woefully inadequate.[15] Whether leased or purchased, cargo animals did not come cheap. The *correos* thereby often incurred debts of their own to pay for transportation and supplies. For *correos* on many routes, carrying only documents—the correspondence of the government and the public— was simply not profitable. Carrying *encomiendas* proved to be the only reliable way of making the journey lucrative.

Allowing *correos* to carry *encomiendas* could potentially work well for the mail system administrators as well. By effectively passing off the cost of the *correo*'s journey to individuals willing to pay for luxury items, medicine, and imported goods, the administration could keep the *correo*'s wages low. For this reason administrators like Larrazábal tended to support *correos* in their campaign to carry *encomiendas*. Larrazábal and other mail officials in Guatemala maintained that the practice of carrying parcels "fuera de valija," or outside of the official mail trunk, dated back to the Guatemalan mail's inception in 1620.[16] Larrazábal insisted that he was doing nothing new by turning a blind eye, claiming that "the practice of carrying and delivering permissible parcels has always been allowed."[17] Administrators could also point to the fact that in 1766, the practice was even formalized to the extent that a set fee was determined for the carrying of *encomiendas* to the provinces: six *reales* per pound to Leon, Comayagua, and Tegucigalpa and four *reales* per pound to San Salvador, San Vicente, and San Miguel.[18]

On the other hand, however, administrators had also to reckon with the potentially detrimental consequences of carrying *encomiendas*, the greatest of which was a tendency to retard the *correo*'s journey. Though in 1773 Larrazábal excused the practice by pointing out that Blas Cabrera had returned from Oaxaca with his *encomiendas* of Chinese cloth two days earlier than expected, Cabrera's load of roughly eighty pounds was lighter than some.[19] Mateo Lopez, for example, carried with him many bulky items on his 1805 journey. Among his parcels were 70 containers of wire, 166 panes of glass from Puebla, and 45 jars of salt from England.[20] And José Rivera, the *correo* embroiled in the grape controversy, eventually lost his employment in 1805 over delays caused by excessive *encomiendas*. Already in his seventies, Rivera perhaps misjudged how much his mule would be able to carry. The administrator in San Salvador complained that "Jose Ribera arrived in this city yesterday the twenty-sixth of the month at ten in the evening being delayed more than a day and a half, according to the route schedule, and he was carrying an excessive load of two-hundred and seventy-five pounds and separately on the shoulders of an Indian sixty-six sacks."[21] The weight and size of the *encomiendas* were such that the pack animal fell several times. Rivera was fired, and the limitations on carrying *encomiendas* were once again reinforced.

The other argument leveled against Larrazábal in 1773 and the *encomienda* practice generally was that it placed an excessive burden on Indian towns along the route. When Larrazábal had the audacity to break the *encomienda* prohibition merely to acquire luxury goods (the Chinese textiles were reportedly for his mother-in-law), the *Oidor Decano* of Guatemala, Don Juan González Bustillo, took the matter into his own hands.[22] He protested that "the Administrator of the Mail should be the most vigilant, precise and punctual in obeying the resolutions of the Crown," but instead of preventing the problematic delays, Larrazábal contributed most to the problem by undermining the mail carriers' regulations. And, he added, the "well-known burden placed by the mail carriers upon the Indian Towns along the route is no small matter, for it is they who provide the mail carriers with mules for their cargo and for themselves." As Bustillo indicated in his letter, these supplies were in theory to be paid for by the *correo* according to predetermined fees (*arancel*); for most of the late colonial period the rate of compensation was half a *real* per league.[23] But, he wrote, "even if they are properly paid according the fee schedule (which I highly doubt), this payment is hardly adequate compensation for the extraordinary amount of work and the degree of danger to which the mules are exposed, conditions which lead to significant deterioration if not complete loss of life."[24] In practice, *correos* often abused the animals, or underpaid for their supplies, or demanded more than the town could provide. When the fees were raised to one *real* per league, the mail administrator complained on behalf of the *correos*, claiming that the correct fees were never actually observed.[25] "Even when the mail service was not run by the crown, the Indians were never paid according to the fee schedule," he insisted. Rather, their assistance to the *correo* was "based on their clear and implicit consent, which has existed from time immemorial and which was evident in the spontaneous generosity of their ancestors observed by the Conquistadors."[26] This complaint resulted in an informal sanction from the administration in Spain, effectively condoning the practice of underpaying the Indian towns for the *correos*' supplies. Needless to say, the Indian towns must have viewed their supposed "spontaneous generosity" toward the *conquistador* and the *correo* differently.

The relationship between the *correo* and the Indian towns along his route was a difficult and often exploitative one. As early as 1764, when the original regulations for the official mail were released in Spain, *correos* were explicitly enjoined not to delay their journey or overburden Indian towns by demanding extra transportation for goods or merchandise. It was ordered that "mail carriers should travel lightly, and should not demand of the Indians more pack animals than are necessary for carrying Letters." Nor, the regulations warned, should they subject them to the "troublesome delays which his Majesty has been informed currently occur when certain said mail carriers exploit their station to play the role of merchants."[27] Many towns along the route claimed to find the passage of the *correo* so taxing that they asked to be excused from any obligation to provide him with supplies. While the town could potentially earn income by providing mules and a *tayacan* (guide), for many the gain seemed not worthwhile. The town of Acala on the route to Oaxaca cited the "misery and calamitous state" of their town in requesting exemption. "As the town of Acala falls on the King's highway," they explained, "and as we are therefore obliged by law to provide food and supplies to travelers, and as this last obligation is indispensable, we ask only that we be excused providing for the monthly mail." Excusing them would be as much a benefit to the crown as it would be to Acala, they argued, pointing out that "it has happened many times that since we do not have sufficient animals to provide him with, he has had to proceed on the route by foot, at great detriment to his Majesty."[28] As Acala's appeal makes clear, travelers of every kind could request (and pay for) supplies according to the *arancel*, but towns along the *camino real* had a particular obligation to the *correo* that often exceeded their means. Relationships with the mail system as a whole, if not with the individual *correo*, were developed over time, and the administration came to expect consistent services from certain towns.[29] Other, similar complaints from the same period indicate that the *correo* frequently took advantage of his position to demand extra supplies not only to accommodate his *encomiendas* but to provide for traveling companions. A *correo* traveling in the vicinity of Lake Atitlán in 1786 demanded supplies for his friends, and when the Indians of the town resisted he attacked them with his riding whip. According to the complaint, such conduct was not uncommon. What is worse, the passage of the *correo* along a given route gave other travelers the opportunity to impersonate the *correo*—usually by tooting a horn upon entry to the town—and demand supplies in his stead. Towns lying on the *correo*'s path had consequently to suffer the double burden of the exacting *correo* and his fraudulent imitators.[30]

Angering the Indian towns along the mail route was decidedly not to the administration's benefit, since the towns provided not only supplies but the crucial guides who led the *correo* along his route. Routes changed over time (and according to the season), making it essential that the *correo* travel with someone who knew the current route and was informed of its particular travel conditions.[31] Certain routes were famously difficult to travel, and in discussing alternatives officials had necessarily to rely on the expertise of Indian guides. The route to Totonicapán, for example, plagued travelers and *correos* continually, and one exasperated official finally suggested changing the route, declaring that, "both have assured me that there is a path known to the Indians, and also to a few Ladinos and Spaniards, by which it is possible to avoid not only this Peak but also Hunger Peak and the infamous Slab Peak."[32] But the precise location of the alternate path was difficult to pinpoint. It was true that a Franciscan, Brother Josef Antonio Sánchez, had traveled the route twice in the company of Indians, and he could confirm that the path was a far easier route to travel than the principal road. But he could not locate the path on his own. The former *alcalde* of Totonicapán, Don Geraldino, had also tried to find it, but, it was reported, "the Indians who were leading him misled him, and got him lost on purpose." The officials proposed different hypotheses as to why the Indians were so secretive: "according to some they did this out of fear that if the King's highway were rerouted along that path it would harm their crops and pastures which they have nearby, or, say others, because they wanted to avoid having to work on building a New road as they were obliged to do in the repairs of the road through Slab Peak." Whatever the reason, Don Geraldino had to return without having accomplished his objective of discovering the secret route.[33] Believing there was much to gain from exploiting the new route, officials in the city demanded that it be located and integrated into the *camino real*. The Indians were duly compelled to identify the path, and as construction on the route began, the *alcalde* confirmed that their concern had been losing the safety of their farmland and pasture.

The motivation the Indians had for hiding the route from Don Francisco Geraldino was this: the Indians have their grazing pasture and ranches in this place, and it is here that they keep their livestock safe from robbers, and they say this will no longer be the case once the road is built and that they will have to evacuate the area. In addition, it upsets the Indians and Ladinos of Sololá that where this route travels downhill to meet the King's highway (near the town of Concepción) it passes through an open expanse about two leagues long, and it is here that the *Naturales* and *vecinos* have planted their crops; if the route is opened through there they will have to cut through good farmland and lose eighteen or more feet of it.[34]

Moments of dispute like this one reveal the other perspective on "dangerous distances" observed by Cortés y Larraz. The freedom he lamented as perilous because it avoided the rule of law clearly had benefits for some.

Almost everyone stood to profit from the new route other than the Indians who had kept the path secret and who soon found themselves working on its construction, destroying their safe pasture in the process. The new route avoided the perilous peaks that had so inconvenienced travelers and *correos* in the past, and as such it benefited not only the mail system but all those who relied on the King's highway. It also economized three to four leagues and almost two hours of travel. Thus the mail system profited greatly from exploiting the hidden path; it could be assured that the new route would bring with it more reliable and more timely mail delivery.

Just how much the royal mail in Guatemala profited in financial terms during these years is somewhat difficult to determine. Consistent data on revenues and expenditures is not available for any year prior to 1810. A report produced in 1804 on the mail service's income over the 1782 to 1803 period suggests significant growth, despite the wartime curtailments in maritime service. From 1782 to 1792, the Guatemalan office brought in roughly 1,760,800 *reales*, while from the 1793 to 1803 period it brought in roughly 2,443,531 *reales*.[35] Since the *correo* paid his travel expenses out of pocket, the mail service's only substantial expense lay in salaries. In the 1790s, the monthly expenditures on salaries for *correos* and scribes averaged only about 450 *pesos*.[36] The central office in Guatemala City had four employees—the administrator, the bookkeeper, the administrator's assistant, and the office boy—and ran on 3,000 *pesos* a year, with the administrator's salary accounting for half of this amount.[37] Detailed accounts for the mid-1790s indicate that after paying salaries and other minor expenses, quarterly profits could range from 5,000 to more than 12,000 *pesos*.[38] To all appearances, the Guatemalan mail service was making a substantial profit.

The administrators throughout the late colonial period were aware, however, that the royal mail was not making as much money as it could have been making. As mentioned previously in Chapter 3, the general public's stubborn insistence on sending private couriers, or what the mail administrators termed *correos clandestinos* (clandestine mail), undoubtedly robbed the royal mail of substantial income. Clandestine mail was defined broadly to include any correspondence not carried by the official *correo* in "la valija cerrada"—the closed trunk. Letters sent with friends and travelers were perhaps considered less egregious because they robbed the crown of less income, but they were equally illegal. Believing initially that a steep fine would dissuade individuals from sending their mail privately, administrators set the fine very high—at 500 *pesos*. However, the fine proved singularly ineffective in deterring the practice of sending clandestine mail. The traffic of clandestine mail continued unabated throughout the colonial period, despite the administration's attempt to create more post offices for people in inaccessible areas. As with the sending of *encomiendas*, mail officials were vexed to discover that many of the individuals sending or receiving clandestine mail were of dismayingly high status. In fact, in 1779 a man was imprisoned for carrying clandestine mail to Archbishop Cortés y Larraz.[39] The cases of *correos clandestinos* are filled with clergy, military officers, or other people of good social standing who decided to circumvent the official mail system.[40]

Encomiendas and clandestine mail alike were usually spotted by a guard at the checkpoint outside of a city, and if the observations of the guard at the San Salvador checkpoint were at all representative, the sending of clandestine mail was a regular occurrence. Juan Cestona reported in an 1805 letter that "counting only the towns in the immediate surroundings of the City, private mail carriers are sent almost daily."[41] In the same year, Faustino de Capetillo, the interim administrator in Guatemala, recommended dropping the fine to 25 *pesos*, as the 500 *peso* fine proved impossible to collect. "Since the year 1780," he wrote, "when I first took office, numerous cases of clandestine mail have passed across my desk, and despite the efforts made by those of us in this office we have not succeeded in collecting more than two of the owed fines."[42] The new fine, eventually set at 50 *pesos*, would be split three ways between the mail administration, the judge who heard the case, and the individual who denounced the clandestine mail. The administration would not earn much, but it would still earn more than it would have in postage.

As long as the fines were paid, then, the mail system stood to profit even from the passage of clandestine mail. In the ongoing negotiation over who would profit most from the mail service, the administrators—and therefore the crown—were the clear winners. Earning substantial profits from postage even during times of decreased traffic, the Guatemalan office kept its costs low, passing much of the burden on to the *correos* and to the Indian towns that sustained them. While the *correos* may have found opportunities to turn an occasional profit by carrying *encomiendas*, Indian towns had few such opportunities. Proportional to their means, they shouldered the greatest financial costs of carrying the mail.

The Cost of Distance

Looking beyond the purely financial costs, however, *correos* stood to lose just as much. While the towns could lose pasture and farmland to a new route or valuable livestock to the *correo*'s carelessness, the *correo* risked his health, his personal safety, and his job on every journey. If the hardships of the road themselves did not end a *correo*'s career, avoiding them often did. Blas Cabrera might have made a small profit from his journey to Oaxaca, had the Chinese cloth not been discovered. As it was, he had to pester the beleaguered Larrazábal for payment of the official mail, and he probably received no payment for the confiscated *encomiendas*. Instead, he received continual visits from city officials attempting to pinpoint the source of the Chinese textiles. Eventually Guatemala City got too hot for Cabrera, and from one day to the next he vanished. Larrazábal sent the other *correos* to Cabrera's house six times in the effort to locate him, but they reported that Cabrera and his wife had simply disappeared.[43]

Blas Cabrera likely knew that many a *correo* had not only lost his job but ended up in jail for getting on the wrong side of officials in Guatemala City. As familiarity with the *fuero* resulted in more paperwork involving *correos* being forwarded to the central administration, the archives amassed a sizeable collection of colorful cases.[44] *Correos* were arrested not only for complications with *encomiendas*, but for trading insults with local officials, for drunkenness, for assault, for carrying illegal arms, and in some cases simply for failing to finish their route. While the genesis of many of these cases can be attributed largely to the preoccupations of Bourbon reformers, they are nevertheless reliable insights into the experiences of *correos*. In other words, the sociopolitical circumstances of late eighteenth century Guatemala were responsible for complicating, and in some cases criminalizing, certain actions and behaviors intrinsic to the *correos'* circumstances.

The most likely penalty facing *correos* was incarceration for inability to finish a route. In some cases this inability was directly attributable to the high travel costs. The *correos* in Costa Rica who protested their insufficient salaries often simply did not have the funds to complete their journey. They were placed in an impossible situation when local officials threatened to imprison them for failure to reach the end of their route.[45] In other cases the *correo* fell ill and had to choose among several bad alternatives: he could continue the route, despite being ill; he could wait to feel better and risk delaying his arrival; he could entrust the mail to another person. Most *correos* chose the first alternative, jeopardizing their health even more in the process. Benito Arrevillaga, a *correo* for the provinces in the 1790s, forced himself to travel in such poor health that he died before reaching his destination.

He began his route in good health, but having arrived in the City of San Salvador, he felt quite ill as I am told by the Administrator, and he did not wish to abandon the journey. Nor did he wish to do so in San Miguel, where he arrived in even worse shape, and without pausing he continued on with the goal of reaching León. But after walking the connecting route, which is about forty-five leagues long, without taking any sustenance whatsoever, he arrived in the Town of Viejo unable to go any farther. There was time to do nothing more than prepare himself for death and receive the sacraments; he died immediately.[46]

The administrator in Guatemala lamented that "this mail carrier has been one of the most respected and accomplished in the Service, a man who with his dedication to work supported a wife and four children," and he recommended giving the family a small allowance.[47] As the account of Arrevillaga's journey makes clear, portions of the route could be grueling, even for a healthy traveler. Relying on the calculations established in Chapter 3, by which a league might be understood as the distance traveled in an hour, forty-five leagues would entail nearly two days of uninterrupted travel. A forty-five league stretch without food would have been taxing regardless of Arrevillaga's condition, and the route to the provinces was replete with such obstacles. Manuel de Mella, sent along the same route to León in 1778, nearly lost his life paddling a leaky canoe out of Conchagua.[48] With long, uninhabited stretches and waterways subject to flooding, the route to León was dangerous under any circumstances. These examples demonstrate vividly how peripheral Guatemalan peripheries really were. Reaching them required a significant investment of funds, time, and energy.

Other *correos* who fell ill chose to wait or hand off the mail trunk rather than imperil their health by continuing. José Romero, a thirty-five-year-old *español* who traveled the route to Oaxaca, initially attempted to follow Arrevillaga's example by continuing to travel while ill. He left Oaxaca in late 1803 with a fever and chest pains, and when he arrived in San Lucas he was unable to continue. He entrusted the mail trunk to officials in San Lucas and returned to Oaxaca for medical attention. Once he had recovered, he returned to Guatemala, where he was promptly arrested for having left the mail trunk "abandoned to the Indians" on the Oaxaca route. The administrator in Guatemala insisted that he should have returned to Oaxaca *with* the trunk and there enlisted the help of the Oaxacan mail administrator. Romero pleaded that he had done what he could, and indeed there seems to have been no good option between delaying the mail by returning to Oaxaca with the trunk or "abandoning" the mail by entrusting it to Indian officials. Romero enlisted the support of the physician who had treated him in Oaxaca, and the officials in Guatemala City finally relented, ordering him to be set free in mid-April 1804, on the condition that he pay a 100-*peso* fine. Utterly unable to pay the fine, however, Romero was forced to remain in jail. After spending four months in jail, Romero begged for six months' time in which to pay off his debt. He had been compelled to sell even his clothes in order to pay for his food in prison, and he was entirely without means. A relative, Manuel Romero, mortgaged his home in order to guarantee the debt, and José Romero was set free. Unfortunately, in 1805, the debt remained unpaid.[49]

It is likely that officials in Guatemala City viewed José Romero and other *correos* who fell ill with skepticism because some "sick" *correos* were actually drunk. Indian towns and provincial officials complained repeatedly of the behavior of drunk *correos*, who disrupted town life in more ways than one. In 1791, *correo* Miguel Custodio was found lying by the side of the road outside of Nejapa, seemingly drunk, while the Indian guide stood by with the animals. The *alguacil* of Nejapa, who found them, escorted Miguel Custodio into town in order to sober him up with food, but upon arriving Custodio began raving that someone had stolen his firearm and his bedroll. He grew so agitated that he pulled out his knife and wounded the *governador.* Custodio was arrested, and the story he gave in his defense echoed that given by many other correos. He had left Guatemala in somewhat precarious health and had worsened on the route to León. After taking the medicine prescribed to him, *vinagre de Castilla* and *limonada* (vinegar and lemonade), he had rapidly improved. But on the return trip he had fallen ill once again.

In the Port of Conchagua he had a recurrence of the pain that he had first experienced leaving this Capital city, and he carried it while walking all the way to San Salvador, where the Administrator of the Mail Service Don Domingo Ferreros voluntarily gave him a drink of *aguardiente*. But since his stomach was empty and he is not accustomed to taking drink, the *aguardiente* went to his head on the journey to the town of Nejapa.[50]

Custodio's claim that he was not accustomed to taking drink was somewhat disingenuous. Other towns had complained of Custodio's conduct before, and his behavior in Nejapa was probably in character, if somewhat more pronounced than usual.[51] In some cases, officials had no difficulty determining the *correo*'s state of intoxication. José Andrade, a twenty-two-year-old carpenter who worked as a *correo* out of Guatemala City, was discovered in a state of undeniable inebriation by the *alcalde* of the Barrio San José, Don Manuel Sánchez. Andrade was reportedly barefoot and wielding a heavy stick against two other men. When Sánchez confronted him, Andrade retorted that the *alcalde* had no jurisdiction over him because he was a *correo*. Sánchez nevertheless threw him in jail, only to release him weeks later when his employment as a *correo* was confirmed by the administration.[52]

The number of cases in which *correos* were involved in violent confrontations is suggestive, and in each case the *fuero* granting special privileges to the *correos* played an important part.[53] While not exactly placing the *correos* above the law—on the contrary, some *correos* found themselves in and out of prison—the *fuero* ensured that all criminal cases involving *correos* would fall under the jurisdiction of the mail administration. Consequently, if a *correo* was arrested by an *alcalde* or other official, he had only to declare that he was a *correo* for the matter to be removed from the official's hands. This tended to inspire the *correos* with a certain degree of confidence—or insolence—when confronted with local officials. *Correos* held another advantage in their confrontations with local officials because of their special permission to carry banned weapons. In 1779, the Guatemalan *Fiscal* determined that employees of the royal mail could carry certain banned weapons as long as they were used purely for self-defense and in the service of the mail. Pistols, daggers, and other weapons that could be easily concealed were not permitted—though Miguel Custodio, twelve years later, carried both a short firearm and a knife.[54]

In some cases, these special privileges prompted *correos* to challenge the growing authority of local officials, as Custodio and Andrade did. The local officials *correos* tangled with in urban areas were contributing to a deliberate and marked tightening of social control in the late Bourbon period. Ana Margarita Gómez's work on the Bourbon military in Guatemala demonstrates that an increased military presence in the late colonial period led to a greater militarization of urban areas and to more invasive social coercion. Though troops were initially necessitated by the foreign wars (alternately with England and France), they were gradually relied upon more for domestic policing. Their duties in transferring the Guatemalan population from Antigua to Nueva Guatemala after the earthquake transitioned easily into urban patrolling, so that by the late colonial period troops in urban areas worked hand-in-hand with *alcaldes* to monitor and disarm the population.[55]

The confrontations between *correos* and local officials therefore in many ways echoed those occurring throughout Guatemala, but the *fuero* gave the *correo* somewhat greater leverage. In 1778, *correo* Manuel de Mella flagrantly disavowed the authority of the *alcalde ordinario* in Guatemala City after an altercation with a merchant. Provoked because the merchant had thrown water on him, Mella threatened him with a knife and then resisted arrest when the *alcalde* arrived, shouting that he recognized no authority other than the mail administrator's and the president's.[56] And in Guatemala City's *barrio del* Perú, two *correos* similarly defied the authority of the *alcalde* of the neighborhood. Don Juan José Soto, the *alcalde*, claimed that the two *correos* had called him (translating loosely) "shorty, a worthless shit, an ass and other names of a similar nature."[57] The two *correos*, both tailors by profession and in their mid- to late twenties, claimed that a ruckus in the neighborhood had already started when they passed by. The *alcalde* had accosted them, wielding a gun and sword and accompanied by three drunk Indians carrying machetes and a pistol. To make matters worse, when the two *correos* invoked the *fuero*, the *alcalde* had scoffed at the badges they wore on their chests, saying "that he shit on them."[58] The confrontation turned violent; being outnumbered four to two, the *correos* were quickly overwhelmed. As often happened with *correo* cases, the two were jailed temporarily before the mail administrator stepped in to release them. The conflict would not necessarily end there, however; as the *Sargento Mayor de Plaza* warned sourly, "a long experience with mail carriers has taught me that on few occasions do their cases allow the truth to be aired, and in general there always remain long-standing grudges and resentments against the testifying witnesses."[59]

In other cases, the *correos* entered into violent conflicts with people other than officials. One rather exceptional but illuminating case concerns *correo* Francisco Anzueto's attacks against his wife in 1805. A twenty-four-year-old mestizo weaver, Anzueto had hit his wife repeatedly on the head but had only injured her so severely because of the weapon he carried: a "narrow, double-edged sword."[60] As a *correo*, Anzueto was entitled to carry such a weapon, ostensibly for self-defense, but in this case as in others the weapon was used instead for assault. Most frequently, *correos* were arrested for assaulting other men, and just as in Anzueto's case, the victim of the assault was more often than not someone well known to the *correo*. In other words, though the special dispensation to carry banned weapons was intended to protect *correos* while they traveled, *correos* turned their weapons against friends, family, and neighbors instead of strangers on the road.[61]

The cost of the *correo's* special privileges, then, was to some extent paid by the people around him. However, the violence that accompanied *correos* at home and on the road cannot be attributed entirely to these special privileges. The violence directed toward *correos* must also have played a part, not necessarily by directly provoking violent behavior in response but by dissuading men who were unwilling to risk physical assault from becoming *correos* in the first place. Men who became *correos* knew that one of the greatest threats came from bandits who assaulted *correos* to steal the silver they carried or, during wartime, correspondence. The risk of falling victim to banditry came with the territory.

Correo Matías Fonseca, for example, was attacked in late 1789 only three leagues outside of the capital at one-thirty in the morning. Four men on horseback approached him, and while two attacked the guide the other two attacked Fonseca, cutting his hand with a sword or machete all the way to the bone. Fonseca was able to see little of his assailants in the darkness: he couldn't tell whether they were *descalzos* (barefoot) or not; and he could only say that the man who attacked him had been tall and wearing a white shirt. The bandits stole the money Fonseca carried for his journey and left. Though "the guide, because he was Indian (and characteristically timid) ran to hide by the side of the road to avoid being assaulted and was only drawn out by the cries of pain from the *correo*," the pair eventually made their way back to the city at six in the morning, where the administrator paid the surgeon to bind Fonseca's hand. The testimony of the guide,

"Jose Toc, Indian-ladino from the town of Chinautla," concurred that the *correo* had not been to blame or—what would have been worse—in collaboration with the bandits. Since the bandits had stolen only what the *correo* carried, leaving the correspondence, Fonseca's spare clothes, bread, and chocolate untouched, the greatest casualty was Fonseca's right hand.[62]

Attacked twenty-one leagues outside the city only three months later, *correo* Lugardo Herrera was less fortunate. At about eight-thirty in the evening Herrera was confronted by eight men wielding swords or machetes, firearms, and heavy sticks. Three attacked Herrera, another three assaulted the guide, and two pursued the mule carrying the mail trunks. Ripping open the trunks, they took all of the money and much of the correspondence. As the trunks contained an entire trimester's worth of revenue from the provinces, hundreds of *pesos* were estimated stolen. When the *correo* was able to find aid, fifty soldiers were sent to the site of the robbery, but they could find no trace of the bandits.[63]

The administration occasionally took steps to prevent such tremendous losses, shifting the dates of departure to avoid planned assaults, but for the most part the *correos* were expected to fend for themselves.[64] Accosted in 1808 by six men who shot at him until he fell from his horse, *correo* Mariano Aroche lost the thirty *pesos* he carried for his expenses, the ten *pesos* he carried in *encomienda*, and his clothes. The official trunks were kept safe because the guide (perhaps more wise than "timid") had fled and hidden off the road. In ascertaining what had occurred, officials interrogated Brother Mariano Pérez de Jesús, who had traveled with the *correo* for part of his journey after the attack. Though in response to questioning Brother Pérez de Jesús confirmed that Aroche was seriously wounded and not drunk, and though Aroche had lost mostly his own money and not the mail administration's, he nevertheless lost his job over the incident. Once again, the mistrust of the administration had proven an even greater liability than the perils of the road.

The *correos* understood distance somewhat differently than did mail administrators and privileged travelers. Where Archbishop Cortés y Larraz saw the long distances and difficult roads as obstacles to spiritual and moral safety, *correos* saw more earthly dangers. And while officials viewed the network of towns across the isthmus as sites for potential income, *correos* saw towns, *haciendas*, and individuals that they counted on for food and supplies. Some elements, however, created shared conceptions. Guatemalan space was understood as principally route-based and organized around central places. In this sense, the archbishop's thorough descriptions of routes and hierarchies of parishes are consistent with the mail officials' construction of route itineraries and tables of hierarchically placed towns. Both map well onto the *correos'* vision of crucial stopping points on a web of intricate, dangerous roads. Peripheries were understood among all to be less policed and more dangerous, not to mention harder to reach; depending on the viewer's perspective, these attributes could represent moral peril, administrative inconvenience, or an opportunity for sizeable profit despite sizeable risks. In the eighteenth century, these characteristics of space and distance dominated local conceptions. In the first quarter of the nineteenth century, the balance began to change: existing ideas about coterminous territories and boundaries became more dominant, while route-based hierarchies became less so.

The Nineteenth Century: A Changing Calculus

During the late colonial period, the mail administration profited at the expense of individual *correos* and the Indian towns that sustained their travel. For Indian towns, the passage of the mail was usually a losing proposition. Poor compensation for the mule and guide, brutal treatment of their animals, and the not infrequent harassment at the hands of unruly *correos* made the passage of the mail a costly nuisance. *Correos* may have stood to gain somewhat more from their middling pay (after expenses) and the carrying of *encomiendas*. But apart from the financial costs they absorbed to pay for supplies—costs that often resulted in substantial debt—*correos* also paid a heavy toll in terms of their personal health and safety.

In the nineteenth century, the stakes were raised significantly for *correos*. The period between 1821 and 1840 was one of intermittent warfare across the isthmus, and the continual crises required officials to rely heavily on special couriers. *Correos* stood to gain tremendously from these emergency trips, which were paid at a higher rate than ordinary travel. At the same time, *correos* were increasingly the target of assaults, as the information contained in the correspondence they carried became potentially as valuable as currency. For the first time, however, the high costs paid by *correos* were increasingly paid by the mail administration as well. Though the Guatemalan office had sent much of its accumulated earnings from the late colonial period on to the peninsular main office, some funds were reinvested in the system, permitting the establishment of new post offices throughout the region. As discussed in Chapter 3, the Guatemalan mail system had expanded significantly by 1820. Regular service linked Oaxaca to Guatemala and Guatemala to the provinces and Omoa. Local post offices had enabled the formation of a regional network, and despite tussles over *encomiendas*, *correos* could be relied upon for reasonably regular delivery. Between 1821 and 1840, the mail system struggled to preserve this system while paying mounting costs for special couriers and absorbing the continual losses occasioned by minimal correspondence and disrupted service.

In 1821, Central America followed Mexico in declaring independence from Spain. Never a whole-hearted commitment, the alliance with Mexico fell apart in 1823 with the overthrow of Agustín de Iturbide, and Central America declared itself a separate republic. Between 1823 and 1826 an uneasy peace among the united Central America states persisted, overseen in part by Salvadoran Manuel Arce, who was appointed president of the federation in March of 1825. As Arce attempted to consolidate the union by creating an army and imposing taxation, towns throughout Central America broke out against him in rebellion. Internal war lasted until 1829, when Honduran Francisco Morazán succeeded in unifying a coalition of Nicaraguan and Salvadoran troops. While Morazán kept a loose hold on the Central American Federation from his base in Honduras and later San Salvador, the state government in Guatemala expanded under Governor Mariano Gálvez. Between 1831 and 1838, Gálvez embarked on extensive reforms, "setting the model for nineteenth-century liberalism throughout Central America."[65] But his later reforms challenging both local political power and clerical power throughout the state went too far. Provoked by the extremity of the reforms as well as by the passage of a deadly cholera epidemic, towns in Guatemala and elsewhere revolted. Rafael Carrera led what would become the most consequential revolt in Chiquimula, between Guatemala and El Salvador. In 1839 the federation of Central American states was abolished, and Carrera continued to skirmish against the remnants of opposition before being formally declared president in 1844.

These political and military ruptures could not but affect the operation of the mail system. The detailed impact of these upheavals is difficult to document, precisely because the normal functioning of the system found itself repeatedly disrupted. Nevertheless, it is clear that the violence of the period impacted the mail service in two main ways: *correos* as individuals found themselves in greater danger on their routes; and routes were reoriented by the mail administration in order to compensate for the observable danger of particular roads and regions. As a result, certain destinations effectively lost communication with Guatemala City while others maintained or improved their communication ties. Initially, after the break from Spain in 1821, the mail system maintained a policy of continuing its established service to Mexico and the provinces, essentially preserving the colonial system.[66] But by 1822, regional offices were receiving a mandate from the central administration to improve mail service throughout the region, signaling a new set of needs: a colonial province's network would not be sufficient for a national and federal system.[67]

Over the next twenty years, the administration attempted to increase the frequency of service and the number of destinations within Guatemala and Central America. In February 1823, an attempt was made to establish three monthly trips to Mexico, departing on the first, tenth, and twentieth of the month.[68] Though the attempt was short lived, it demonstrated the administration's intention to sustain more frequent communication with the important cities in the region. But by 1824, these important cities lay southeast, rather than north, and the system consisted of "two trips on horseback per month to Oaxaca, three of the same to the Eastern Provinces, two trips on foot to Chiquimula, Zacapa, and Gualan, two to Verapaz and Peten, and two to Antigua Guatemala."[69] Destinations within the state of Guatemala were serviced twice a month and the provinces to the southeast could expect mail from Guatemala City three times per month. The expenses incurred by special couriers were already, by this time, putting the mail administration in Guatemala in the red, and the cost-cutting measures suggested in 1824 by the administrator indicated a new set of priorities. Antonio Batres y Nájera recommended a range of options: paying the special couriers as ordinary *correos*; eliminating one of the trips to Oaxaca; eliminating one of the three trips to the provinces; or, lastly, sending the mail to Oaxaca only as far as the border between Guatemala and Mexico.[70] As it is the first mention of a *correo* handing off mail at a border, the final recommendation bears notice. It suggests a new conviction that the responsibility for the documents carried by the *correo* might cease at a specific, politically determined place along the route. And, of course, it indicates that the connection with Mexico was no longer the most vital, to be preserved at all costs.

In 1824, the administrator also attempted to create a special mail service between Guatemala City and Antigua Guatemala, calling it the *correo de gabinete* (cabinet mail service). Since the authorities of the Guatemalan state resided in Antigua and the authorities of the Central American Federation resided in Guatemala City, a constant communication was required between them. Batres y Nájera established service departing Antigua on Mondays, Wednesdays, and Fridays, and returning to Guatemala City on Tuesdays, Thursdays, and Saturdays.[71] The two cities thereby created a communication link that must have been experienced as a tremendous contraction of temporal and spatial distance. In 1826, before warfare disrupted service further, the state government recommended expanding this close communication network by creating more regular service to the "interior" of the state.[72] This suggestion was abandoned for three years, during which warfare necessitated the frequent and expensive use of special couriers. Then, beginning in 1830, attempts were once again made to solidify communications within Guatemala and the Central American Federation. A proposal was made to link the long-neglected capital of Verapaz, Salamá, with a direct service to the capital. A weekly mail was established with Quetzaltenango, and every other week a *correo* would travel from the capital to Chiquimula and Cobán.[73] In 1831, the state government advised the Central American government that regular service should be established to Petén.[74] Despite a number of setbacks, weekly service between Guatemala and Chiapas was established in 1835, and in the same year proposals were made for providing a regular delivery of mail carried on horseback to San Salvador and León.[75] The temporary relocation of the Central American government's capital to San Salvador in the 1830s made the route southeast of particular importance. Clearly, the reforms were intended to enable a more consistent and above all more frequent flow of information among the important cities and towns of Central America.

These ambitious efforts to provide Central America with more regular internal communication were plagued increasingly by warfare, cholera epidemics, and a lack of funds. In the year following its establishment, the mail to Chiapas had to be suspended due to insufficient funds, and the cholera outbreaks in the early 1830s and again in 1837 had the effect of paralyzing communication with Chiapas.[76] The epidemic had been controlled in 1834, but an outbreak in Belize in 1836 could not be effectively contained, resulting in a devastating 17% rate of illness and 5% fatalities.[77] Most scholars credit the 1837 cholera epidemic at least partially for provoking the rebellions that broke out after 1838.[78] During those years, Guatemalan Governor Mariano Gálvez was forced to abdicate, the Central American Federation was abolished by the Guatemalan state government, and then Central American President Francisco Morazán was called on to contend with Rafael Carrera and other leaders of rebellions across Guatemala. Necessarily, the pace and pattern of communication changed dramatically. The mail administration struggled to remain functional and was forced to entirely refocus its energies. Chiapas, previously one of the most important locations on the crucial route to Oaxaca, became one more outlying *departamento* in the eyes of the central office. By 1840, the administrator did not even consider the eighty-*peso* trip on horseback to Chiapas worth reestablishing, so paltry was the correspondence it carried.[79] While service to Chiapas, Verapaz, Petén, and other northern destinations continued sporadically, the Guatemalan government and the mail administration concentrated their attention and funds heavily on the route to the southeast, particularly to El Salvador. A city that had previously oriented itself primarily northward, emphasizing communication with Oaxaca and, beyond it, Spain, Guatemala became if not cut off certainly distanced from Chiapas and Mexico, reorienting itself to the southeast.

As the Central American conflict nucleated between the Guatemalan and Salvadoran capitals, the trip to San Salvador became the single most important information corridor between 1838 and 1845. Costing forty-two *pesos* and three *reales* for the roundtrip, the ordinary mail was rarely sufficient, though it was intended to travel weekly.[80] Special couriers were repeatedly required to communicate with officials in Chiquimula, Santa Ana, and El Salvador. The very importance of the communication they carried ensured that *correos* on the southeastern route became the targets of frequent assaults. Rafael Carrera himself assaulted the mail in September of 1839 near Jalpatagua, and in 1840 Salvadoran troops assaulted the mail in Quetzaltepeque and at the Río Paz.[81] As the route to El Salvador grew in importance, it inevitably became more dangerous. Salvadoran troops became a frequent presence on the route, occasioning injury or even death for *correos* such as Julián Pacheco, who was killed in Santa Isabel, near Santa Ana, in 1840.[82] The motives for assault had become decidedly strategic. As the presence of troops on the route grew and the number of assaults increased, the nature of the terrain changed. The routes were not only more dangerous; they had become politicized. For the first time, *correos* were forced to try alternate routes, not because of weather or the complaints of Indian villages, but to avoid confrontations with troops.[83] It is perhaps not too great a stretch to characterize the *correo*'s role, in this period, as quasi-military.

The strategic nature of the assaults is itself an indication of the kind of correspondence carried by *correos* during the period of turmoil in the late 1830s and early 1840s. The general dysfunction of Central American commerce and government during the 1837-1844 period makes it likely that the official mail dwindled during this period to correspondence relating directly to the political situation. In fact, even the *correo* on the crucial Guatemala–El Salvador route frequently returned to Guatemala without any correspondence at all.[84] And so, in a self-reinforcing cycle, the absence of correspondence prevented the reestablishment of consistent (solvent) mail service, which in turn made it impossible for people outside of the highest political circles to rely once again on the mail. Well into the 1840s, then, while the *correo* partly occupied his former role as a courier for the government and the public, he simultaneously functioned as a military messenger. Requiring safe-conduct papers and facing the likelihood of assault from hostile troops, the *correo* traveled a politicized and necessarily more dangerous route.[85]

While ongoing challenges to Rafael Carrera's leadership continued in the early 1840s, attempts were made to restore the mail service. A report prepared in early 1840 by Mariano Córdova, the Guatemalan mail administrator, gives some sense of the existing structure. Post offices in the state of Guatemala were located in Nueva Guatemala, Antigua Guatemala, Chimaltenango, Amatitán, Escuintla, Salamá, Zacapa, Chiquimula, Gualán, and Izabal. Córdova proposed sending and receiving mail according to the schedule shown in Table 4.1.[86]

TABLE 4.1.

Incoming and outgoing mail schedule for Guatemala City, 1840

Departures	Destination
Tuesdays at 2pm	Antigua Guatemala, Chimaltenango, Amatitán, Escuintla, Salamá
Fridays at 2pm	San Salvador (connecting with Honduras, Nicaragua, and Costa Rica)
Saturdays at 2pm	Zacapa, Chiquimula, Gualán, and Yzaval (connecting with the maritime mail)
3rd and 18th of the month at 2pm	Los Altos, Soconusco, and Mexico
Arrivals	*Point of origin*
Mondays	Antigua Guatemala and Chimaltenango
Tuesdays	San Salvador (with the mail from Honduras, Nicaragua, and Costa Rica)
Thursdays	Zacapa, Chiquimula, Gualán, Amatitán, Escuintla, and Yzaval (with the maritime mail)
16th and last of the month	Los Altos, Soconusco, and Mexico

Source: Derived by the author from documents at the Archivo General de Centroamérica

Córdova attempted to launch this schedule despite the persistence of occasional assaults and the more than occasional absence of correspondence. He purchased new trunks for the mail routes within the state and gradually commenced weekly service to the more far-flung destinations. But after only a year and a half of following this schedule, Córdova was forced to admit that the routes were scarcely solvent. In an illuminating report written in 1841, Córdova declared that "the only routes I consider necessary and productive are those passing through the Department of Chiquimula, which channels the correspondence from overseas and the Port of Izabal and is therefore of value to commerce."[87] In fact, the route to the port via Chiquimula was not only the sole profitable route: the revenue from the route financed all the others in Guatemala. The weekly mail to Antigua, which had become necessary to government officials and businesses alike, brought no profit but at least paid for itself. Meanwhile the routes to Salamá, Amatitán, Escuintla, and Los Altos barely brought in enough to cover a third of their cost. As Córdova argued, "this demonstrates that they are unnecessary, as there are very few people in them who even write."[88] The old difficulty of finding enough writers to finance the passage of the mail had resurfaced once again. Despite the existence of a functional network and the capacity to deliver mail frequently, relatively few correspondents in Guatemala required the services of the system.

The mail system found itself in a paradoxical situation. While the Bourbon-era reforms had succeeded in creating a foundation for a relatively effective communications system, the two decades of internal conflict had dried up the sources of correspondence. Over the course of seventy-five years, document travel had become both faster and more frequent. In the absence of any significant technological change in the means of transportation, the mail system had nonetheless managed to create a network that reached more destinations more often and more quickly. These changes had the effect of creating a temporal and spatial contraction—of shortening distances. The mail system had also, in part, become more functional and maneagable because the territory it covered had become dramatically smaller. Distances had, then, also become *literally* shorter. *Correos* who had previously traveled hundreds of leagues north and south to Oaxaca and Costa Rica now traveled only as far as Chiapas and El Salvador. And Guatemala was no longer oriented as it had been toward Mexico and Spain.

This altered pace and orientation accompanied new conventions for the production of documents, resulting in a virtual end to the creation of "composite" documents. Documents written in Guatemala after the first quarter of the nineteenth century are more likely to be authored by a single person at a particular place and time than by several authors along a temporal and spatial route. Documents accumulated at each end of a correspondence, rather than circulating and concluding in a single place. While bureaucratic practices, the quality of and access to paper, and the reorganization of administrative offices doubtlessly played some part in restructuring document form, it seems clear that the new pace and systematization of communication had an impact as well.

The changing correspondence between Guatemala City and Chiquimula helps explain how composite documents transformed as communication improved. In 1769, the newly appointed mail administrator in Guatemala generated correspondence with other officials about establishing a monthly route that would pass through Chiquimula on the way to Honduras. The resulting thirty-page composite document involved nearly twenty distinct instances of writing or signing by officials in Guatemala City and Spain, and it was composed over the course of 1769 and 1770.[89] They determined that the mail would travel monthly through Chiquimula on the way to Honduras.[90] By 1795, the monthly mail route had made possible a fluid correspondence (discussed further in the next chapter) about the custodianship of an *escribano* archive in Chiquimula. The composite document about the archive was initiated in Chiquimula; it traveled to Guatemala City early in the month of August; and it returned to Chiquimula with the officials' replies by the end of the month.[91] Yet the adoption of an even more frequent mail delivery schedule would change the possibilities for this kind of composite document. By 1822, Chiquimula sent a *correo* to the capital every two weeks. The mail administrator wrote several letters to his superior in Guatemala City with every dispatch: individual letters that accumulated in the capital in files according to their subject and place of origin.[92] The new mail schedule made it possible for the office in Chiquimula to communicate in greater volume and with greater speed, but both made it difficult to pursue the continuous chains of communication required to create composite documents. The increase in speed and volume made the free-form correspondence more practical. By the 1840s, the correspondence of the mail administrator to other officials rarely contained marginalia. Comments that would have gone in the margin of Córdova's letter (Figure 4.1) were sent to him separately. The itinerary model and the radial model of correspondence, upon which colonial knowledge was built, were being replaced by a network formed of closed circuits.

These changes in communication and in the perception of distance were part and parcel of how Guatemala and the Central American states understood themselves to be taking shape politically. The conception of key places linked by routes necessarily contended with the conception of the new Central American states as bounded spaces. With the determination of boundaries came a new emphasis on demarcating space beyond that occupied by important roads and towns. For *correos,* dangers were no longer exclusively tied to treacherous routes and distant peripheries; dangers emerged from the politicization of regions and borders. The conception of bounded space had always been present, but it had not dominated the local perception of space and distance as it came to in the nineteenth century. At the highest administrative level, this was reflected in the first effort to create cartographic representations of the Guatemalan state. The recurrent military threat in different parts of what had formerly been the Kingdom of Guatemala necessitated more information than that provided previously by charts, tables, and *relaciones geográficas.* "Without maps, without tables, without surveys we cannot presently estimate the value or potential power of our province," protested the director of the *Sociedad Económica de Amantes de la Patria* (Patriots' Association of Economists), José Cecilio del Valle. He demanded the publication of "less inexact maps of our province . . . so we can at least have these drafts while the ones we should have are created."[93] Valle knew of only five maps of the region, all of them inaccurate, and he hoped to have at least three maps: "one, of Indian Guatemala; another, of its Spanish political subdivisions; and a third of its post-independence departments, with a report on the resources of each one."[94]

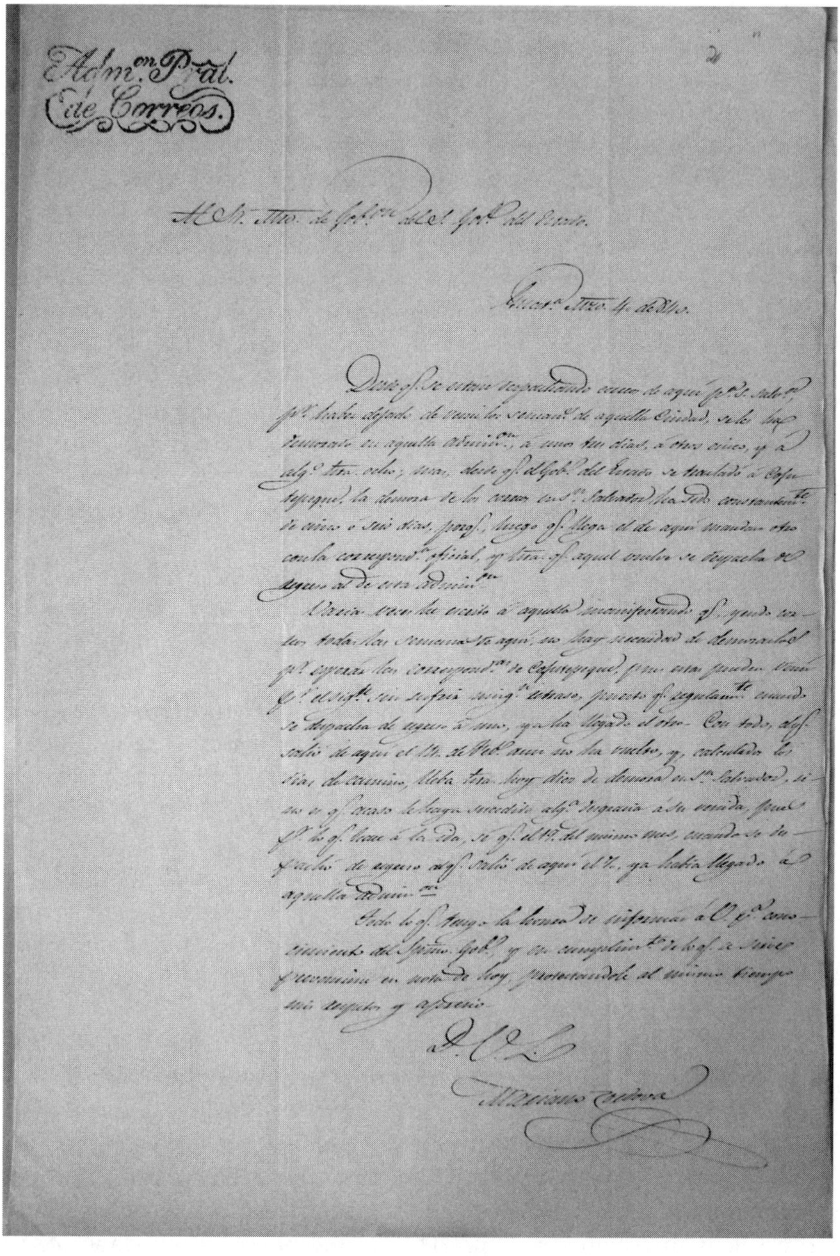

FIGURE 4.1. Mariano Córdova letter from 1840
Source: Archivo General de Centroamérica. Photograph by the author.

José Felipe Mariano Gálvez commissioned the improved maps in 1831 and received them in 1832. The maps, executed by Miguel Rivera Maestre, are the first official cartographic representation of the state of Guatemala created in the region, and they reveal a remarkably altered landscape.[95] Though they were created for Gálvez in 1831-1832, when Guatemala was part of the Central American Federation, they specifically delineate only the "state of Guatemala in Central America." This is hardly accidental; as Raymond Craib posits in his study of nineteenth-century Mexican state formation and cartography, the re-formulation of space in cartographic form served a political purpose. Craib argues that regional conflicts in Mexico "confounded any comforting thoughts of a unified national space and repeatedly raised the specter of total national disintegration." Countering such disintegration, "a national map refuted such troublesome realities by visually affirming what supposedly already existed . . . Even simply delineating where Mexico ended and other nations began could be significant at a time when established boundaries and territorial cohesion were increasingly regarded as integral features of the modern nation-state."[96]

In the Guatemalan case, the shifting political relationships with Mexico and the states to the south necessitated a delineation of Guatemalan territory. As the Rivera maps make clear (Figures 4.2 and 4.3), territory was perceived as a measured, bounded landscape marked by topographical features, routes, and place-names. At this time and for these purposes, it made sense to use cartographic representations rather than itineraries. A first plate shows the whole of the state, bordered by the otherwise blank territories of "State of Honduras," "State of Salvador," "State of Chiapas," "Tabasco," and "Yucatán."

The remaining seven plates detail of each of Guatemala's new "departments," including limited topographical markers (volcanoes, rivers, and rough elevations), towns, political boundaries, and roads. The maps rely on longitude and latitude, creating a landscape that is measured—and bounded—by a grid, as the map of Chiquimula demonstrates.[97]

The Guatemalan landscape was clearly being represented in new ways. But to what extend do such representations reflect an end to colonial conceptions? Though these maps contrast sharply with the representations of space evident in the itineraries used by colonial mail officials, authors of geographical reports, and travelers, they should be interpreted as the culmination of gradual change and a shift in emphasis rather than a radical break with colonial notions. The altered political landscape of the nineteenth century foregrounded another dimension to the conception of Guatemalan space, but preexisting notions of distance, routes, and space remained in place as underlying elements.

The early nineteenth-century writings of José Arjona demonstrate aptly that there were as many continuities as there were changes. In a sense, the orders given to *Capitán de Ingenieros* José Arjona in 1826 were centuries old. He was asked to survey the newly independent states by traveling to Soconusco, Chiapas, Belize, Guatemala, and then farther south: another request for *relaciones geográficas.*[98] Yet some aspects of Arjona's orders and his reports differ sharply from the conversation among colonial writers. Arjona's orders were to provide a "military survey" of the region, and he obligingly provided a "military glimpse of the border—or rather a plan of defense for each of the contact points between departments." Mirroring the cartographic depictions from the 1830s above, he emphasized the "demarcation of the dividing line, statistical sketches of the districts on either side of the line, and itineraries of the routes that lead to it." Arjona set out to survey the Central American states just at the moment when they were beginning to fracture along the lines he described. From March to July of 1826, he traveled through the region and wrote detailed reports that belie the difficult circumstances of their composition. Arjona did not travel with a retinue and ecclesiastical privilege, as did Cortés y Larraz; nor did he have the obligatory support of townspeople as did the officials who composed *relaciones geográficas* in the colonial period; he could not even count on the basic supplies afforded to the mail carriers.

The difficulty of his task made itself evident in the questions he communicated to his superiors at the beginning of his journey to Chiapas.

Upon examining the weighty commission assigned to me, I have had the following doubts: First, if I should cover the entire province of Chiapas up to the old border (*antiguos límites*) between this state and Mexico. Second, if I should travel in private and if I should conceal all aspects of my purpose in making surveys and inquiries. Third, if I should observe the same behavior in acquiring information in this district as I did in the region of Soconusco. Fourth, if in some of the towns I may ask for assistance from the authorities, be it for a guide, supplies, or for information about the region.[99]

Arjona's doubts present a clear image of a man planning to travel with a low profile—if not, precisely, in disguise—and in a possibly hostile terrain. His would clearly not be a composite document; on the contrary, he was acutely aware of his isolation in completing his assignment. The note appended to his letter, which falls at the end of his portfolio, points to the dangerous nature of his work. Creating a secret code for the correspondence sent between him and the minister of war, Arjona implied the possibility that his documents might be stolen or read by enemy eyes. He may have been describing the same geographical region described by previous writers, but he was nonetheless describing a distinct social, political, and military terrain (Figure 4.4).

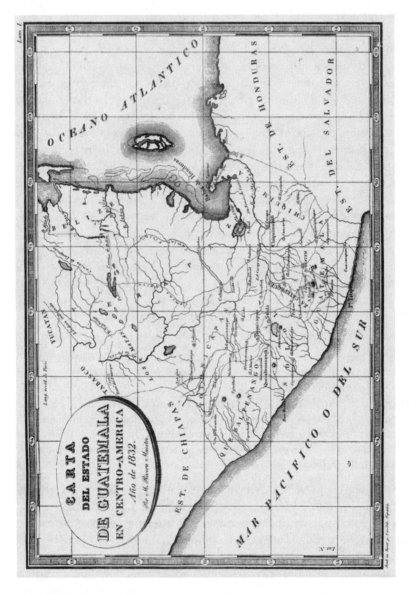

FIGURE 4.2. Rivera Maestre's map of Guatemala

Source: Miguel Rivera Maestre

FIGURE 4.3. Rivera Maestre's map of Chiquimula
Source: Miguel Rivera Maestre

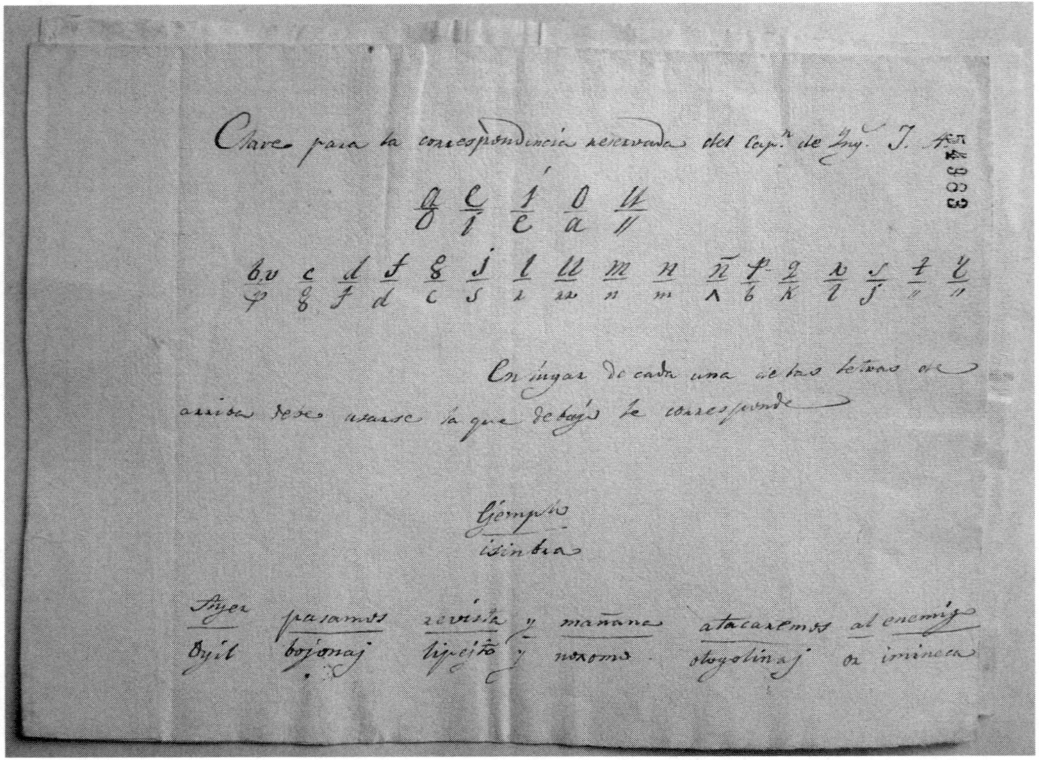

FIGURE 4.4. José Arjona's key to the code

Source: Archivo General de Centroamérica. Photograph by the author.

The altered political landscape—a landscape that in Arjona's time was also a militarized landscape—initially appears to be completely altered from the network of towns and parishes visited by officials in the eighteenth century. Borders matter in ways that they did not before. Both Arjona's means of travel through the potentially hostile peripheries of the region and the objective of his descriptions are distinctive. They are not without precedent, however; instructions from mainland Spain during the colonial period placed intermittent emphasis on determining the military potential of roads, forts, and urban defenses. And upon closer inspection, it becomes clear that Arjona relied on assumptions common to the colonial period: "The long and extremely difficult communication existing between this district and the other points along the frontier will not permit a single officer (*jefe*) to govern its defense: it is therefore indispensable that this section be assigned to one separately."[100] Though his concerns were military rather than spiritual, Arjona echoed Archbishop Cortés y Larraz, emphasizing the poor roads and the difficulty of governing a single area. The parallel becomes more striking in the description of the two routes into Soconusco: one had only two small, impoverished towns along a forty-eight league stretch; the other one ran along the coast. Arjona pointed out that "the towns from which we must draw resources lie at a great distance," and he was worried about "the great misery of these towns and the tremendous obstacle posed by the roads, the weather, and the swarms of mosquitoes . . . that would all greatly debilitate the troops."[101]

Arjona was clearly focused on a potential military campaign rather than on the spiritual health of the region's people, but in many ways his observations echo those written by Cortés y Larraz more than fifty years earlier. The routes were poor and difficult to travel; the population was dispersed; the terrain was such that any governing individual would have to focus on a small area. Evidently the landscape in certain peripheries had not changed so radically. Arjona also described routes in detail, once again echoing Cortés y Larraz and the authors of geographical reports from the colonial period.

What of the use of spatial/temporal measures? Accompanying Arjona's meticulous descriptions of the route and his travel along it are tables that seem to borrow from the colonial distance-interval charts and offer new improvements (Table 4.2).[102] Arjona not only provided his measurement of the intervals listed in the left-hand column; he also detailed precisely his method of calculation. Describing a league as six thousand paces, or the number of two-and-a-half foot steps taken along a flat road in an hour, he provided an exact calculation for each segment of the journey. Segments running uphill or downhill were accounted for accordingly. In some sense, he was following the instructions sent from Spain fifty years earlier in the

TABLE 4.2.

Portion of José Arjona's distance measures

Itinerary of longitude and latitude from the River Petacalapa to Sesecapa calculated in leagues of 5000 varas or 6000 paces of two and a half feet which on a regular road are taken in one hour

Notable landmarks	Paces on a road that is . . .			Total leagues and paces		Observations
	Flat	Rising	Descending	Leagues	Paces	
From the River Petacalpa	3000					Before the River Petacalpa lies the *hacienda*
To the River Masacate	3000					by the same name, on the descent to the river, which is some twenty paces wide . . .

Source: Derived by the author from documents at the Archivo General de Centroamérica

1776 questionnaire that requested variable measures for different terrain (as described Chapter 1). His careful accounting leaves no doubt that he relied on a temporal/spatial measure for distances along the routes he traveled. It is also worthwhile noting that he titles his documents "itineraries."

Thus, despite Arjona's unique military and political agenda specific to 1826, the tools and perspectives relied upon in his report are in many respects colonial in origin. The other portions of his report confirm this. Arjona provided detailed demographic tables listing "souls, men, households" for each town, and he reported on local production of maize, rice, and beans, the livestock holdings of each town, and the number of cacao trees.[103] For Belize (*Walize*), he listed the number of whites, free *pardos*, free blacks, slaves, and soldiers.[104] These charts are not unlike the colonial tribute tables and the geographical reports compiled by colonial officials. In other words, Arjona's methods for taking stock of the regions he visited were essentially colonial methods.

There is nothing surprising about this overlap, if we consider that Arjona and his contemporaries were only recently "national" rather than "royal" subjects. It seems natural that they would rely on the practices that they had perfected over many decades. Even the apparent novelties of his approach have their roots in the late colonial period. The most notable novelty of Arjona's account is the way in which it treats centers and peripheries. Spain, of course, is no longer a center at all. Mexico looms large as an absence.

Guatemala, as center, is the vital place he corresponds with and returns to. And while peripheries are described in similar ways—hard to govern, hard to reach, slow to access—not all former peripheries remain peripheral.

How new is this, really? By considering the changes in the mail system alongside the new representations of space in the national period, it becomes clear that this novelty is in fact a colonial novelty. In the 1750s, as this and the previous chapter have shown, Guatemala City corresponded with various points within its administrative boundaries on an irregular, occasional basis. Within the *reino*, every place other than Guatemala City lay at a great distance, in terms of communication and travel. But by 1800, Guatemala City communicated with many locations monthly and with some places weekly. Quetzaltenango, Chiquimula, San Salvador, and Omoa, among others, were no longer as peripheral as they had been. Moreover, places other than the capital within the *reino* communicated with one another more easily and frequently. Some internal peripheries acquired a greater importance and facility of access than they had previously enjoyed. After independence, mail administrators essentially attempted to preserve and in some cases improve upon this colonial achievement. While certain places, such as those described by Arjona, remained peripheral, others had become regional centers. The facility of communication with internal peripheries added a new density and complexity to Guatemala City's network as a whole. Gradually, Guatemala had become a place with peripheries that lay at less of a distance.

Part Three

5   *The Distant Archive*

I hereby order that from now on all decrees and letters . . .
be stored in the archive of the *audiencia* and that a book be
made to keep an accurate inventory of them so that they
may be understood and obeyed with the greatest facility.[1]
—King Philip II, 1597

As Guatemalan peripheries shifted, distancing Spain and bringing formerly
marginal places to the fore, a concurrent and related change occurred
in how documents were stored. Chapter 4 has argued that while routes
remained important to the imagining of places linked by distances, the
perception of Guatemalan space into coterminous territories defined by
political boundaries came into focus. It has also argued that conventions
in correspondence changed, as the denser and more efficient mail system
facilitated the creation of local correspondence "circuits" where previously
the far-flung itinerary and radial modes of document travel had entirely
dominated. As the next two chapters argue, the related manner of storing
documents transformed as well, beginning in the late colonial period and
continuing in the national period.

In the colonial period, the documents carried by Guatemalan *correos*
traveled to the desks of ecclesiastical authorities and merchants, to the
homes of individuals, and to officials in every corner of the Spanish empire. But once documents had traveled a particular spatial-temporal route
through the *audiencia,* their travels did not end. Many of the official documents carried by *correos* traveled across the Atlantic or to a neighboring
audiencia only to be stored for short or long periods of time in archives.
These two stages of the document's voyage were not unrelated; indeed,
a pause in an archive was often simply a resting point in the creation of a
composite document. The *escribanos* who kept colonial archives were also
crucial to their composition and movement. Yet in the national period,
the gradual transformation of composite documents made for documents
with shorter life spans. Documents traveled from point of origin to point
of receipt and remained there, their single journey complete. The archivists who replaced *escribanos* had less of a role in document creation and

spatial movement: they primarily stored and organized sedentary paper. Archives, therefore, went from being nodes in the process of document creation and travel to being purely document repositories. Or, considered in a different light, archivists became custodians exclusively of a document's temporal travel.

To reveal this transition, Chapter 5 focuses on the colonial period and argues that document travel and document storage were closely related practices. The organizational framework for document travel closely mirrored and complemented the framework for document storage. Correspondence inventories or indexes, in use even in the sixteenth century, were relied upon to organize documents sent between Guatemala and Spain. Similarly, the crown ordered that document inventories would form the necessary structure for official archives. "Books" were created to periodically inventory and index the contents of regional and central administrative offices. Additionally, the officials assigned to organize and safeguard archives, *escribanos*, had a close relationship to the mail system. As the official secretaries and scribes at various levels of government, *escribanos* were responsible not only for storing documents but also for discharging and receiving them. The principal *escribano* (*escribano mayor*) for the *audiencia,* for example, had the task of copying and disseminating mandates from the Guatemalan president, the king, and the Council of Indies.

This chapter also considers, relatedly, how *escribanos* acted as keepers of documentary "treasure" in their capacity as archivists. While documents created locally were certainly of importance, archives fulfilled the vital purposes of storing mandates that had traveled from central authorities. Decrees and letters sent by administrators in Spain were crucial to effective governance, and it was essential for the king to be assured that *escribanos* would protect, preserve, and disseminate his word in distant archives. The *audiencia* archives preserved orders from Spain, and regional archives preserved orders from the Guatemalan capital. Likewise, the *audiencia* preserved the gathered replies from its provinces, and the documentary storehouse in Seville preserved replies from every corner of the empire. Archives organized and directed the hierarchical movement of documents.

Treasure from Afar: Early Archival Practices

Essential to the granting of land titles, the writing of contracts, and the execution of justice, *escribanos* were critical to the early days of the *cabildo* and, later, the *audiencia*. More than mere scribes (*escribientes*), *escribanos* could be secretaries, notaries, witnesses, and archivists who oversaw the entire production of official documents.[2] In light of their multiple responsibilities relating to document production, *escribanos* might also be considered the essential agents of standardization in processes that were necessarily composite.[3] As multiple authors in various places contributed to a document's formation, the presence of an *escribano* ensured that the document would follow prescribed guidelines and remain valid. Certainly the *escribanos'* legal imprimatur was as important—if not more important—than their technical skills. Without the *escribano's* signature or stamp, documents could not become official instruments. Angel Rama has written that *escribano* documents laid the groundwork for the future of American cities, stating that "before becoming a material reality of houses, streets, and plazas, which could be constructed only gradually over decades or centuries, Latin American cities sprang forth in signs and plans, already complete, in the documents that laid their statutory foundations and in the charts and plans that established their ideal designs."[4] Nevertheless, despite the crown's reliance on the *escribano* as a stamp of legitimacy and an insurer of standardization, *escribanos* were "not disinterested bystanders," as Kathryn Burns has pointed out.[5] *Escribano* work did not always proceed "by the book," and "words got to paper through a complicated relay process, one that might involve several people and considerable filtering and rewriting." But it is precisely this composite relay process that made the *escribano* so essential.[6] As producers of documents, *escribanos* necessarily determined many aspects of their creation, treatment, and storage.

The importance of *escribanos* was such that by 1529, the Guatemalan city council already relied on three, and in 1535 the Council of Indies requested detailed information on any additional *escribanos* in the province.[7] From early on, an effort was made to ensure that *escribanos* were, as Burns puts it, "as Castilian as possible."[8] Guatemalan records indicate that legislation sent from Spain prohibited *mestizos* and mulattoes from becoming *escribanos*.[9] They were subject to other constraints as well: as of 1619 in Guatemala they were not permitted to engage in commercial ventures, and they were generally not permitted to leave their jurisdiction.[10] This was due in part to how *escribanos* were distributed throughout the *audiencia* and appointed at different ranks. *Escribanos reales* (royal scribes), not assigned to particular jurisdictions, could be further distinguished as ecclesiastical scribes, as *escribanos de cámara y gobierno*, or as *escribanos* for the city council, the province, or the *audiencia*.[11] The *escribano público del número* (notary scribe), which Jorge Luján Muñoz likens to present-day notaries, were assigned to particular jurisdictions. It is worthwhile noting that *escribanos* in heavily Indian regions had to be repeatedly reprimanded for poor treatment of Indians, such that in 1605 the bishop in Guatemala requested that Spanish *escribanos* be removed from *pueblos de indios* for causing so many disputes.[12] It is unclear whether this recommendation was followed, but in 1638 at least one position was created specifically for an Indian *escribano*, evidently because the *corregidor* believed him more capable of carrying out the necessary tasks.[13]

Legislation from the sixteenth century indicates that the crown considered the document repositories created by *escribanos* in the Americas equally vital to effective governance. A 1525 decree ordered that *escribanos* in the Caribbean periodically deposit indexes of any notarized documents with the newly created governing bodies of the islands.[14] The organization and protection of archives was addressed in a 1536 *real cédula* sent to Guatemala mandating that all orders and decrees be stored in the council safe and be organized according to an inventory. The *cédula* urged that the council should "take great care" of the documents, and even went so far as to say that if "any of the stated provisions and ordinances that have previously been sent cannot be located in the province," official copies would duly be made.[15] Evidently knowledge of the contents of the decrees was not enough; their physical embodiment, certified and on paper, had its own significance. A *real cédula* sent several decades later to the Guatemalan *audiencia* further clarifies this intention. In 1566, the crown explicitly ordered that copies of *cédulas*, certified letters, and other mandates be stored in the cities and towns of the *audiencia*.[16] The dissemination of such official copies would ensure both that the word of the king would be present throughout the *audiencia* and that his subjects would have recourse to local copies.

Certain *escribanos* had a particularly important role to play in ensuring that this procedure was followed. The *escribano de cámara* had a special obligation to not only copy and store such official mandates but also to be present for their initial receipt. A 1587 *cédula* reprimanded the officials of the *audiencia* for opening the correspondence from Spain without the *escribano de cámara* present. A *cédula* dated only a week later took the Guatemalan *audiencia* president to task for having sent a letter penned by a common servant rather than by the *escribano de cámara*. The *escribano* thereby played a unique role in legitimizing every aspect of how a document was handled. He had to supervise a document's creation, he had to be present when official documents from Spain were received, and he had to be involved in a document's subsequent storage and, if necessary, duplication.[17]

The *escribano*'s role as intermediary between the processes of sending and storing documents appears to have been entirely by design. The archive played a key part in both processes. As a 1596 *real cédula* makes explicit, the archive was conceived in early legislation as a kind of safety net (or, to mix metaphors, a "backup" system) for the process of exchanging correspondence. The brief *cédula* is worth quoting fully, as it explains precisely the rationale linking document travel and document storage.

President and high judges of my royal *audiencia* in the city of Santiago in the province of Guatemala it being convenient and Necessary that a register be kept there of the letters sent to me from that *audiencia*, and it being my understanding that this is not done, I Order that from now on, all letters sent to me from that *audiencia*, regardless of what matter they pertain to, be copied and a register of them be kept and that you the president and high judges who write them keep a record of them in bound books because it is my wish that you have such books there and because it is also convenient that all provisions, decrees and letters sent from here be carefully safeguarded from now on. And in order for this to be done with the proper clarity and order, I Order that that they be placed in order in the archive of that *audiencia* and that there be a book where they shall all be recorded to the letter, and So that they may be found and obeyed easily they should be organized according to topic and a table should be made of them because it could happen that if some of the orders in them are not made known they will not be obeyed. And once this book is made you shall send me a copy with an account of the decrees it contains and which have been obeyed and which have not and why this is so.[18]

This *cédula* succinctly combines the imperative to see ingoing mandates logged, copied, safeguarded, and obeyed with the need to see outgoing correspondence copied and accounted for. Philip II leaves no doubt that these two forms of record-keeping were meant to be stored in the same place. The *audiencia* archive therefore had the double task of storing copies of outgoing correspondence and storing books of incoming decrees and mandates. As the *cédula* clarifies in its final section, Philip also wished to have sent back to him a copy of the book storing his own decrees. Perhaps the distant archive in Guatemala can be more clearly conceptualized not as a safety net or a backup system but as a mirror: a documentary reflection of the paperwork on the other side of the Atlantic. In its ideal form, the archive in Guatemala would have mirrored the correspondence sent to Spain and the book of *cédulas* would have mirrored Philip's own collection of decrees. At the heart of the *cédula* lay the objectives of good governance. Acknowledging that orders could not be fulfilled if they were not well and widely known, the *cédula* characterized the archive as a place that would both safeguard and, crucially, make accessible the decrees and provisions sent by the king.

The archive had consequently to protect information and provide information at the same time. To this end, *escribanos* were charged with duplicating documents that might be required by officials while guarding their originals. From early on in the colonial period, officials attempted to "borrow" documents from the archive, a practice the *cédulas* from Spain strictly prohibited. A 1587 *cédula* castigated one of the *audiencia* judges for taking the safe filled with *cédulas* and *provisiones* to his home. Protesting that a stray document could easily be lost in this manner, the *cédula* ordered that officials were to request only the specific document they needed.[19] Some decades later, the practice was amended to prevent even a single document from leaving the archive. In 1621, a high judge in the *audiencia* had an entire bundle of papers sent to the office of an *escribano público*, a notary outside of the *audiencia* office. This prompted an order stating that no original was to leave the archive; rather copies were to be certified and witnessed for consultation outside the archive.[20] The clearest articulation of what would become standard policy came only a few years later, in a 1624 *cédula* that decried the rumors of documents floating free outside the archive and insisted, "because of the danger that they may be lost or damaged . . . I do order that the books and papers be stored in the archive . . . under two locks and that none shall be taken from it but rather when necessary they shall be viewed in the archive and copies made there."[21] The archive safe of the Guatemalan *audiencia* was from then on kept under lock and key.

As access to the archive was strictly controlled, so did control over its papers become contentious. In 1626, a Guatemalan *regidor* (councilman) demanded that he be given one of the keys to the archive, since the officials who held the keys appeared to treat the documents carelessly. The councilman found one of the "ancient books pertaining to the founding of the city" missing, and upon inquiring was coolly informed that another official was keeping it at home. He protested that this would not do, since there were "ancient documents that must be protected as they guard secrets that should not be known by anyone."[22] The documentary treasure, then, consisted not only of more recent *cédulas* and mandates from Spain essential to effective governance but also ancient documents considered vital to the city's foundations. What made them valuable, in the councilman's eyes, was their "secret" content and their pertinence to the city's establishment.

Implicitly, however, what made them particularly valuable was their status as originals. In other words, they were valuable as material objects apart from their content. The solution to protecting the valuable material objects in the archive while making their content accessible to officials therefore relied heavily on *escribanos* and their compliance in providing certified copies (*traslados* or *testimonios*). *Reales cédulas* repeatedly stressed that *escribanos* were obliged to copy documents faithfully, even if they had not authored the originals. In 1643 *escribanos* were exhorted to take greater care, as their copies of documents penned by others were observed to be "not very faithful or legal."[23] As control of archives—particularly the *audiencia* archive under the charge of the *escribano de cámara*—grew more effective, their documents were both safer and harder to access. *Escribanos* could either readily provide faithful copies of archive documents or, on the contrary, refuse to provide copies or provide sloppy copies. In the late seventeenth century, the Guatemalan *Fiscal* himself had difficulty extracting documents from the *escribanos*, prompting him to level a fine against the *escribano de cámara* and certain *escribanos de provincia*.[24] Writing from Spain, the king found himself apologizing for the *escribanos* to the *Fiscal* while demanding that they comply with his requests. He recognized that *escribanos* occupied positions of unusual power. They provided the vital protection for archives and the equally vital stamp of validity for documents, but as keepers of both their lack of co-operation could potentially obstruct the entire flow of paperwork that allowed the transatlantic empire to function.

Archives and Escribanos in the Eighteenth Century

Throughout the eighteenth century, Guatemalan *escribanos* continued to play a crucial role in the organization and safekeeping of documents. Efforts were made to improve Guatemalan officials' accessibility to archival documents, such as in the creation of a central depository for the documents of deceased *escribanos* and in the greater emphasis on the *escribano*'s obligation to provide copies of documents under lock and key.[25] But this did little to change the *escribano*'s role as the principal overseer of document production in eighteenth-century Guatemala. Likewise, *escribano* archival practices changed little during this period.[26] The principal tool relied upon by *escribanos* for the organization and safekeeping of documents continued to be an inventory or index.

Echoing the 1596 orders, the king reprimanded his Guatemalan *audiencia* in 1710, saying "the Council of Indies has received various documents of yours, and there was not an index accompanying them, as is customary." Even when the index traveled in the same ship with the indexed letters or decrees and therefore ran the same risk of loss or theft, it was seen as a necessary safeguard.[27] Indexes were likewise relied upon for the ordering of archives, as the early *cédula* quoted at the beginning of the chapter and many later decrees demonstrate.[28] Lest this identical method of organization seem a superficial similarity, it should be noted that the rationale for indexing archival contents was the same as the rationale for indexing correspondence. Indexes of archival contents were necessary to account for "lost" documents. As an early eighteenth-century set of instructions for re-ordering the Guatemalan *ayuntamiento* archive makes clear, the intent was to avoid the "very evident risk as is today lamentably manifest in the loss" of documents. The official complaining of the archive's deplorable state pointed to the absence of important volumes and demanded that "an inventory be made of all the papers in the archive, which . . . should be executed by the *escribano* of the *ayuntamiento*."[29] The archive contained a great deal of documentary treasure, as the official was careful to point out.

Internal complaints were echoed by later decrees sent from Spain and elaborated by *audiencia* officials. In 1761, the king wrote to the *audiencia* upbraiding its officials for the poor state of their archives. Pointing directly to the difficulties posed by distance, which precluded his subjects from consulting with him directly, the king stressed the need to not only keep *cédulas* and mandates in order but to also keep careful records of all documents produced by the *audiencia*.[30] The *audiencia* officials put the king's orders into effect by addressing the "disorder" of the archive papers and noting that a loose *cédula* was too easy to misplace ("traspapelarse") or steal. The Guatemalan *Fiscal* admitted that in the *escribanía de cámara* "many cannot be found, either due to poor organization or to carelessness." He reminded the *audiencia* that the correct procedure was for the *escribano* to keep a "book of copies" of the decrees, so that the original might be kept safe. He also called for the decrees to be indexed, "as was done in the past": a lapsed practice that the *Fiscal* insisted the *escribanos* adhere to.[31] Much like correspondence that might be ruined by water, lost during travel, or stolen as it changed hands, documents in the archive ran analogous risks due to poor storage conditions, poor organization, and theft. While proper procedures were crucial at each stage to minimize these risks, the most reliable way to both prevent and account for lost documents was to keep rigorous inventories and indexes of every single document received and produced by the *audiencia*.

The indexes of Guatemalan *escribanos* testify to their efforts in fulfilling these mandates. *Escribanos* duly kept copy books of all decrees, as well as log books of all document traffic (*libros de conocimientos*), draft books with notes and rough copies of letters, and books recording incoming correspondence.[32] The *libros de conocimientos* kept by the *escribano de cámara* could span several years, listing each document acted upon by the office.[33] Separate books recording correspondence with subordinate offices were in some cases organized based on location, as, for example, a notebook initiated in 1771 recorded all correspondence with the administration in Tuxtla. Noting the date of the incoming correspondence, the *escribano* also indicated when a reply had been sent, thereby giving a clear sense of the pace of communication. Receiving on average one or two pieces of mail from Tuxtla each month, the *escribano* in Guatemala usually took two weeks to a month to reply.[34] Demonstrating once again the *escribanos'* role in the movement of documents, the itinerary for *cordilleras* in Table 5.1 suggests that the Tuxtla book would have been one among many. With a circulation route in mind, the escribano would keep correspondence books for each location.[35]

TABLE 5.1.

Late colonial itineraries for escribano documents

This central office [of the *escribano de cámara*] and the real *audiencia* have always observed the following itinerary for the dispatch of *cordilleras*:

First Cordillera	Second Cordillera
Sacatepequez	Vieja Guatemala
Escuintla	Chimaltenango
Chiquimula	Solola
Castillo del Golfo	Vera Paz
Omoa	Castillo del Peten
Sonsonate	Totonicapan
San Salvador	Quesaltenango
Comayagua	Suchitepequez
Tegucigalpa	Soconusco
Realexo	Tuxtla
Subtiava	Ciudad Real
Leon	
Castillo de San Juan	
Nicoya	
Matagalpa	
Costa Rica	

But now an effort will be made to reform these itineraries, since the *cordilleras* customarily take an entire year to circulate. The *cordillera* itinerary might be revised as follows:

1st cordillera	2nd cordillera	3rd cordillera
Alcalde ordinario	Escuinta	Leon
de esta capital	Sonsonate	Subtiava y Realexo
Sacatepequez	San Salvador	~~Castillo del Peten~~
Chiquimula	Tegucigalpa	Masagalpa
Castillo del Golfo	Comayagua	~~Nicoya~~
	Truxillo	Nicoya
	Omoa	~~Matagalpa~~
	~~Tegucigalpa~~	Costa Rica

4th cordillera	5th cordillera	6th cordillera
Totonicapan	~~Vieja Guatemala~~	Vera Paz
Quesaltenango	Chimaltenango	Castillo del Peten
Suchitepequez	Solola	
Soconusco		
Tuxtla		
Ciudad Real		

Source: Derived by the author from documents at the Archivo General de Centroamérica

With such an active role in document circulation, the *escribano* naturally incorporated the organization of document circulation into the organization for document storage. Other volumes grouped correspondence
from various locations but organized the documents geographically within
the volume. A 1767 book of correspondence with tax collection offices
throughout the *audiencia* subdivided the correspondence with Omoa,
Golfo, Chiquimula and Zacapa, Sonsonate, Quetzaltenango, Totonicapán, Sololá, Escuintla, Verapaz, Mazatenango, Sacatepéquez, and the
capital.[36] Adhering to the rule of keeping even their rough drafts logged,
the *escribanos de cámara* kept books of their office's preparatory work,
thereby providing some insight into the less official side of their workday.[37]
The book preserved the doodles, drafts, and idle musings of *escribano* staff
over a forty-year period, from which the cover of this book is taken. Burns
has observed a similar, more extensive "menagerie of fanciful creatures" in
the colonial archives of Peru, and such pages offer brief, distorted glimpses
into the many aspects of *escribano* work that was not preserved, cataloged,
and indexed.[38]

The *escribanos* in regional offices were charged not only with overseeing
the production and storage of documents in their district, but also with co-
ordinating their documents with *escribanos* at other levels of government.
A set of guidelines sent from Spain in 1768 outlining the procedures for
writing and storing mortgages at the regional level highlighted the methods
of organization and archiving demanded of local *escribanos*.

It will be the obligation of the *Escribanos* of the municipal governments to keep
one book or several with separate registers for each of the towns in the district,
with their corresponding log, such that there is a clear account of which mortgages
exist in which town, and the logs should be organized by year, so that updates
might easily be made, and they should be paginated and bound in the same manner used by *Escribanos* for their notary books, and if the mortgages be located in
more than one Town, they should be registered in the books for each corresponding place.[39]

The instructions emphasized a method of organization that was primarily spatial and secondarily temporal. They also specified which documents
were to be archived by the *escribano*, stating that "the legal instrument
that should be exhibited at the mortgage Office, should be the first copy
made by the *Escribano*, which is called the *original*, except when it is an
ancient document that has been misplaced or lost, in which case it should
be a copy certified by a competent Judge."[40] While the latter instructions
placed greatest emphasis on the safety of the document and its status as an
original copy, the former focused on ease of access. The guidelines took
the matter of locating documents further, specifying that in addition to

organizing the mortgages by location and year, *escribanos* were to keep separate indexes.

To facilitate locating documents, the municipal government's *Escribanía* should have an index Book or general Register, in which according to the letters of the alphabet the names of the Signatories to the mortgages and the districts or parishes where they are located should be listed, and next to each should be noted the page where the document regarding the given mortgage, person, parish or territory is to be found: by this means it will be possible to find any mortgage that needs to be located by three or four different methods; and to facilitate the creation of this general alphabetical index, whenever the document is created it should be entered in the Index.[41]

The instructions indicate clearly that the documents were stored not only for their value as originals but also for their continued use as legal instruments. The emphasis on being able to locate documents easily and by various routes suggests that the *escribanías* anticipated a fair amount of traffic from people who wished to see copies of mortgages. In other words, the archive was now constituted in the instructions not as a treasure house of untouched documents but as a living archive frequently consulted by officials and other individuals. "Since the conservation of public documents is so important to the State," the instructions continued, "all the *Escribanos* throughout the region should send to the Judge or District Governor an annual register of the legal instruments existing in their notary books, so that it be stored in the *Escribanía* of the municipal government."[42] The index would permit the official and the *escribano* to identify any missing document not registered in the logbook. In a manner exactly parallel, then, to the system promoted for keeping track of correspondence, the guidelines sought to create matching indexes in two places that would mirror each other and signal the absence of missing documents. Just as the king expected to receive an index of correspondence matching the index of sent mail in Guatemala, the district governor or judge would receive an index of documents ideally matching the register held by the local *escribano*. Indexing thus served the dual purpose of facilitating "way-finding" within an archive and preventing document loss.

The other, complementary method of facilitating way-finding and document safety was to promote centralization and consolidation of archival material. Already, the structure of composite documents inherently encouraged both. When a single matter was initiated and elaborated in multiple sites, then sent to a central office for approval, the composite document reflecting all of these steps would naturally be stored in its final destination—the central office. Thus places like the *Casa de Contratación* in Seville or the Guatemalan *audiencia* effortlessly accumulated documentary material on matters large and small. But the range of institutions and the presence of regional notaries complicated this centralization. Just as the mail service kept its own archive, so did the *escribano* in Totonicapán keep his own *protocolos*. Beginning early in the colonial period, efforts were under way to consolidate document holdings in both Spanish America and Spain.

The Simancas archive, founded by Philip II between 1540 and 1545, became a primary site for document collection in the eighteenth century. A 1726 manuscript by Agustín Santiago Riol, titled "Report on the waste and loss of political papers belonging to Spain and remedies that should be followed for their conservation," lamented that foreign invasions and the habits of a traveling court had resulted in many documents being lost or destroyed.[43] Riol observed, giving due credit to internal strife and rapacious royal councilors, that by the early eighteenth century archives found themselves in a truly sorry state. He felt obliged to point out that the king's effort in 1718 to transfer documents to Simancas had not improved the situation. "In 1718," he wrote, "your majesty ordered taken to the Archive of Simancas all the papers of the Councils and Offices for which there was already a given place, but this was done with such careless haste that it left no occasion for the offices to inventory which documents were taken."[44] Riol did his best to counter these adverse circumstances by surveying the state of existing archives.

The report demonstrates clearly that royal offices in Spain each continued to keep their own archives in the first quarter of the eighteenth century, and it was his belief that this had in part permitted the very uneven treatment—and consequent occasional neglect—of royal documents. The Council of Castile's papers, for example, suffered from similar indignities to those experienced in Guatemala, where officials withdrew documents whenever and however they saw fit.[45] The papers at the archive of the Presidency of Castile, Riol protested, "have been treated with such neglect that I have seen them many times thrown on the floor of the room, exposed to the view of anyone and everyone. Their state is so grave and they require great care," he insisted, due to the important "secrets" that they contained.[46] The Inquisition, by contrast, had kept its archives in very good order, such that "the Inquisition has a great advantage over other councils in that it can easily determine what has transpired to its benefit in the past because its papers are in better order than those of the others."[47] Thus by 1726 official document troves found themselves in varied conditions, and no small part of the confusion was due to the fact that their contents had already been partly transferred, either informally and gradually by officials or by direct order in larger chunks. Riol pointed to the fact, for example, that he had written his brief account of the Inquisition for his report based on documents found at the Simancas archive.[48]

Their consolidation would, in theory, make it simpler to consult related documents pertaining to a single issue or branch of government. As various documents were transferred to Simancas in 1718 and other document caches were combined, the task of finding them was potentially made easier. Riol repeatedly argued, however, that consolidating archives was no substitute for careful inventorying. Writing of the office of the *Cámara de Gracia*, for example, an archive that had its origins in medieval record-keeping, he observed that some documents were not inventoried at all and others were inventoried poorly.

The manner in which its papers are kept is not in so disorderly a fashion as with the other offices, but it is still confusing and obscure, because while the case documents and others are inventoried, the inventories are so minimal that they only list the names of the interested parties, and when one looks for a document it is difficult to find it without knowing its date.[49]

Other portions of the archive had no inventory at all, and when he recognized that "it would be very important to make an Index of them" because the time-consuming project had never been accomplished, he took on the task himself. "I began to silently make a few notes along an alphabetical index of some particulars," he wrote, "and realizing that there was no unimportant document among those precious pages I thought to embark on a fundamental and universal work treating all of them without omission."[50] Riol's report is thus not bent wholly on the goal of archive consolidation. Transferring papers to Simancas was a worthwhile goal, he implied, as long as this was done by preserving and properly indexing them.

In Spanish America, these priorities were reflected in both the mandates received from Spain and in the consequent reforms carried out in official archives. Tamar Herzog, in her study of *escribanos* and archives in Quito, also places the initial stages of archival consolidation early in the seventeenth century. Herzog characterizes the early formation of archives in Spain as an effort to wrest control from *escribanos* who held a monopolistic control of documents, rather than as an effort to preserve documents.[51] She indicates that later on in 1780, a concerted effort was made in Quito to gather government-related documents in a central location. It seems that in Guatemala—consistent with Riol's manuscript—efforts at consolidation were more concerned with preserving documents than with wresting control from *escribanos*. Luján Muñoz points to the 1699 mandate in Guatemala to create an archive in the *ayuntamiento* for the records belonging to deceased *escribanos*.[52] And he points to a case in Veracruz in which an *escribano* attempted to retain the notary books of a deceased colleague and was overruled.[53] Similarly, an *escribano* for the Guatemalan city council was ordered to return certain books and papers within three days when they were found missing from the archive in 1755. The official complaining of the missing documents pointed out that they were not bequeathed to the *escribano* by his predecessor for him to do as he liked.[54] So while an *escribano* maintained control of his documents during his lifetime, the central administration effectively absorbed his documents after his death. Nonetheless, *escribanos* were still trusted more than other officials with document holdings prior to their eventual incorporation.

Stray papers were repeatedly ordered back into the *escribano's* care in Guatemala. In 1769, for example, an order was given for papers found in the office a deceased official, Pedro Ortiz de Letona, to be handed over to the *escribano*. The official giving the order agreed that these documents were necessary for bookkeeping purposes, and he demanded that the *escribano* create a proper inventory of the papers "for their improved organization."[55] Similarly, after the 1773 earthquake, efforts were made to restore to the *escribano mayor's* care papers abandoned in the ruined capital. Ordering that the abandoned documents be restored to the *escribano* within fifteen days, the decree lamented the state of the archive, emphasizing that it contained "the most sacred deposit of treasures and public writings, which preserve the most ancient contracts and the wise decrees of the king spanning more than two centuries." Languishing in the ruined capital, they lay "on the floor, exposed to dampness, rot, and vermin."[56] Once again, the welfare of the city's documentary treasure—at least among certain officials—prompted efforts to consolidate stray papers.

The efforts at archive consolidation can be seen as corresponding with and reinforcing the continued emphasis in the eighteenth century on prohibiting original documents from leaving official archives. Since *escribanos* were the established custodians of archives, this resulted in a consistent and enduring privileging of the *escribano's* control of important papers. The matter could not have been put more clearly than it was in 1764, in a decree sent from Spain responding to rumors of documents being withdrawn from the Royal Treasury in the Philippines.

> I have resolved, that under no pretext may the books or papers archived in my Royal Offices be withdrawn, nor may they be handed out for any reason by their custodians; and only in very exceptional cases may Viceroys, Presidents, and Governors send an *audiencia* minister from the district accompanied by a government *escribano*, to make any copy that might be necessary.[57]

Curtailing even the power of his highest officials in Spanish America, the king placed the safety of the documents above all other concerns. But as the decree makes clear, the intent was not to empower *escribanos* but to assure that documentary treasure was kept secure. In the attempt to obey these orders, officials in Guatemala in the eighteenth century placed their *escribanos* in command of archives that were increasingly consolidated and well organized.

The Keys to the Archive:
Disputes over Custodianship of Guatemalan Documents

Disputes over archival materials in eighteenth-century Guatemala are relatively rare. The numerous and explicit decrees from Spain and the long tradition of assigning custodianship to *escribanos* left little doubt as to the rightful place of official documents. Most documents pertaining to archive management in the eighteenth century address the problem of stray papers and the persistent tendency among high-ranking officials to withdraw original copies from the archive. To a lesser extent, Guatemalan officials echoed Riol's call for greater tidiness and organization. The disputes discussed below that did occur, however, are particularly illuminating, as they shed light on the question of ownership versus custodianship.

In the 1720s, a bitter personal dispute between the district governor of Sonsonate and the district's *escribano*, Juan Antonio de Torres, led the *escribano* to seek an injunction against the district governor and his family. Traveling to Guatemala to seek the injunction, the *escribano* necessarily abandoned his post, a circumstance which prompted the district governor to take a radical step. "The papers and books of his archive were taken from the house of the *escribano*" and placed in the central office. The district governor claimed that the *escribano* had essentially forfeited his post and his right to the archive by abandoning his position and traveling to the capital. The dispute made its way all the way to Spain, where the king weighed in on the question of whether the *escribano* had neglected his duties. In 1728, Torres was ordered back to Sonsonate and was charged with a fine for having temporarily abandoned his post. However, it was also ordered that he be fully restored to his position as *escribano* "quickly and without delay and that the district governor and the council return to him all the papers pertaining to his office and that in the future they treat him respectfully and without giving cause for any complaint."[58]

The dispute provides a glimpse into the surprising enmity that occasionally arose between officials, but it also offers telling indications of the *escribano*'s position as the custodian of official documents. It is worth noting that the documents were originally kept in Torres's house (identified, quite explicitly, as his "casa"), which demonstrates that he probably conducted his business as official *escribano* for the district from his home.[59] The district governor's abrupt removal of the documents during Torres's absence may have been motivated largely by spite, but it nonetheless suggests that the papers were of continuing use to officials in Sonsonate; or, at the very least, it was plausible that the papers would be of continuing use and had therefore to be made accessible. Even when

Torres was found to have been to some degree at fault for neglecting his post, he was considered the rightful custodian of the documents. The emphasis of the 1728 document, with its composite parts written in Guatemala and Spain, is clearly directed toward the restoration of the *escribano* office. The 1728 document was stored in the Guatemalan capital under the heading, "Ordering that the district governors of Sonsonate return and restore to Don Juan Antonio de Torres, *escribano*, all the papers and legal instruments belonging to his archive with all due accounts, and that they execute the other matters discussed herein."[60] Written as a matter of course, the title's mention of "*his*" archive is nonetheless worth noting.[61]

A similar case occurred in the late eighteenth century in Chiquimula. The *corregidor* for the province of Chiquimula and Zacapa, Tomás de Mollinedo y Villavicencio, complained that the *escribano*, one Enrique Girón Alvarado, had attempted to transfer the archive to his house.

The *escribano* of this province, Don Enrique Girón, wishes to have the Archive presented to him so that he may move it to his house, a wish that I, your *corregidor*, have not agreed to. In the first place because the archive should remain in the building that belongs to the Royal office, and said *escribano* should assist in the archive at least three hours in the morning and three in the afternoon to attend to any tasks that might arise.[62]

Mollinedo y Villavicencio went on to claim, in the second place, that the archive had always customarily been held in the royal offices and in the power of the *corregidor* because of the "bad consequences that have resulted on occasion." While in the power of the *corregidor*, he argued, the archive was made available to the *escribano* by granting him a key that would permit him free access to any papers he needed for the fulfillment of his obligations.[63] Mollinedo y Villavicencio concluded by asking his superiors in Guatemala City to clarify the obligations and privileges with regard to the archive.

The *escribano*, Enrique Girón Alvarado, simultaneously wrote to officials in Guatemala protesting that the archive had been withheld, despite the fact that his *real título*, the document bearing his license and notice of his appointment, indicated that the archive would be his responsibility. "It was denied me," he wrote, "on the pretext that said archive should remain in the charge of the *corregidores*, when in fact it should be the contrary, since it has been the custom from time immemorial that the Archives have been and are in the charge of the *Escribanos*, as it is to them that their custody corresponds."[64] The opposing interpretations of the *escribano* and the *corregidor* appear to have been motivated by causes other than personal enmity—at least initially. Girón evidently was a recent appointment to the post in Chiquimula, and Mollinedo y Villavicencio was a veteran official who had only lately arrived in the region.[65]

The response from officials in Guatemala was in some degree surprising. The *Fiscal* stated that "if the archive is situated in the house of the *corregidor* it does not cease to be the responsibility of the *escribano*."[66] The *audiencia*'s final verdict suggested a compromise, since it gave some responsibility to both the *corregidor* and the *escribano* but by doing so it created space for contradictory interpretations.

It is ordered that the archive should exist in the room designated for it: that the *escribano* should be presented with all the papers pertaining to his office accompanied by a formal inventory, and he should have in his power a key permitting him to attend the office during the hours determined by the *corregidor* for the transaction of business.[67]

By ordering that the archive should be kept "in the room designated for it," the officials either unwittingly or intentionally left the precise location of the room unspecified. Perhaps the instructions stating that the *escribano* was to be given a key were suggestive, indicating that room would not be his; but this implication was not sufficiently transparent. Mollinedo y Villavicencio wrote back at once, promising to put the orders into effect, and evidently interpreting the orders heavily in his favor.

The dispute over the archive did not end there. A full four years later, Enrique Girón Alvarado wrote to the officials in Guatemala again, protesting that the *corregidor* had failed entirely to present him with the papers of the archive as ordered. Girón took a particular view of the orders sent from Guatemala, which he cited as stating that "it falls to me to have the Archive."[68] Instead of presenting him with the papers as ordered, Girón argued, the *corregidor* had followed his own "capricious system" and denied him the papers for all of four years. Girón claimed to be most disturbed by the state in which Mollinedo y Villavicencio kept the archive.

This is not the worst, Sir, as the Room in which the archive is kept is also used as a Storeroom or Dispensary where rifles and even comestibles are kept. And these naturally attract insects, rats, and other pests that eat the papers, a fact I can testify to as I have had occasion to see the door casually left open. There are many documents, lying unused, that have been eaten by moths and rats, for where hygiene and care are lacking this often occurs.[69]

As if to provide damning evidence of the poor treatment of documents in Chiquimula, all the papers pertaining to the case—including Girón's—were duly eaten away (Figure 5.1).

The troubling state of the archive, Girón wrote, impelled him to write once again to the officials in Guatemala. He could not be responsible, he protested, for the poor state of the papers when they were handled by the *corregidor*, his family, and others who had no sense of how to treat valuable documents. He begged the officials to insist with the *corregidor*,

FIGURE 5.1. A document from Chiquimula, eaten by vermin
Source: Archivo General de Centroamérica. Photograph by the author.

so that the archive might be turned over to him. In a brief postscript, he asked the officials to request the intervention of higher authorities in Chiquimula. The *corregidor*, having been informed on the first occasion that Girón was pursuing retrieval of the archive, had taken revenge by incarcerating one of the *escribano*'s domestics.[70] Girón's letter reached Guatemala, and the officials of the *audiencia* ordered that an inquiry be made into the situation in Chiquimula. They sent a letter to the *corregidor,* and they sent an official, Don Juan de la Paz, to investigate, but nothing further is known of where the archive remained or who took responsibility for its care. Perhaps the state of the documents themselves speaks most clearly as to their probable fate.

The decision taken by Guatemalan officials in the Chiquimula case was clearly not the only opinion rendered on the custodianship of archives, so it would be a mistake to generalize too broadly based on the dispute. However, a few points might be safely inferred. The reaction of the officials in Guatemala in response to the Chiquimula dispute, whatever ambiguities it may have permitted, clearly privileged the *escribano* as the custodian of the archive under any circumstance. The *Fiscal* emphasized that even were the archive to be situated in the *corregidor's* own rooms, the *escribano* would still bear responsibility for the archive. Seen in this light, the ambiguous instructions to place the archive in the "room designated (*destinado*) for it" appear to convey the message that the room itself was irrelevant: wherever the designated room might be, the archive was the responsibility of the *escribano*. The important question was not ownership so much as custodianship.

The decision—or, rather, the follow-up to it—also makes apparent the officials' continued concern with the safekeeping of documents. No doubt Girón expected to strike a chord with his vivid description of documents carelessly strewn in a storeroom, prey to insects and rats. The officials' decision to send a representative in person surely testifies to the seriousness of their response. Lastly, the original instructions from Guatemala also place a distinct emphasis on the use of an inventory for the transferal of documents. Their orders stating that the archive should be presented to Girón with a "formal inventory" were intended to ensure that the papers were presented according to protocol. The transfer of documents—and other materials—by inventory constituted one important step in the transfer of office between officials.

A transfer of archival papers beyond the office of *escribanos* will help to demonstrate the importance of the inventory as an instrument in "moving" papers. The Guatemalan mail office did not hire its own *escribano*, but it nonetheless relied on an extensive archive that included legal documents, correspondence, and logbooks of incoming and outgoing mail. In the 1770s, the Guatemalan mail administrator Simón de Larrazábal found himself still deprived of the archive held by his predecessor, Joseph Melchor de Ugalde. The death of Melchor de Ugalde had left the archive and the contents of the office in the hands of the interim administrator, Andrés Palomo, who had failed to deliver them. The documents and other effects were found in Melchor de Ugalde's house, kept and cared for by his widow. In 1774, a formal inventory of the archive and other contents of the office was finally created by an *escribano*, Don Joseph Sánchez de León, who was attended by several witnesses. A clean copy of the inventory, destined for the mail administration's archive, was written on *papel sellado*. Beginning the list of "papers and furniture," he inventoried the "books" found in Melchor de Ugalde's care. Notebooks containing accounting information, logs of incoming and outgoing mail, communication with regional offices, and other important paperwork were described in terms of their contents and number of pages. The inventory made note of blank pages and the frequent absence of signatures on many of the documents in the notebooks.[71]

Several pages inventorying documents were followed by a list of furniture. The office contents offers both a detailed visualization of the mail office and a clear explanation for why the documents and "furniture" were equally important to the transfer of office. Melchor de Ugalde's office included generic items, such as six metal candleholders, two narrow cedar-wood tables, and a large writing table. But it also contained a collection of items without which it would have been difficult to execute the receipt and delivery of mail at all. His office contained a scale, crystal inkpots, two wooden seals bearing the inscriptions "Yndias" and "Guathemala," a mailbox for the receipt of local mail, a sign with a coat of arms for the office door, numerous large and small mail trunks with their chains and locks, and an office safe.[72] The inventory concluded that "there are no additional papers, letters, or furniture belonging (*pertenecientes*) to the Administration."[73]

The retrieval of the documents and furniture reveals the various levels of custodianship. Melchor de Ugalde's widow, who had implicitly cared for the documents and furniture since October of 1770, when her husband passed away, had no claim upon the objects she had housed for four years.[74] Andrés Palomo was their temporary custodian, as is made clear in the questions put to him about the contents of the office safe. Their ultimate custodian was Simón de Larrazábal, but they "belonged" to the Administration. Just as Palomo and Melchor de Ugalde's widow would not have dreamed of keeping the seals, the mail trunks, and the office safe, they made no claim to the documents written by Melchor de Ugalde—the archival documents essential to the effective management of the mail system.

The "delivery" of the archive by means of an inventory highlights the use of the inventory as an instrument for safekeeping. It also points to the similarities between the risks of moving documents across extended spatial distances and the risks of moving documents across shorter distances: from one office to another, or from one custodian to another. During transportation to Mexico or Spain, documents might be lost, stolen, or destroyed by poor weather. Similarly, as the Chiquimula dispute makes evident, documents might be destroyed or misplaced while stationary. The use of an inventory permitted accountability and therefore greater safekeeping. As the numerous *cédulas* sent throughout the colonial period make evident, the safety of documentary treasure continued to be a concern even when documents were nominally under the *escribano*'s lock and key. Certainly it was essential to facilitate access to useful documents, but preventing loss or theft was paramount. The archive inventory provided both, creating ease of access and ensuring—theoretically—the safety of each listed document.

6 *The Inventories of Guatemalan Archivists*

> Despite my continuing poor health, I have gone to the Customs Office to review the ancient archive of the *escribanía de cámara*, which is currently a mountain of scrap-paper piled in a room; it has been moved to a large storeroom within the customs house, and the bundles have been placed on skids so that the necessary sorting might begin.[1]
> —Miguel Talavera, Guatemalan archivist, in 1836

In the nineteenth century, the role of *escribano* changed. While *escribanos del número* (otherwise known as *escribanos de provincia*) essentially continued their work as public notaries, certain government *escribanos* found their work divided and distributed among various officials. In some cases, the position of government *escribano* was dissolved, to be replaced by a secretary or archivist.[2] After 1825, government *escribanos* were appointed as national *escribanos* at the federal level or state *escribanos* at the state level.[3] Throughout the 1820s and 1830s, as the colonial bureaucracy was recast and to some extent replaced by the bureaucracies of the federal and national governments, the tasks previously delegated to *escribanos* fell largely to secretaries, archivists, and notaries. Archives had been nodes of communication in the colonial period. They now became repositories of stationary documents whose only travel would be temporal. Divorced from the processes of creating and moving documents relating to political affairs of the moment, archivists became custodians of the past.

The formal transformation of the *escribano* position and, more importantly, the changing political boundaries of the former *audiencia*, left Guatemalan archives in a state of considerable disarray. However, despite the period of chaos caused by the wars for independence, which prevented the smooth transfer of papers from *escribanos* to *archiveros* (archivists), continuities of method are evident. Two comprehensive efforts were made to organize the government archives in the Guatemalan capital, the first in the 1830s and the second in the 1840s. These attempts at organization mark the beginning of Guatemala's national archival system. The early archivists of Guatemala's national archives both preserved and modified the practices of colonial *escribanos*. One important continuity was the reliance on document inventories. As late as the end of the nineteenth century,

Guatemalan bureaucrats charged with organizing the nation's paperwork relied on inventories to catalog documents, facilitate access, and improve accountability.

This chapter takes a broad view of the changes that occurred from the late colonial period to the mid-nineteenth century. As Central America separated from Spain and then Mexico, as the provinces of the *audiencia* became states of the Central American federation, and as the states became independent nations, documentary treasure became national treasure. Disputes over which government had claim to particular documents erupted as states solidified their spatial—and documentary—boundaries. Furthermore, while efforts to consolidate and centralize archives continued, these efforts were systematically undercut by new document forms. No longer composite, documents amassed separately at each node in a correspondence network. Local archives accumulated paper, and central archives stored more fragmented pieces of document conversations.

This chapter also attempts to follow one particular set of documents as it "traveled" from the early colonial period into the national period. The archive inventory of Ignacio Guerra y Marchán, the Guatemalan *escribano de cámara* in the late-eighteenth century, provides an exemplary archive inventory of official documents ranging from 1600 to 1782. This archive, containing valuable documents from the colonial period, was safeguarded by Marchán until his death. Marchán's inventory and the inventories of later archivists permit some insight into how one *escribano*'s domain became the contents of the Guatemalan national archive: how documents traveled safely from the colonial period to the present.

Escribano de Cámara, Ignacio Guerra y Marchán

Ignacio Guerra y Marchán was appointed to the *escribanía de cámara* in July 1777.[4] As the principal *escribano* in Guatemala City, he had close contact with the highest members of government in the capital and important duties as not only a clerk and archivist but also a disseminator of official information to the provinces. His name and rubric appear on documents well into the early nineteenth century.[5] Whether because they had the fortune of being better preserved or because Guerra y Marchán was an *escribano* of particular diligence, his archive inventories provide some of the most complete accounts of the *escribanía*'s document collection.[6] Guerra y Marchán's inventory of documents written between 1600 and 1782 provides not only an invaluable sense of which documents his archive contained but also how the *escribano* conceptualized the organization of his archive. The first several pages of Guerra y Marchán's two-hundred-page inventory provide two separate tables of contents. On the inside cover of the inventory is a general list of the number of pages pertaining to each category. The categories used in this list, clearly the first place consulted in the inventory, include both regional designations and administrative departments. This brief index bears some similarities with the contemporaneous place-name indexes created by mail officials and described in Chapter 3. Neither are "maps" and yet both fulfill the purposes of a map. While considering archival content rather than geographical locations, the archive inventory was similarly intended to designate "places" within the archive and, more importantly, to facilitate way-finding. As the index corresponds to the ordering of entries within the inventory, Guerra y Marchán would have turned to this page to locate a section on, for example, documents from León (Figure 6.1).

A more detailed table of contents following the brief index divides the documents by administrative department. Separated into numbered bundles (*legajos*), the documents are listed by date and with reference to how many documents each date range contains.[7] The inventory entries following the two tables of contents begin with "*indiferentes*" or miscellaneous documents and proceed to list the documents for the various regional jurisdictions and departments of the *audiencia*. Each subsection is ordered chronologically, according to the *legajo* divisions indicated in the second table of contents. The documents are numbered and then described in two to four lines, giving a sense of the document's subject and the parties involved.

The structure of the inventory suggests that region and governmental department were both important organizational tools for the *escribano*'s archive. Guerra y Marchán, in attempting to classify (and afterwards, locate) a document in his archive, would consider either geographical jurisdiction or departmental jurisdiction. The structure of the inventory also suggests a secondary but nevertheless important emphasis on date—or, more precisely, chronology. Once "within" a department or region, Guerra y Marchán would have considered the date in order to find a document, and in some cases he crossed out or inserted document entries that had been previously entered under the wrong year.

The content of the inventory is also instructive. Archive inventories were only one kind of *escribano* inventory among many. During Guerra y Marchán's tenure, various logbooks and indexes kept track of the archive's content. Several *libros de conocimientos*, or receipt-books, logged document production within his office.[8] He kept logbooks of documents provided to *audiencia* and city council officials, such as the Guatemalan treasurer.[9] A register (*protocolo*) inventoried documents deposited in the archive and placed in the *escribano*'s care.[10] Guerra y Marchán kept a

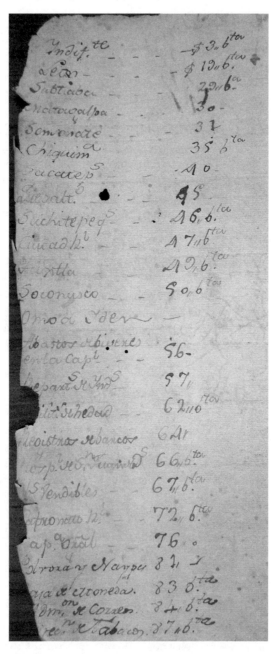

FIGURE 6.1. Ignacio Guerra y Marchán's archive inventory
Source: Archivo General de Centroamérica. Photograph by the author.

book in which the office's drafts and notes for a roughly ten-year period were stored.[11] And, confirming the point made in Chapter 5 regarding the *escribano*'s ties to the mail system, Guerra y Marchán also kept inventories of replies received to decrees from Spain that he had copied and sent by circular to the provinces.[12] However, none of these various inventories, lists, or logbooks provided a comprehensive account of the *escribanía*'s content. The inventory listed above was Guerra y Marchán's effort to account for all of the important documents in his possession, primarily the finished versions of legal instruments. As Kathryn Burns describes in her study of colonial Peruvian archives, the official archive omitted as much as it included. Drafts, accounts, preparatory correspondence, and other supplemental materials were never inventoried and were rarely kept.[13] According to Guerra y Marchán's definition, only a portion of the papers contained in his office qualified as archival materials.

To consider, for example, a selection of documents that should now be familiar, Guerra y Marchán inventoried on six pages the documents in his archive pertaining to the mail system. Beginning with the year 1770, the *escribano* listed cases involving administrators such as Melchor de Ugalde and Andrés Palomo as well as *correos* such as José Rivera. Documents pertaining to route revisions, "clandestine" mail, paperwork prepared for the payment of *extraordinarios*, and the occasional criminal case against a *correo* are all listed. Among them are documents that clearly remained central to the archive's collection. Under the year 1774, for example, Guerra y Marchán listed the case pertaining to the transfer of papers from the deceased Melchor de Ugalde to Simón de Larrazábal discussed in Chapter 5. The *escribano* had previously and incorrectly entered the case of the *correo* archive under the year 1782 in his inventory, and the cramped entry at the top of the page demonstrates the effort at revision. At the bottom of the same page, listed under the year 1777, Guerra y Marchán made note of the case relating to the "little crate of grapes" carried by the *correo* Joseph Rivera. The case, discussed in Chapter 4, which caused such controversy over the delivery of *encomiendas*, remained one of the roughly fifty documents pertaining to the mail administration that Guerra y Marchán preserved in his archive.[14]

It seems at first perplexing that Guerra y Marchán created no additional inventory during the thirty-odd years that he remained in his post after 1782, but it seems less surprising when the circumstances of the inventory's creation are considered more closely. During Guerra y Marchán's time in office, he and other officials in the new capital of Guatemala struggled to restore documents that had been left behind in the ruins of Santiago de Guatemala after the 1773 earthquake. Efforts to fully recuperate all the documents from the former capital apparently took years. In 1780, the officials in the new capital ordered that the long-overdue recovery be immediately effected.

Concerning the fact that the secret archive of the council, the archive of the Office [of the President] and the register-books of deceased *escribanos* all find themselves still in the ruined city of Guatemala, although it was ordered that these be brought here long ago, because they are needed here in the Capital, where they ought to be: and they should be within sight in order for them to be cared for and so that they do not fall into decay. Let it be made known to the *Escribano Mayor* . . . so that they might be brought.[15]

The statement by the crown attorney on this occasion was somewhat more specific, demanding in September of 1780 that "a city councilman, with the assistance of the *escribano* . . . conduct all the Papers, and archive them according to an Inventory in this capital, providing verification that this has been completed within two months."[16] It appears that the task of recovering the archive and creating the inventory were first assigned to Joseph Manuel de Laparte, the *escribano de cabildo,* or city council secretary. But in May 1781, Laparte had still not complied with the council's orders. "The papers still lie abandoned in his office," the council protested, "and he has several of those belonging to the secret Archive locked away, depriving the Council of access to them."[17] They demanded that Laparte put the orders into effect or designate someone to take his place so that the papers be organized and made available.

Laparte's eventual reply in November of 1781, more than a year after the initial orders were issued, gives some sense of the difficulties posed by the task of organizing and inventorying the archive. Writing to Councilman Juan Manrique, he stated that he wished to point out to him "the great amount of work that has been done with the papers from the council archive that were brought from Guatemala. You yourself, Sir," he protested, "saw the lamentable condition in which they were packed and delivered." The chaotic condition of the papers was due, he explained, to how they had been hauled off of the shelves and packed out of order. Bound documents had come undone, making it difficult to determine how papers corresponded to one another. "Once we had returned," he wrote, "we began to organize them, putting them into categories in order to gain greater clarity, and we spent the entire winter wading through that confusing labyrinth."[18] Laparte protested that he was doing everything in his power to organize the archive and provide the needed inventory.

In December, the council's attorney (*síndico procurador*), Josef Fernández Gil, offered a scathing response to Laparte that gives a clear sense of how Guatemalan council officials envisioned the responsibilities of the *escribano* in relation to the archive. He summarized indignantly the injury to the public that resulted from withholding archived documents. It was according to the law and in order to preserve good order that "the papers of the secret archive are in the power of the *Escribano mayor*," he wrote. "These should be kept under three locks, for which purpose two cabinets were purchased and placed in that office." But it was not enough to keep them safe, he explained. "At every turn it is necessary to have various documents within sight, and they are required for providing reports concerning diverse matters." He protested that the difficult work of hauling the papers from the ruins of the former capital and organizing them into topics or subcategories was already complete. "The same cause that necessitated moving the documents to the new seat of the council," he went on, "necessitates the formation of an Inventory, since being already in bundles, tied and numbered, there can be no doubt that it will be easier to create it." He was certain that Laparte had no motive for postponing the creation of the inventory other than to waste time, and he demanded that the *escribano* be fined one hundred *pesos* if he did not immediately comply.[19] Fernández Gil prioritized both the archive's safety and its ready access to Guatemalan officials, but his emphasis on the *escribano*'s failure to complete the inventory demonstrates without any doubt that the inventory, not only the recovery of papers from the ruined capital, was thought essential to these objectives.

Later that same month Laparte was duly fined for failing to complete the inventory, but even this was not enough to provoke him into providing the much-sought document.[20] The *escribano de cámara*, Ignacio Guerra y Marchán, signed the orders on Christmas Eve of 1781 to provide Laparte with a final ultimatum. Laparte's name is signed beside Guerra y Marchán's, where the *escribano de cabildo* acknowledged receipt of the papers served to him by his colleague. But why he still did not comply does not form part of the record. Guerra y Marchán was doubtlessly assigned the task that Laparte did not fulfill, because it is his name on the cover of the 1782 inventory. And in 1798, the correspondence documenting Laparte's signal failure was found among his papers after his death. Guerra y Marchán signed the documents once again to acknowledge their receipt and admit them into his archive.[21]

The inventory that the Guatemalan officials clamored for so urgently in the early 1780s was seen to serve the purpose of recovery and reorganization. The fact that an inventory was thought essential in 1780 but no revision or new inventory was required during Guerra y Marchán's tenure suggests that the inventory was considered primarily a tool for periods of transition. In this sense, the inventory might be seen as a kind of "stock" inventory rather than an updated catalog. This does not mean, of course, that the content of the archive managed by Guerra y Marchán and the other *escribanos* remained stagnant or stable after the creation of the inventory. On the contrary, the late eighteenth century and early nineteenth century appear to have been periods of intense paperwork production. The *libros de conocimiento* and other indexes in Guerra y Marchán's office kept track of the document content produced after 1782.

An order sent from Spain in 1802 gives some sense of how vast the paperwork of the *audiencia* and council in Guatemala had grown. Having received news, the orders indicated, that the office of the president in Guatemala required additional employees for its effective management, a new *archivero* (archivist) position was created with an annual salary of three hundred and sixty *pesos* per year. The two *escribientes,* or scribes, in the office had their salaries raised from two hundred to three hundred *pesos* per year. The orders simultaneously confirmed the appointments of Don Alexandro Ramírez as secretary, Don Miguel Talavera as *oficial mayor,* and Don José Ramón Barberena as *oficial segundo,* all of whom were already employed in the office.[22] While the creation of the *archivero* position is significant, it is also important to note that the appointment took place in the president's office and not in the office of the *escribano de cámara,* Ignacio Guerra y Marchán.

However, the changes to Guerra y Marchán's office were not far off. In 1812, the Cortes de Cádiz altered the role of *escribanos* significantly and, to a lesser extent, modified archival practices. In 1812, the Cortes replaced the office of *escribano de ayuntamiento* with a general secretary, and they abolished the sale of office for *escribanías.*[23] Existing appointments could be maintained, assuming the *escribano* passed inspection and met with official approval.[24] The Cortes de Cádiz also issued the first regulations concerning the submission of printed materials to a central archive or library.

It is decreed: 1. Printers and Publishers of the Court shall present two copies of all printed works and papers that are printed to the Court Library. 2. These copies shall be presented without fail on their day of publication, under penalty of a fifty ducat fine. 3. The Librarian of the Court shall sign a receipt for the copies he receives. 4. In the Capitals of the Provinces the copies shall be presented by the printer to the Head of State (*Gefe Político*), and in the other Towns they shall be presented to the District Governor in the same manner and subject to the same penalties. 5. The District Governors will direct these copies with all possible promptness to the Heads of State, and these will forward the copies through their Secretaries of Peninsular Government, who will have them immediately transferred to the Library of the Court. 6. The Heads of State and District Governors will give receipt to the printers of the copies they receive. 7. The Heads of State will remit monthly to the Court . . . a list of the works and papers that they have sent or that remain in their hands due to the failure or delay of the Mail.[25]

Notably, the preamble to these articles describes the repository to which the copies will be sent as the "Archive and Library." The orders from the

Cortes de Cádiz reflect both innovations and continuities with previous practices. The hierarchical system of communication, the reliance on the mail system, and the use of an inventory (here, "list") all echo the long-standing methods of bureaucratic communication practiced during the colonial period. However, the emphasis on printed materials is new. Similarly, a distinction might be made between the effort in 1812 to gather exhaustively materials printed throughout Spanish America and the earlier, more circumscribed efforts by the Council of Indies to recoup correspondence and replies to official paperwork. As described in Chapter 5, efforts at consolidation of archives were well under way in the eighteenth century. The attempt in 1812 to centralize in the Spanish library all printed materials regardless of subject or origin seems qualitatively different.

The corresponding changes to *escribano* offices were not immediate. Despite the 1812 changes, which in any case appear to have had little effect on the *escribanía de cámara*, Guerra y Marchán continued to maintain his own archive until his death in approximately 1815. It is unclear when Guerra y Marchán died, but in April 1815, the king conceded the *escribanía de cámara* and the contents of Guerra y Marchán's office to his widow, María Petronila de la Cerda. The office was granted to her and her children, though at a fourth of its former value (two thousand *pesos*).[26] There is little to document how María Petronila de la Cerda fared as custodian of the *escribanía* during the following years, but a plaintive appeal made in the 1820s suggests that the political upheavals taking place in Guatemala made effective management of the *escribanía* difficult. The break with Spain and then with Mexico in the 1820s entailed a rapid reorganization of government, and Cerda complained that the changes had placed a great strain on the *escribanía*. She asked to be assigned some assistance in maintaining the office and restoring it to order.[27] As it happened, the difficulties experienced by Cerda were occurring everywhere in the maintenance of government archives. A few short years and a series of political realignments had served to render the archives almost unmanageable. In the 1820s, the long-term effort to reconcile the historical archives of the *audiencia* of Guatemala with the paperwork of the administration for the existing state of Guatemala began.

Government Archivists: Victoriano Grijalva and Miguel Talavera

The government of the independent state of Guatemala in the 1820s did not take long to discover that the archives in its possession required urgent attention. One portion of the project was assigned to Victoriano Grijalva, who began the arduous task of sorting through the government archives in

1823.[28] Part of the difficulty lay in the fact that there was not one archive but many archives. The newly established state government in Guatemala ordered that the archives of each "department," corresponding to the former provinces of the *audiencia*, be reclassified. The orders were to divide each regional archive into three subcategories: *político* (political affairs), *hacienda* (domestic or internal affairs), and *guerra* (defense).[29] Correspondingly, Grijalva and his newly appointed assistant, Francisco Flores, were ordered to organize the documents in the state's capital, creating an "archive of the old administration."[30]

Beginning in the 1820s, Grijalva worked to restore the archive of the "old government," collecting stray documents that were scattered in the hands of individuals and regional offices and creating the all-important inventory that would take stock of the archive's content. While few traces remain of Grijalva's work during that period (beyond his inventories), the scant evidence indicates that he was consolidating documents from throughout the former *reino*. The effort at consolidation initiated in the eighteenth century continued in the nineteenth century, as valuable documents were collected from *escribanos*, defunct offices, and private individuals. The original documents by Fray Francisco Ximénez documenting the history of San Vicente de Chiapas and Guatemala, for example, were demanded for inclusion in the archive from Francisco García Pelaez, author and later archbishop of Guatemala.[31] Documents were collected from the offices of *escribanos*, who presented their documents to the archivist with inventories.[32] Similarly, Grijalva also collected the documents belonging to the former commerce bureau (*consulado de comercio*), absorbing them into the main archive.[33]

Efforts at centralization, as distinct from consolidation, were also under way. The newly incorporated state of Los Altos sent its papers to Grijalva, indicating that the archive in the state's (or federation's) capital was seen as the suitable depository for documents from regional peripheries.[34] An attempt to recover the archives of towns situated on the shores of Lake Izabal in the early 1830s makes evident the motives of this centralization. An official was sent to recover the archives of villages near Lake Izabal and the Polochic River in 1834, and he reported that "he recovered several documents, that is to say the archive of the villages that existed on the shores of the lagoon of Izabal and the river Polochic, and since the History of the State is being written, these might provide some material for it."[35] While the notion of writing chronicles with the aid of historical documents was certainly not new, the emphasis on recovering and centralizing documents for the purposes of writing Guatemalan state history was.

Centralizing colonial documents would be easier than centralizing newly created documents. As discussed in previous chapters, composite documents from the colonial period had an inherently cumulative quality that nineteenth century documents did not. Dissociated conversations in paper resulted in burgeoning local archives that, moreover, remained essential to ongoing local governance. But even the more feasible centralization of colonial documentation was complicated by the shifting location of the region's centers.[36] From 1824 to 1839, there were both states (corresponding roughly to the former colonial provinces) and a Central American federal republic, and centralization occurred at both levels. Once the state boundaries of the Central American federation were determined, for example, orders were issued in 1824 to recuperate all papers pertaining to the state of El Salvador.

The Congress of this State being installed and finding itself prepared to address matters in all aspects of its administration, including civil, military, and ecclesiastical matters, it has been resolved that you [the secretary of the Congress], as a representative of this people and of the national assembly, shall recover from whichever archives in which they might be found and with use of an inventory all the documents and papers in the assembly or Supreme Government, as well as in the subordinate tribunals, that correspond to the stated Congress.[37]

This was separate from the attempt to centralize papers in the Federation's capital. As political conflicts erupted throughout the 1820s and 1830s, the appropriate location for particular documents and entire archives came into question. From 1824 to 1834, the Federal capital remained in Guatemala, but in 1834, the capital for the federal republic was forcibly moved to El Salvador. After residing briefly in Sonsonate, it was moved to San Salvador, where it remained until 1839.[38] During this period, federal authorities in San Salvador made repeated efforts to transfer whole archives to the new capital. In 1835, for example, federal authorities in San Salvador wrote to the state government in Guatemala ordering that the *consulado* (merchant tribunal and guild) archive be transported to the federal capital. The letter dated August 6 makes the noteworthy claim that apart from being necessary to the resolution of several administrative matters, the archive "belongs to the federation."[39] The orders indicated that the archive was to be presented to Miguel Talavera in Guatemala, who would then facilitate its transportation to San Salvador.[40]

Soon after sending for the *consulado* archive, the federal authorities in San Salvador went even further, requesting all of the archives pertinent to the federal government. On September 11, 1835, Miguel Talavera requested assistance for the massive project of organizing and transferring the archives to San Salvador.

In accordance with orders from the national Government I am commissioned by the Intendancy to arrange and remit to San Salvador all its archives. I have made clear that I cannot complete the arrangement of the archives on my own without the assistance of a person who has knowledge of how to handle documents. And though two have been named, neither assignment has taken effect.

Over the course of the ensuing year, Talavera embarked on a project of reorganization that strained his weak health and met with only partial success. The orders issued from San Salvador required not only a simple inventory and transfer but an internal redistribution of documents. Focusing on the archive of the former captaincy of Guatemala and the *escribanía de cámara*, the Salvadoran authorities agreed to grant the Guatemalan state's demands for the "documents that pertain to the towns governed by it." To effect this division, Miguel Ignacio Talavera was assigned "to inventory all that which belongs to the said archive, making divisions of the documents that pertain to the former provinces, today states, excluding from these divisions those documents in which the national government may have some interest."[41] The somewhat offhand instructions sent by the federal authorities must have struck Talavera as either disingenuous or entirely ignorant: anyone familiar with the archive of the *capitanía* and *escribanía* would have known that even to inventory and transport them was an enormous labor. Orders to sift through them, making regional divisions and weeding out the documents pertinent to the various levels of government, would have struck any archivist as nearly impossible.

Talavera's plaintive reply to these orders implied that this was the case, though he ascribed his inability to complete the orders to other causes. Citing ill-health, Talavera wrote that he doubted whether "I can dedicate myself (for now) to the arrangement of the disorganized voluminous archive of the old *escribanía de cámara*; since one of the causes of my current illness was a similar task, which I have successfully completed." Talavera protested that "after completing this extraordinary service, it is not possible for me to begin another even more difficult one which would certainly aggravate my illness." Citing his forty-seven years of honorable service, Talavera begged to be assigned some task more in keeping with his precarious health. The marks of revision in Talavera's letter, where he qualified his unwillingness to work on the archive by adding "for now" and replaced "disorganized" with "voluminous," testify to the delicate line he was walking: on the one hand he could not brush off the authorities' request, however unrealistic; on the other hand he wished to avoid what he knew to be a nearly impossible task.[42] The reply from San Salvador sent only a few days later indicated that Talavera would be granted a two-month respite from his labors so that he might regain his health, but that after the two months ended he was to begin at once upon the inventory and divisions of the archive.[43]

Talavera replied none too graciously on June 10, writing to the authorities in San Salvador, "As soon as I succeed in recovering from my current illness, I will go to the Tax Office to review the archive of the old *escribanía de cámara*, the arrangement of which the Supreme Government has seen fit to assign me." He promised to report on the state of the archive and any necessary resources he would need to begin his work. "This new service that I am willing to offer," he wrote, "despite my limited strength and weak state of health, shall be a test of my respectful deference and obedience to the commands of the Supreme National Government. And that is all I can reply for now."[44]

Realizing, no doubt, that the work at the archive was now inevitable despite his pleas, Talavera visited the archive three weeks later to take stock of the task that lay ahead. On June 30, he wrote the words cited at the opening of this chapter, exclaiming in horror at the state of the precious documents. He went on, saying, "This voluminous archive, which as far as I am able to ascertain ranges from 1600 to the present, finds itself in such turmoil and disorder that its outdated inventories are useless to its current condition." Talavera stated that he needed "able and intelligent" hands to assist with the archive's preservation. He mentioned two possibilities, public servants who had experience "handling documents," and indicated that he, too, would do whatever possible despite his poor health.[45] While it is unclear when, precisely, the *escribanía* archive left the hands of María Petronila de la Cerda, the widow of *escribano* Ignacio Guerra y Marchán, it is clear that between her request for assistance in 1825 and Talavera's assessment of the archive in 1836, the documents had been poorly cared for. The various archives found in the Guatemalan capital in the 1830s were numerous enough and substantial enough for Victoriano Grijalva to pursue systematization and consolidation with one portion of the nascent state archive while other portions of it fell into decay and disorder.

In July, Talavera was granted the services of an assistant, and it appears that with his aid Talavera began to make headway with the mountain of paper he confronted. He wrote early in the month to the authorities in San Salvador, making general mention of a new system of organization that he intended to propose as an alternative to the method expected by the federal government. On three pages, Talavera outlined the internal organization that he recommended for the archive, relying on both regions and government offices as categories.

Talavera's projected organization of the archive is worth considering in detail because it laid the foundations for the structure that would remain in place for the Guatemalan state archive—and that is still evident today at the AGCA. First, he recommended the division of the archival materials into six regional sections: Guatemala, San Salvador, Comayagua (Honduras), Nicaragua, Costa Rica, and Chiapas. The *separaciones de asuntos*, or thematic subdivisions, roughly accorded to the colonial government's

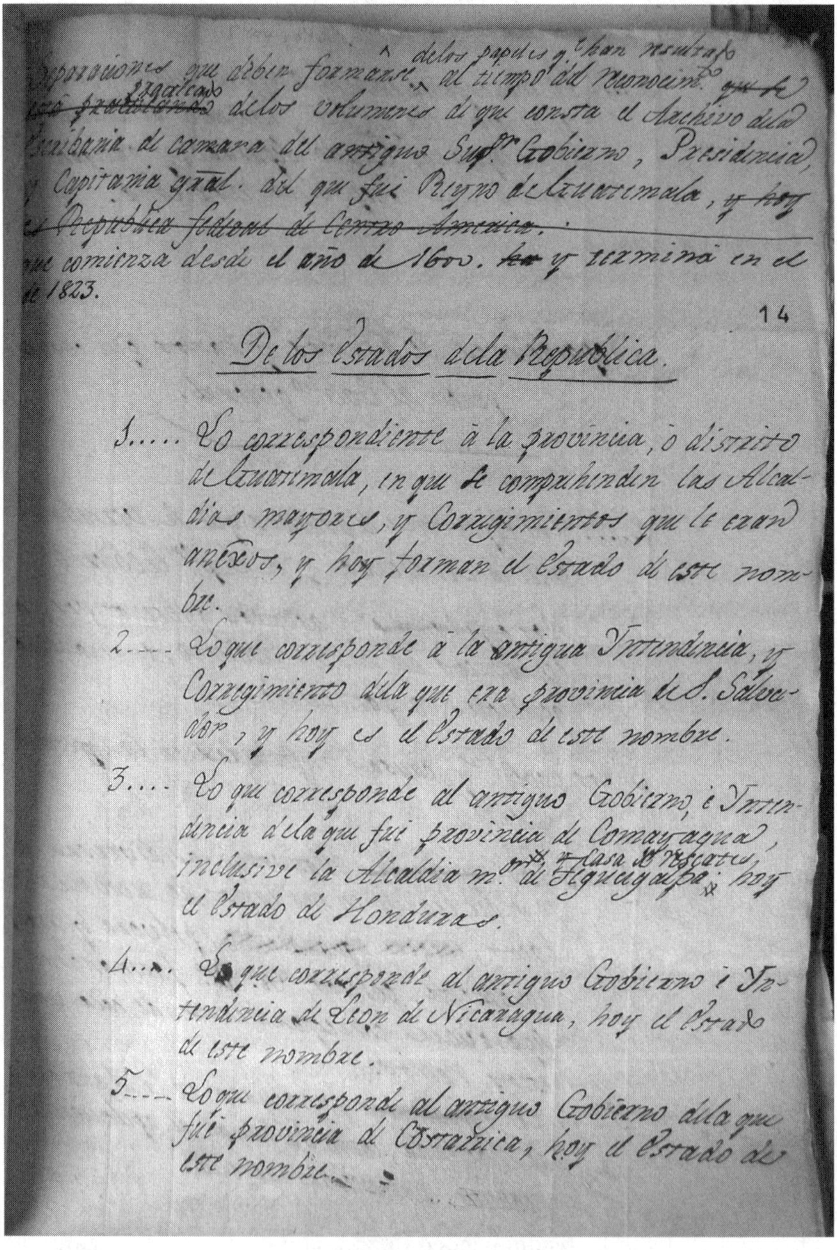

posiciones que deben formarse... delos papeles q.e han resultado
... ugalcaos delos volumenes de que consta el Archivo dela
Escribanía de camara del antiguo Sup.r Gobierno, Presidencia,
y Capitanía gral. del que fue Reyno de Guatemala, y hoy
es República federal de Centro America.

que comienza desde el año de 1600. y termina en el
de 1823.

14

De los Estados dela República.

1..... Lo correspondiente á la provincia, ó distrito
de Guatemala, en que se comprehenden las Alcal-
días mayores, y Corregimientos que le eran
anexos, y hoy forman el Estado de este nombre.

2.... Lo que corresponde á la antigua Intendencia, y
Corregimiento della que era provincia de S. Salvador, y hoy es el Estado de este nombre.

3.... Lo que corresponde al antiguo Gobierno, é Intendencia della que fué provincia de Comayagua,
inclusive la Alcaldía m.r de la casa de Reales, hoy
el Estado de Honduras.

4... Lo que corresponde al antiguo Gobierno é Intendencia de Leon de Nicaragua, hoy el Estado
de este nombre.

5.... Lo que corresponde al antiguo Gobierno della que
fué provincia de Costarica, hoy el Estado de
este nombre.

FIGURE 6.2. Archive organization recommended by Miguel Talavera, page 1
Source: Archivo General de Centroamérica. Photograph by the author.

internal organization. Branches of government such as the *audiencia* and the royal treasury were granted their own sections. And Talavera designated separate sections topically, such as those pertaining to the University of San Carlos, the granting of *encomiendas*, and the *patronato real*.[46] In his attached letter to the authorities in San Salvador, Talavera explained that the regional subdivisions were essential and that the thematic subdivisions would permit the federal government to identify the documents that were "of interest" to it. By this means, he avoided the thorny task of picking through the entire archive for documents relevant to the federal government's interests, as the authorities had requested. The recommended organization would create twenty-four subdivisions within the archive.[47]

Considered side by side, Talavera's outline and Guerra y Marchán's index to the archive inventory have much in common as way-finding documents. Talavera's structure contained twenty-four subdivisions; Guerra y Marchán's contained twenty-five. Both began with regional subdivisions and continued with thematic subdivisions. And, necessarily, both were self-conscious reflections of the colonial administrative structure. One important difference lies in the emphasis placed upon regional divisions. While Guerra y Marchán relied on a dozen regional designations, separating Ciudad Real from Tuxtla, for example, Talavera reduced these categories to six, framing the divisions around the existing states of the Central American Federation (as well as Chiapas, which by then formed part of Mexico).[48] The eighteenth-century political landscape allowed for much smaller regional units; by the time Talavera created the organizational scaffolding for the archive of the Central American Federation, the cities and districts of colonial Guatemala had become more encompassing, bounded states.

Talavera's proposed method of organization was approved, and the archivist began the long labor of putting the projected divisions of documents into effect. The concerns that occupied him at the beginning of this process give some sense of what the "archive" must have looked like. Lacking even the most basic equipment, Talavera had to negotiate to purchase shelves for the documents, which were lying in piles on the floor. In September 1836 he was able to report that the more well-preserved documents were gradually finding their way, bound and marked in *legajos*, onto the new shelves, but that the papers he found "eaten through and incomplete and thereby useless, these being even worse than those that are torn and dirty" were still piled on the floor due to an absence of proper shelving and other tools.[49] He lacked even basic equipment such as paper, pens, a penknife, and scissors, for which he had to request a small petty cash fund.[50] Talavera's work, as he represented it, was not so much to reorganize the archive but to essentially create it from the ground up.

As the months passed and Talavera continued the slow process of sorting, cleaning, and shelving the documents, the authorities pressed him for the documents "belonging" to each regional government. In December 1836, Talavera found it necessary to explain at length why he was not able to simply turn over the pertinent papers for each state government and the federal government. While the sorting was continuing apace, he wrote, it was simply not feasible to present the archive with a complete inventory as requested.[51] As his later correspondence demonstrated, part of the difficulty lay in making what was essentially an artificial distinction between "regional" matters and "national" matters. Talavera must have encountered this problem repeatedly, but in January 1837 he wrote to the federal authorities with concerns about one particularly complicated issue. What was he to do, he asked, with the papers pertaining to the transfer of Guatemala City from Santiago to La Hermita after the 1773 earthquake? On the one hand, "all of those administrative and economic measures were taken by the general government then in power," but, on the other hand, all of the documents clearly pertained to places and monuments within the new state boundaries of Guatemala. He asked the federal authorities to inform him whether these documents were better set aside for the state's archive or if they were of interest for the history of the Republic.[52] The new spatial and political organization provided a constant, recurring dilemma. Talavera persisted as best he could.

In an undated draft of a letter to San Salvador, Talavera listed the subsections of his archive that would each require an inventory. Allotting one notebook for each subsection, he gave every indication of having completed the first comprehensive effort at organizing the archives of the Central American States. A document from 1838 confirms this; Talavera presented to the Guatemalan authorities an index for the organized archive, which adhered more or less to the structure he had projected in 1836. The index included the number of *legajos* pertaining to each subsection. As expected, the subsections reflected the colonial administrative structure. The regional divisions into states mirrored the colonial division of provinces, and the thematic division of *rentas* kept intact the documentary production of colonial government bureaus. The notes appended to the index also mentioned that nearly two hundred *legajos* remained as yet unsorted. Their poor condition required more intensive cleaning and restoration.[53]

In 1840, the organizational work performed by Talavera was put to the test when the dissolution of the Central American Federation prompted another relocation of archival documents. The former members of the federal republic had become independent states, and as such the Guatemalan state sought to recover many of the documents that had been sent to San

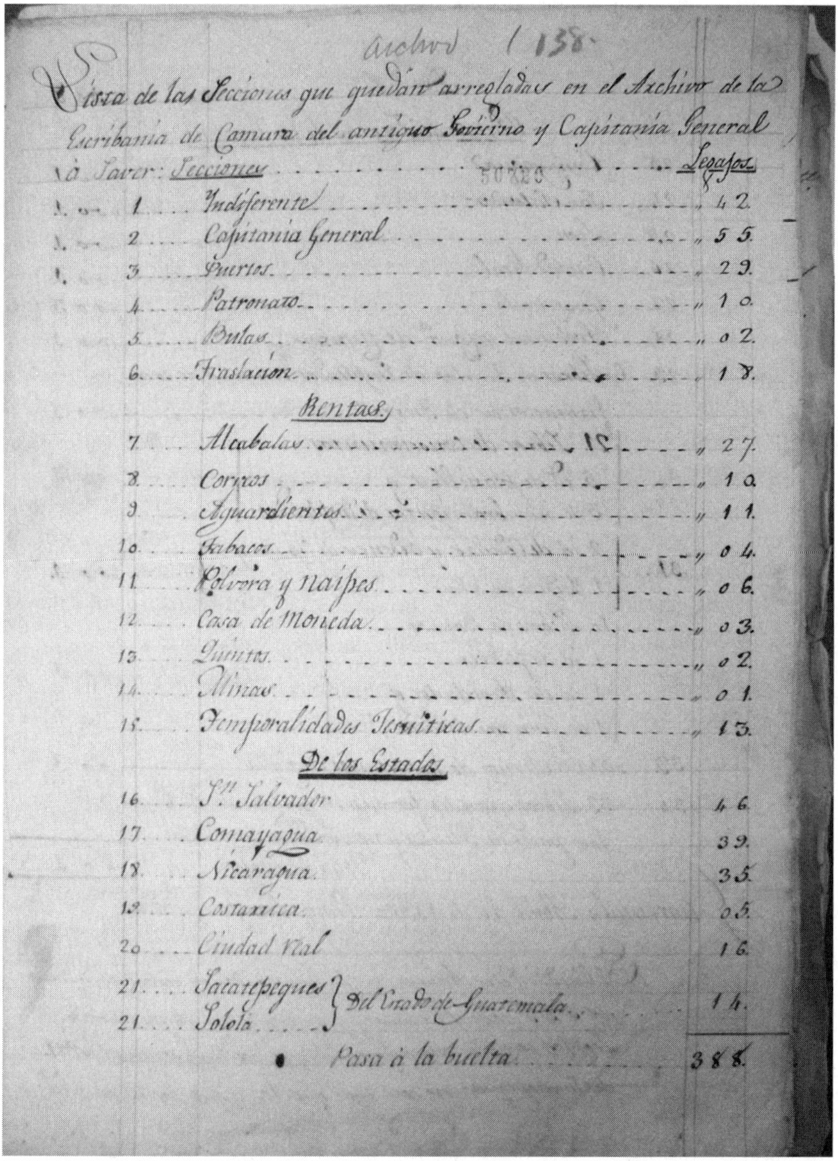

Archivo 1 158.

Vista de las Secciones que quedan arregladas en el Archivo de la
Escribanía de Camara del antiguo Gobierno y Capitanía General
à saver: Secciones . . . . Legajos

1 . . . . Indiferente . . . . „ 42.
2 . . . . Capitanía General . . . . „ 55.
3 . . . . Puertos . . . . „ 29.
4 . . . . Patronato . . . . „ 10.
5 . . . . Bulas . . . . „ 02.
6 . . . . Traslación . . . . „ 17.

Rentas.

7 . . . . Alcabalas . . . . „ 27.
8 . . . . Corpos . . . . „ 10.
9 . . . . Aguardientes . . . . „ 11.
10 . . . Tabacos . . . . „ 04.
11 . . . Pólvora y Naipes . . . . „ 06.
12 . . . Casa de Moneda . . . . „ 03.
13 . . . Quintos . . . . „ 02.
14 . . . Minas . . . . „ 01.
15 . . . Temporalidades Jesuiticas . . . . „ 13.

De los Estados

16 . . . S.n Salvador . . . . 46.
17 . . . Comayagua . . . . 39.
18 . . . Nicaragua . . . . 35.
19 . . . Costarrica . . . . 05.
20 . . . Ciudad Real . . . . 16.
21 . . . Sacatepeques } Del Estado de Guatemala . 14.
21 . . . Solola . . . . . }

● . . . Pasa à la buelta . . . . 388.

FIGURE 6.3. Talavera's final table of contents for the archive
Source: Archivo General de Centroamérica. Photograph by the author.

Salvador. While no precise inventory remains of which documents were transported to San Salvador in the 1830s, it seems clear from Talavera's work that documents pertaining to the former Guatemalan *audiencia*, which governed the region's colonial provinces, were considered foundational for the federal republic, which governed the same region in the form of the Central American states. When Guatemala became an independent state, its government had some grounds for claiming that the *audiencia* had been situated in Guatemala and therefore the *audiencia*'s documents belonged to Guatemala.

Beginning in May 1840, the Guatemalan government pursued the recovery of archival collections that had been only recently sent to San Salvador.[54] In 1841, for example, they requested the return of the *consulado* archive discussed above. The Salvadoran authorities replied, stating that the question of redistributing the archive was a difficult one, "as it belongs to the entire nation," but if the president of Guatemala himself promised to take responsibility for responding to any requests for documents that might emerge from San Salvador, they would agree to send the archive back to Guatemala.[55] The Guatemalan authorities replied that the archive would be cared for and put "at the service of the other states, so that they may take from it the information that is necessary."[56] As if to clarify this intention, a note was made internally among Guatemalan officials of the solemn obligations of the archive's custodianship.

The Department of Commerce of this State promises to preserve under its custodianship the archive that it has solicited: in the care of this department it will be subject to national authority, whose orders it will obey, and finally at all times the stated archive will be at the service of the other states so that they may take from it the data and information that they find necessary.[57]

The comments emphasize the obligation to share the documentary sources among the states. And they make explicit the custodianship of the archive: held by the department of commerce, which answered to state authorities, the archive lay ultimately in the hands of the Guatemalan national government. It hardly requires mention that by this point there was no question of an *escribano* custodianship; the documents belonged indisputably to the Guatemalan state. This point was made even more explicitly some years later, when the Guatemalan authorities requested additional documents pertaining to general governance. Ranging from the 1750s to the 1830s, the documents were packed in four crates and presented to a representative of the Guatemalan government in 1847 with an appended "Inventory of papers belonging to Guatemala."[58]

After 1840, then, it is possible to trace a history of separate archives in the Central American states. As the transfer of documents in the 1840s suggests, many of the colonial *audiencia* documents that had left Guatemala were quickly restored to the Guatemalan capital. There is no mention of Miguel Talavera after 1840, and it seems likely that at some point during or just after the dissolution of the republic, Talavera succumbed to the illness that had for so long made his work at the archive difficult. The archivist who re-emerged after 1840 is Victoriano Grijalva, who as "archivist of government offices" was not directly involved with the restoration of the *escribanía* archive but had never entirely vanished from the scene. In 1843, orders were given for all government-related documents to be handed over to Grijalva.[59] The Guatemalan state archivist presumably attempted to organize the collections of documents that became his responsibility, but an unexpected difficulty arose. Grijalva was called to offer military service, and several requests were made throughout the 1840s for him to be excused so that the crucial work of maintaining the archive could continue.[60] Despite these requests, Grijalva was obliged to serve in 1844.[61] His resulting absence appears to have been disastrous for both the archive and the daily functioning of the office in which he was engaged. José Palomo, an official writing to a government minister in July 1845, protested that "the general government archive finds itself in a state of such chaos that it complicates and delays our work, resulting in a grave loss of time and excess work for not only the archivist but the entire office."[62] The state of the archive was due, he went on to explain, to its transfer from its former location to the offices in the government palace and, moreover, to Grijalva's absence "during the campaign of Jutiapa," which, as a battalion officer, he was obliged to take part in. The abundance of incoming work served to make matters worse, Palomo wrote, so that day by day the office fell further behind.[63] Though the minister conceded so far as to assign Palomo a replacement archivist, Grijalva was not excused from military service, and it appears that during his campaigns the Guatemalan archive fell once again into decline.

Continuities and Changes in the Nineteenth Century

Archival practices in nineteenth-century Guatemala were, necessarily, in some regards different from those that endured throughout the colonial period. While *escribanos* continued to play a vital role as notaries and official scribes, in some of their duties they were gradually replaced by secretaries and archivists. The tasks performed by these bureaucrats in the national period were not identical to those of the colonial *escribano*. The most evident change is the division of the *escribano* office into separate responsibilities for the government secretary and the government archivist.

In the nineteenth century, the position of archivist appears to have grown gradually more specialized.

Necessarily, the changing political boundaries of the region led to parallel changes in how document ownership was conceived. As the transfer of documents to and from San Salvador in the 1830s and 1840s demonstrates, document collections were understood to "belong" to federal or state authorities, depending not so much on their authorship but on their content. Talavera consulted the authorities in San Salvador in order to determine whether documents pertaining to the transfer of the capital after 1773 should belong to the state or federal archive, thereby signaling that documents were thought to belong to the government organ they described. The shifting location of the document collections and the accompanying work by Talavera and Grijalva point to a much deeper transformation in the notion of ownership and custodianship. Neither archivist would have dreamed of claiming that the archive "belonged" to anyone but the government. While notaries outside of government may have continued to keep their own document collections, archivists and secretaries in local and national government clearly maintained the archives for the government they served. The days in which a government *escribano* might tussle over custodianship of "his" archive had passed.

Despite these significant changes, there were also remarkable continuities in the practices of *escribanos* and archivists. To begin with, many of the individuals who were present in the colonial period continued their work in the national period. Miguel Talavera was assigned a role as government archivist in 1802, and he continued his important work well into the 1830s. This inevitably led to many continuities of method. The understanding of the archive as a storehouse for treasure—documentary and otherwise—continued and evolved over the nineteenth century as well. A document from 1821 discusses the safekeeping of three handkerchiefs marked by María Teresa de la Santísima Trinidad, religious relics that the government officials paid to preserve in the archive.[64] Equally revealing and no doubt more typical was the treatment by government authorities of the original manuscript by Bernal Díaz de Castillo. In 1853, a publisher was authorized to borrow the manuscript in order to create a printed copy, and in 1872 Guatemalan authorities facilitated the loan of the manuscript to permit the government of Mexico to obtain a copy.[65] Over the following decades, the movements of the manuscript were closely monitored as copies were made and researchers—such as Hubert Howe Bancroft—sought to consult it.[66] The manuscript was undoubtedly considered documentary treasure, and there could be no question that it belonged to the Guatemala government. Its proper place was thought to be the government archive or, later in the nineteenth century, the national library. Yet the circulation of the manuscript among publishers and copyists indicates a subtle shift in how documentary treasure was preserved. In the nineteenth century there were no complaints and responding strictures regarding the withdrawal of documents from the archive. The repeated injunctions in the colonial period to prevent original documents from leaving the archive appear to fade away by the nineteenth century. The archive remained, clearly, a place to store important documents and a prioritized site of preservation. The efforts of archivists such as Talavera and Grijalva speak to the importance placed on archival maintenance. Protocols developed later in the nineteenth century also testify to the continued sense that document were to be protected. In 1875, for example, two notaries were forbidden from using archival documents for a study of *escribanía* methods.[67] But there appears to have been some relaxation of the rules governing whether and under what conditions documents could circulate. While the sense of the archive as a treasure storehouse and the need to protect its documents continued, practices and customs of archive use were not constant.

One practice that did continue well into the nineteenth century was the use of inventories. Inventories of various government archives were created in every decade until the end of the century.[68] The inventory remained a vital tool for taking stock of archival content, and these inventories thereby continue to reflect colonial ways of organizing knowledge. As the recurrence of organizational forms, identification numbers, and document tags indicate, these inventories were composite documents: they relied heavily on the work of past archivists and *escribanos*. The significant labor required for organizing archival materials created in the inventory a kind of gravitational pull; elaborating an entirely new system and breaking away from the creation of a composite inventory would have compounded the already extraordinary work involved in updating archival contents. So the form endured. In the late nineteenth century, the massive project of inventorying the entire contents of the colonial-era archive was once again attempted. The numerous notebooks created in the process of forming the inventory indicate that a project as large or larger than Talavera's was in progress. One of the archivists involved—he was likely one of many—left his signature on a draft notebook created over a four-year period.[69] The volume created by Eugenio Amaya cataloged a subset of the archive: documents that had been gathered and bound prior to their storage. The documents ranged from 1561 to 1900. Using strips of paper glued to the binding and crossing out his entries repeatedly, Amaya attempted to create a finished catalog of the archive's collection of bound documents.

The multivolume archive inventory that emerged from these labors accounted for all the documents in the national archive's collection. Despite being repeatedly abandoned, moved from one state to another and one

FIGURE 6.4. Portion of the catalog by Eugenio Amaya of archival collections showing revisions

Source: Archivo General de Centroamérica. Photograph by the author.

building to another, many—some unknown proportion—of the documents had survived. Documents that had formed part of the archive inventory by Ignacio Guerra y Marchán more than one hundred years earlier were listed in much the same way. The transfer of the *correo* archive from Don Andrés Palomo to Don Simón Larrazábal in 1774 was listed as document 2776. On the following page, the 1777 case of the rotted grapes carried by *correo* José Rivera was listed as document 2781. These numbers, devised at the end of the nineteenth century, correspond to the *expediente* numbers used today for these documents at the AGCA.[70]

The documents were ordered in *legajos* and identified by date and subject in the inventory. Someone wishing to find a document had only to search by region or subdivision and then by date. Consultations by the government and the public were possible and may even have been common, if a regulation prohibiting the use of tobacco and the wearing of hats within the archive is any indication.[71] It would appear that by the early twentieth century, the difficult task of creating a comprehensive inventory for "way-finding" within the archive had been achieved. That the archive remained a vital tool for way-finding of all kinds is evident in a piece of correspondence sent to the Guatemalan archivist in 1902. The secretary of foreign relations in Mexico urgently requested any "documents or titles" pertaining to Mexico and Chiapas in the colonial period. He added that "their acquisition is all the more urgent since, at the moment, we are attempting to fix the borders of this State with the adjoining ones, and the said documents are indispensable."[72] The archive may have found its fixed place in Guatemala, but the borders it helped to create were still uncertain.

Epilogue

In the summer of 1993 I began a long stay in Tucurrique, Costa Rica, a town I had lived in for some years as a child but could not remember. A Costa Rican friend later laughed at the mention of Tucurrique, saying that though he had never heard of the town, the word meant something like "that out of the way place" or "that corner in the middle of nowhere." And, in fact, Tucurrique felt to me on that trip like a place in the middle of nowhere. I flew to San José, took a bus to Turrialba, waited for a bus connection, and then took another bus to Tucurrique. We passed more than one mud slide on the winding dirt road, and the River Reventazón, as the name suggests, was swollen to bursting with muddy water. The months I spent in Tucurrique were profoundly disorienting in the way an extended dislocation always is the first time. On the one hand I found myself in a kind of earthly paradise, a valley where you could pick fruit off the trees and then in the afternoon watch the clouds roll in to dump rain of biblical proportions on the corrugated aluminum roofs. On the other hand, being among habits and livelihoods so new to me threw off my inner compass, so that I could no longer remember why certain things mattered and others didn't. Every few weeks I visited friends in San José and reminded myself, vaguely and not too persuasively, of what the world had previously been like. Even there, it was difficult to remember. The Miami airport where I'd made my connection months earlier seemed a hazy, fictional place that I might have imagined.

When, many years later, I read the geographical report by engineer Luis Diez de Navarro, who in 1744 traveled throughout the Kingdom of Guatemala reporting on the state of the provinces, I was astonished to see Tucurrique lying, seemingly unchanged, in the middle of his description. "Going along the latter [route]," he wrote, "one finds two Villages of Indios Talamancas called tucurrique and Attirro, which are overseen by Franciscan friars from the Province of Nicaragua." He also noted that he passed a "famous River" that was "more than one hundred paces wide."[1] Finding the obscure but familiar Tucurrique in a colonial document housed at the AGCA had a strangely foreshortening effect, so that for a moment I had the sense that I knew this Diez de Navarro and had walked alongside him on that winding route inland through Costa Rican valleys. And I experienced a similar foreshortening in 2004, when, in the last paper letter sent to me from Tucurrique, a friend suggested we correspond by email. She gave me her email address as if it were the most natural thing in the world, and I found the prospect of an immediate exchange with that remote place curiously disturbing. The document in the archive abridges temporal distance with as much facility as the electronic document, now, abridges spatial distance. But the disorientation lingers.

Carlo Ginzburg's collection, *Wooden Eyes: Nine Reflections on Distance*, is more about critical distance and metaphorical distance than about spatial or temporal measures, yet its concern with distancing, as a crucial tactic for the historian, offers a useful perspective for the kind of distance considered here. Ginzburg writes of "making it strange"—the need to dispel the illusion of a familiar past by infusing it with some estranging, distancing element.[2] Viewed in this light, the historian's work is entirely about distance. Some documents, during the research process, seem impossibly remote: inscrutable and all too foreign. At other moments it is too easy to overlook the countless ways in which the author of a document—like Diez de Navarro tramping through Tucurrique—is unfamiliar, distant, and unknown. The historian has to reckon with the illusion of proximity on the one hand and the illusion of insurmountable distance on the other.

The chapters in this book attempt to follow Ginzburg's advice in "making it strange." Distance, as we understand it today, and whether we measure it in meters or yards, is too easily projected onto the minds and habits of past subjects. In colonial Guatemala, distance was "strange"; at the very least it was different. Bound to a particular geographical, political, social, and economic context, it was conceptualized and represented in ways that are unfamiliar and worth understanding. Distance was thought to connote pejoratively, and distant places—whether distant from Spain or Guatemala City—were considered beyond the reach of secular and ecclesiastical authorities. Administrators in Spain strained to see and govern the Americas, sending and gathering paper in growing volume. Their Guatemalan counterparts in the *audiencia* capital despaired of reining in those distant places like Costa Rica that were separated by so many of leagues of uninhabited terrain: places where spiritual and moral dangers abounded and the word of the king was a distant echo. The spatial movement of documents from peripheries to centers and their temporal movement through archives reveals, like a dye poured into a network of waterways, the trickle and rush of these efforts.

Reforms in the late eighteenth century began a process of change that would result in a radically different structure for knowledge production. The strain to reach the edges of empire was no longer so great. Mail reforms allowed places within regional peripheries, like Guatemala, to communicate with one another more often and more quickly. Local networks had denser traffic, and document patterns changed. The results of these changes are today most evident in how archives operate. To study the colonial period, historians of the former Kingdom of Guatemala visit the central archive in Guatemala City (AGCA) or the *Archivo de Indias* (AGI) in Seville, where composite documents carrying the cumulative writings of peripheral and central authors came to rest. There is a politics to this that we are all aware of but that we do not always draw onto the pages of our historical writings: what we do today as historians builds on colonial practices of organizing knowledge. The argument here, I hope, matters for people beyond Guatemala and beyond the Spanish empire: the structure of colonial archives reveals something about the structure of colonial knowledge production. And understanding those modes of organizing knowledge allows us different insights into all of the documents we use as colonial historians. For Guatemala, informing the Spanish center, knowledge was built radially and along routes. Thus the bulk of Guatemalan official documentation lies in the former seat of the *audiencia* and the former seat of the Council of Indies. Documents from Guatemala look the way they do and say the things they do partly because of this.

For the nineteenth century, the picture looks very different. To study the period after independence, historians travel to local archives scattered through the Central American states, where regional officials amassed boxes of correspondence, legal documents, and account books. Their half of the conversation lies in Guatemala City, more often than not, but the replies from the center are diffuse and scattered.[3] Partly this underscores the obvious point that knowledge in the colonial period was centralized, and knowledge following independence was more localized. But the surprising corollary is that central knowledge in the colonial period was peripheral: created by peripheral authors and informed by peripheral knowledges. Does it follow that in the national period it was less so? I think this remains an open question, but there is no doubt that knowledge production worked differently in the national period; and it works differently today, because peripheries have a different significance and documents operate differently. Administrators in Spain held peripheral knowledge close, no matter how obscure its origin. By enabling local peripheries to draw closer to places like Guatemala City, administrators in Spain changed not the meaning of distance but who was distant. Once proximate and looming, even in the most remote corners of empire, Spain receded.

Notes

INTRODUCTION

1. John Gillis's elaboration of "remoteness" examines, along similar lines, how spatially near places can be contextually remote. John R Gillis, *Islands of the Mind: How the Human Imagination Created the Atlantic World*, 1st ed. (New York: Palgrave Macmillan, 2004).

2. *Case against Magdalena Durango, María de la Cruz, María Candelaria and Michaela Gerónima*. Bancroft Library, BANC MSS 72/57 m, Box 4, 1704.

3. Peter Sahlins, "Centring the Periphery: The Cerdanya Between France and Spain," in *Spain, Europe, and the Atlantic World: Essays in Honour of John H. Elliott*, ed. Richard L. Kagan and Geoffrey Parker (Cambridge: Cambridge University Press, 1995), 230. See also Peter Sahlins, *Boundaries: The Making of France and Spain in the Pyrenees* (Berkeley: University of California Press, 1989).

4. Christine Daniels and Michael V. Kennedy, *Negotiated Empires: Centers and Peripheries in the Americas, 1500–1820* (New York: Routledge, 2002). Amy Turner Bushnell and Jack P. Greene posit in their Introduction that "the concepts of *center* and *periphery* may be usefully applied to the historical understanding of colonial centers and their peripheries in the early modern Americas" (3). They add that "many colonial scholars have yet to exploit the potential of center-periphery concepts for analyzing the internal organization of Europe's early modern American empires" (7). In this endeavor, the editors frame more current work as building on Shils's conception of centers "less as a physical place than a socio-intellectual construct," but departing from Wallerstein's scheme, which "grants too much power to European cores [and] is too exclusively focused on the creation of international trading systems and other broad economic developments . . ." (3–5) D. W. Meinig's influential work does not adapt what he calls a "simple core-periphery or metropolis frontier concept," but his study of the shape of empires' growth across the Americas also in some respects acknowledges peripheries implicitly. His notion of "distance decay," for example, in North America posits that "imperial power declined with distance from the European capital until it became feeble and indirect in the interior of North America where it was represented by European seasonal agents and Indian allies." Incorporating the idea of distance into his framework, he suggests that some places were partly beyond imperial reach. D. W Meinig, *The Shaping of America: A Geographical Perspective on 500 Years of History* (New Haven: Yale University Press, 1986), 265. Though he does not rely on the terms *periphery* and *center*, Edward Said's conception of imperialism and colonialism do rely on distance: "the term, 'imperialism' means the practice, the theory, and the attitudes of a dominating metropolitan center ruling a distant territory; 'colonialism'. . . is the implanting of settlements on

distant territory." Edward W. Said, *Culture and Imperialism* (New York: Knopf, 1993), 9.

5. A.J.R. Russell-Wood has demonstrated the limitations of spatial distance as a defining variable, pointing out that "although distance may be a factor, this is not a sine qua non. Brazil provides numerous examples of regions that were peripheral in that they were separated from their cores not by distance but by topographical features." A.J.R. Russell-Wood, "Centers and Peripheries in the Luso-Brazilian World, 1500–1808," in *Negotiated Empires: Centers and Peripheries in the Americas, 1500–1820* (New York: Routledge, 2002), 123.

6. Susan Migden Socolow and Lyman L. Johnson, Colonial Centers, Colonial Peripheries, and the Economic Agency of the Spanish State, ed. Christine Daniels and Michael V. Kennedy (New York: Routledge, 2002), 60.

7. Authors recognize the flexibility of these qualities, citing, for example, the waning of Portobelo, in present-day Panama, after the 1720s and the transformation of Cuba into a "vital center of empire" in the eighteenth century. John Jay TePaske, "Integral to Empire: The Vital Peripheries of Colonial Spanish America," in *Negotiated Empires: Centers and Peripheries in the Americas, 1500–1820* (New York: Routledge, 2002), 38.

8. Russell-Wood, "Centers and Peripheries in the Luso-Brazilian World, 1500–1808," 106.

9. See, for example, Emil Volek, *Latin America Writes Back: Postmodernity in the Periphery: (An Interdisciplinary Perspective)* (New York: Routledge, 2002). Volek observes that "too much U.S. research on Latin America moves in circles and is written for local consumption," and he is troubled by how to find Latin American authors outside of this circle: "In my search for the Latin American perspective(s) I recognized the nomadic nature of intellectual work today, and although I felt that it might be preferable if the contributors actually *lived* in Latin America, this wish did not seem to me to be the determining factor. Many live there and write happily mimicking the North or Europe" (xvii, xv). As Volek does not explicitly examine the notion of "periphery" and what it constitutes, he implicitly suggests that it is these authors—those who do not mimic—who form the periphery.

10. Enrique Dussel, "The 'World-System': Europe as 'Center' and Its 'Periphery,' Beyond Eurocentrism," in *Latin America and Postmodernity: A Contemporary Reader* (Amherst, N.Y.: Humanity Books, 2001), 104.

11. This seems especially true of "internal peripheries." See, for example, Lowell Gudmundson and Justin Wolfe, *Blacks and Blackness in Central America: Between Race and Place* (Durham, N.C.: Duke University Press, 2010). In Ida Altman's formulation, the movement toward regional studies is an effort to consider peripheries—illuminate the center by looking elsewhere. Ida Altman, "Reconsidering the Center: Puebla and Mexico City, 1550–1650," in *Negotiated Empires: Centers and Peripheries in the Americas, 1500–1820* (New York: Routledge, 2002), 44.

12. TePaske, "Integral to Empire: The Vital Peripheries of Colonial Spanish America," 33. A similar instinct is evident in Peter Sahlins's essay, cited above, on "centring the periphery." Sahlins, "Centering the Periphery: The Cerdanya Between France and Spain."

13. "Periferia" appears in dictionaries of the mid-nineteenth century, but earlier sources, such as the *Diccionario de autoridades* and the *Tesoro de la lengua castellana* make no mention of the term. Sebastián de Covarrubias Horozco, *Tesoro de la lengua castellana o española según la impresión de 1611*, ed. Benito Remigio Noydens and Martín de Riquer (Barcelona: S. A. Horta, 1943); Pedro Felipe Monlau and José Monlau y Sala, *Diccionario etimológico de la lengua castellana*, 1881; Real Academia Española., *Diccionario de autoridades*, vol. Ed. facsímil. (Madrid,: Editorial Gredos, 1964).

14. One notable example is *Carta sobre lo que debe hacer un príncipe que tenga colonias a gran distancia* (Philadelphia: s.n., 1803).

15. Jerry Brotton makes an interesting application of Waldo Tobler's first law, seeing it as a metaphor for the Internet. The argument here about colonial Guatemala does not exactly refute Tobler's law, but it does complicate it; surely colonial Guatemala is not the only place in which physically distant places are perceived as near while physically proximate places register as "peripheral" and "distant." Jerry Brotton, *A History of the World in Twelve Maps* (London: Allen Lane, 2012), 428–429.

16. W. George Lovell and Christopher H. Lutz, "Core and Periphery in Colonial Guatemala," in *Guatemalan Indians and the State: 1540 to 1988* (Austin, Texas: University of Texas Press, 1990), 35–51; Murdo J. MacLeod, *Spanish Central America: A Socioeconomic History, 1520–1720*, vol. California library reprint (Berkeley: University of California Press, 1984).

17. Centers include the present-day departments of Sacatepéquez, Chimaltenango, Guatemala, Jalapa, Chiquimula, El Progreso, and Zacapa as well as portions of the Mexican and Salvadoran Pacific coasts. Peripheries include the present-day departments of Huehuetenango, El Quiché, Alta Verapaz, Izabal, and Petén.

18. Maya—later *Indian*, in Spanish legal terms—centers and peripheries overlapped to some extent with Spanish centers and peripheries but also differed, forming various centers over the course of the colonial period. In 1500, the Maya population in Guatemala was concentrated in highland and lowland areas that in some cases were deemed "peripheries" in the Spanish conception one hundred years later. While the region mainly populated by the Cakchiquel came to form the site for the Spanish colonial capital (later Antigua), the Quiché stronghold in the northern highlands became a Spanish periphery. The center of Pipil society, Cuscatlán, was located to the southeast in what would be become El Salvador. Pre-Columbian social, political, and economic life across the region is beyond the scope of this book, but for a succinct depiction of Mesoamerican settlement patterns around 1500, see Carolyn Hall, Héctor Pérez Brignoli, and John V. Cotter, *Historical Atlas of Central America* (Norman: University of Oklahoma Press, 2003).

19. For a thorough and cogent discussion of Spanish American legal and administrative institutions, see Matthew Campbell Mirow, *Latin American Law: A History of Private Law and Institutions in Spanish America* (Austin: University of Texas Press, 2004).

20. Initially, most of modern-day Guatemala and El Salvador formed part of the Audiencia of Mexico, while Honduras formed part of the Audiencia de Santo Domingo centered in the Caribbean, and the Audiencia of Panama began as far

north as Nicaragua. In the mid-sixteenth century, the Audiencia of Panama briefly stretched even farther north to include much of El Salvador and all of Honduras. A visual summary of these transitions is well presented in Hall, Pérez Brignoli, and Cotter, *Historical Atlas of Central America.*, 32–33.

21. Lovell and Lutz, "Core and Periphery in Colonial Guatemala," 38.

22. *Encomienda* grants for the period between 1525 and 1550 were heavily concentrated in the region from the Pacific coast inland and from Tecpán in the north to Cuscutlán in the south. After 1550, the Spanish population expanded into other regions, including Comalapa, Chimaltenango, Sumpango, and Amatitlán, as well as farther south and east. Ibid., 71.

23. Ibid., 41.

24. See MacLeod, *Spanish Central America: A Socioeconomic History, 1520–1720*. The cacao boom was initially centered in Soconusco, an area between Guatemala and Mexico on the Pacific coast.

25. Indian slavery was officially abolished in 1550. On uses of Indian labor, see Lovell and Lutz, "Core and Periphery in Colonial Guatemala"; MacLeod, *Spanish Central America: A Socioeconomic History, 1520–1720*.

26. These estimates vary. High estimates for all of Central America (the region encompassing Chiapas to Costa Rica) range from 10.8 to 13.5 million; the lowest estimate is 800,000. Lovell and Lutz's more detailed data for regions within the area show a precipitous decline in Costa Rica (400,000 in 1520; 1,343 in 1682) but recovery beginning in the 1680s. (In Guatemala, 2 million in 1520; 128,000 in 1625; 242,020 by 1684.) W. George Lovell and Christopher H. Lutz, "Anexo o apendices a perfil etno-demográfico de la Audiencia de Guatemala," *Revista de Indias* LXIII, no. 229 (2003): 759–764; Hall, Pérez Brignoli, and Cotter, *Historical Atlas of Central America*, 76.

27. Christopher Lutz, *Santiago De Guatemala, 1541–1773: City, Caste, and the Colonial Experience* (Norman: University of Oklahoma Press, 1994), 88.

28. Ibid., 95. For a more detailed discussion of the turn-of-the-century crises, see Miles L. Wortman, *Government and Society in Central America, 1680–1840* (New York: Columbia University Press, 1982), 88.

29. Carol Smith demonstrates that the term *ladino* began to acquire its modern meaning during the nineteenth-century coffee boom. See Carol A. Smith, "Origins of the National Question in Guatemala: A Hypothesis," in *Guatemalan Indians and the State: 1540 to 1988* (Austin: University of Texas Press, 1990).

30. Hall, Pérez Brignoli, and Cotter, *Historical Atlas of Central America*, 88–89.

31. "De las [respuestas] de Cartago, Capital de Costa Rica, que no llegan, hasta pasados tres o cuatro meses, a causa de la corta correspondencia, y de la mucha distancia que hay a Granada, que es donde se introducen, para su conducción a esta Capital." AGI, Correos 90B, February 29, 1768 letter by Joseph de Garayalde. A 1766 letter from Pedro Ortiz de Letona which summarizes the state of communications to the provinces makes the point even more starkly, describing all of Nicaragua and Costa Rica as only tenuously linked to the Guatemalan capital. This situation changed only gradually in the late eighteenth century. AGCA Sig. A3, Leg. 137, Expediente 2754.

32. In 1768, the governor of Costa Rica proposed for the first time the creation of a mail route overland into South America and as far as Peru. AGCA, Sig. A3, Leg. 2885, Expediente 42100.

33. AGI, Audiencia de Guatemala, Cartas de Cabildos Seculares, Guatemala 44B, N. 71.

34. AGI, Audiencia de Guatemala, Cartas de Cabildos Seculares, Guatemala 44B, N. 75. Costa Rica's proximity to Panama is described elsewhere in these documents as "tan cerca de ella que solo hay veinte y cuatro o treinta horas de camino por la mar y cuarenta y ocho leguas por tierra." It is worth noting that this summary and the one quoted at length, written by officials in Spain to summarize the points of the cabildo's complaint, cast Guatemala and Panama as "tan lejos" and "tan cerca," respectively. This does not reflect the cabildo's usage, which states that "la provincia de Costa Rica está distante de la ciudad de Guatemala." The passage quoted above from 1625 similarly describes the province of Costa Rica as "tan lejos de" Guatemala. Which place is cast as distant depends on where the author is located; from Spain, Guatemala might be cast as "distant," whereas within the *audiencia*, authors describe Costa Rica as distant.

35. For population figures, see MacLeod, *Spanish Central America: A Socio-economic History, 1520–1720*, California library reprint:131–133.

36. Wortman, *Government and Society in Central America, 1680–1840*, 77.

37. For growth of cacao in Costa Rica see MacLeod, *Spanish Central America: A Socioeconomic History, 1520–1720*. Wortman cites specific examples of smuggling through Costa Rican ports: Wortman, *Government and Society in Central America, 1680–1840*, 99.

38. Murdo MacLeod describes its trade and communication network as linked south and east: "The Matina Valley on the Caribbean coast of Costa Rica . . . was tied commercially and culturally to the Cartagena, Portobelo, Panama, complex of ports. (As we have seen, Costa Rica felt much more affinity for nearby Panama, or Tierra Firme, than it did for distant Guatemala, throughout the colonial period.) Consequently its economic history belongs only marginally to that of the Audiencia of Guatemala." MacLeod, *Spanish Central America: A Socioeconomic History, 1520–1720*, California library reprint: 330.

39. Ibid., California library reprint: 156. Karl Sapper describes in detail the travel conditions along roads in the Verapazes, which in some cases have not changed significantly even today. Humidity and high altitude add further challenges to roads that are steep, narrow, and muddy during the rainy season. Creating patches of "bottomless" mud, the rain along a route can delay travel by several days. Karl Sapper, *The Verapaz in the Sixteenth and Seventeenth Centuries: A Contribution to the Historical Geography and Ethnography of Northeastern Guatemala* (Los Angeles: Institute of Archaeology University of California, 1985), 7–11.

40. Wortman, *Government and Society in Central America, 1680–1840*, 80–83. Rabinal, in Baja Verapaz, was the site for Bartolomé de las Casas's attempt at peaceful conversion in the mid-sixteenth century. The region's former name, Tezulután, was changed to Vera Paz—true peace—in recognition of what appeared initially to be a successful conversion effort. Sapper, *The Verapaz in the Sixteenth*

and Seventeenth Centuries: A Contribution to the Historical Geography and Ethnography of Northeastern Guatemala, 2.

41. AGCA, Sig. A3, Leg. 147, Exp. 2945. 1805 Letter by Faustino de Capetillo.

42. AGCA, Sig. A1, Leg. 4792, Folio 25. 1770 letter by Joseph Salvador de Cassares. "Asi mismo la distancia que regula de la cabezera al referido Partido devo decir . . ."

43. Before this period Comayagua had been primarily a cattle-ranching region. See Wortman, *Government and Society in Central America, 1680–1840*, 84–85.

44. Lauren Benton, "Spatial Histories of Empire," *Itinerario* 30, no. 3 (2006): 19–34; Lauren Benton, *A Search for Sovereignty: Law and Geography in European Empires, 1400–1900*, 1st ed. (Cambridge: Cambridge University Press, 2009).

45. To some extent, these maps echo the visualizations created by D. W. Meinig for the Atlantic World. Though the maps created by Meinig are self-consciously a modern reader's interpretation, there might yet be points of synchrony with the visualization of contemporaries. Meinig's description of the Spanish Atlantic as "not a broad diffusion of ships across the ocean as in the north, nor a simple axis, but as a circuit along a relatively narrow routeway" confirms the image of a fairly narrow maritime route depicted above. Meinig, *The Shaping of America*, 59.

46. Angel Rama, *The Lettered City*, trans. John Charles Chasteen (Durham, N.C.: Duke University Press, 1996), 10.

47. Hall, Pérez Brignoli, and Cotter, *Historical Atlas of Central America*, 128.

48. Henry Kamen, *Empire: How Spain Became a World Power, 1492–1763*, vol. 1st Perennial (New York: Perennial, 2004), xxiii.

49. Mirow, *Latin American Law: A History of Private Law and Institutions in Spanish America*, 19.

50. Ibid., 32.

51. ". . . Repetidos casos cuya urgencia no permite, por la distancia, el recurso a mi Real Persona." AGCA, Sig. A1, Leg. 4622, Folio 134.

52. "Lo . . . hago manifesto a VSS para que su piedad nos alivie en la mayor parte que puedan de las notorias urgencias en que nos hallamos constituidos." AGI, Correos 90A, August 1, 1773 letter from Simón de Larrazábal.

53. Harold Innis's study on the role of communications in empire building treats empire broadly, considering pre-modern civilizations and the emerging technologies of parchment, paper, and printing. Harold Adams Innis, *Empire and Communications* (Oxford: Clarendon Press, 1950). Scholars writing since the publication of Innis's work have considered the role of communications in more recent periods, including the eighteenth century. Kenneth Banks's study of the French Atlantic concentrates on how "the challenges posed by transatlantic communications impinged on, modified, and increasingly undermined the French state's control over its colonies during the first half of the eighteenth century." Kenneth J. Banks, *Chasing Empire Across the Sea: Communications and the State in the French Atlantic, 1713–1763* (Montreal: McGill-Queen's University Press, 2002), 13. Other studies have expanded and sharpened the treatment of "communication" to include gossip, surveillance, intellectual production, and other forms of social or institutional information. C. A. Bayly's study on "empire and information" in India between 1780 and 1870 explores a wide range of information networks, permitting a tex-

tured and concrete investigation into sources of colonial "knowledge." The emphasis on colonial knowledge evident in Bayly's study reflects a broader interest in framing and localizing sources of colonial "power." C. A. Bayly, *Empire and Information: Intelligence Gathering and Social Communication in India, 1780–1870* (Cambridge: Cambridge University Press, 1996).

54. John Elliott calls the statement by the bishop "prophetic," arguing that "one of the secrets of Castilian domination of the Spanish Monarchy in the sixteenth century was to be found in the triumph of its language and culture over that of other parts of the peninsula and empire." J. H. Elliott, *Imperial Spain: 1469–1716* (New York: Penguin, 2002), 125. Similarly, Henry Kamen stresses that "Castilian speech was a crucial focus of identity because it became in some measure the language of empire. Spaniards used it everywhere in order to communicate with other Spaniards." Not unaware of the importance of the written text as an extension of this linguistic spread, he states that "Castilian literature also crossed the Atlantic, to a continent where the art of writing was unknown, and where it definitely shaped the early American mind." Kamen, *Empire: How Spain Became a World Power, 1492–1763*, 1st Perennial: 336.

55. Rama, *The Lettered City*, 6–8. Other scholars have expanded Rama's formulation, which sets the written word in opposition to the spoken word, pitting "text" against "speech" and "image" alike. Walter Mignolo's treatment of "the colonization of languages, of memories, and of space," casts writing as a driving imperial force which non-textual aspects of Amerindian culture labored under and in some cases resisted. Walter Mignolo, *The Darker Side of the Renaissance: Literacy, Territoriality, and Colonization* (Ann Arbor: University of Michigan Press, 1997), 1–5. In Mignolo's rendering, the European conception of the category called "writing" privileged a single form, causing images, memory, and oral culture to suffer as result. While less stark in its characterization of this oppositional relationship, Serge Gruzinski's study of images in the Americas also argues that "Indians did not share the Spanish conception of the image." The Spanish did not recognize that "when the Indians painted they designed shapes that were both illustration and writing, graphism and iconicity." Serge Gruzinski, *Images at War: Mexico From Columbus to Blade Runner (1492–2019)* (Durham, N.C.: Duke University Press, 2001), 49–50.

56. Bouza recognizes that writing "became identified with the arrival and continuance of the early modern period," but he resists the historiographical tendency by which "writing the history of communication in the early modern period amounted fundamentally to tracing the 'progress' of reading and writing from the fifteenth to the eighteenth centuries." Fernando J. Bouza Álvarez, *Communication, Knowledge, and Memory in Early Modern Spain* (Philadelphia: University of Pennsylvania Press, 2004), 6. Bouza's work also speaks to a related line of research focusing more on personal correspondence as a form of communication than print culture. These might be seen as indirectly confirming the growing emphasis and reliance upon writing as a culture form in the early modern period across Europe. Eve Tavor Bannet, *Empire of Letters: Letter Manuals and Transatlantic Correspondence, 1688–1820* (Cambridge: Cambridge University Press, 2005); Roger Chartier, Alain Boureau, and Cécile Dauphin, *Correspondence: Models of Letter-Writing from the Middle Ages to the Nineteenth Century* (Cambridge: Polity Press, 1997).

57. This story offers a secondary but essential background. See, for example, Roger Chartier, *The Order of Books: Readers, Authors, and Libraries in Europe Between the Fourteenth and Eighteenth Centuries* (Stanford, Calif.: Stanford University Press, 1994); Maxime Chevalier, *Lectura y lectores en la España de los siglos XVI y XVII*, 1st. ed. (Madrid: Turner, 1976); Elizabeth L. Eisenstein, *The Printing Press as an Agent of Change: Communications and Cultural Transformations in Early Modern Europe* (Cambridge: Cambridge University Press, 1979); José García Oro, *Los reyes y los libros: La política libraria de la corona en el siglo de oro, 1475–1598* (Madrid: Editorial Cisneros, 1995); Carlos Alberto and González Sánchez, *Los mundos del libro: medios de difusión de la cultura occidental en las Indias de los siglos XVI y XVII* (Sevilla: Diputación de Sevilla: Universidad de Sevilla, 1999).

58. Annelise Riles, *Documents: Artifacts of Modern Knowledge* (Ann Arbor: University of Michigan Press, 2006), 7. Recent studies by sociologists and anthropologists consider documents in both Foucaultian terms as objects that "produce the very persons and societies that ostensibly use them" and in Weberian terms as "crucial technological elements of bureaucratic organization" (9, 10). Both approaches acknowledge the importance of bureaucracy and institutions surrounding—or created by—document use.

59. Peter Burke, *A Social History of Knowledge: From Gutenberg to Diderot* (Cambridge: Polity, 2000), 55.

60. Ibid., 61.

61. Ibid., 13–14.

62. Karl H. Offen, "Creating Mosquitia: Mapping Amerindian Spatial Practices in Eastern Central America, 1629–1779," *Journal of Historical Geography* 33 (2007): 254–282. Barbara Mundy lengthens and gives complexity to this argument in her study of the *relaciones geográficas*. Barbara E. Mundy, *The Mapping of New Spain: Indigenous Cartography and the Maps of the Relaciones Geográficas* (Chicago: University of Chicago Press, 2000).

63. Roger M. Downs and David Stea, *Maps in Minds: Reflections on Cognitive Mapping* (New York: Harper & Row, 1977), 104–5.

CHAPTER 1

1. AGCA, Sig. A1, Leg. 4502, Exp. 38311.

2. AGCA Sig. A1, Leg. 193, Exp. 3934: 1809

3. As Harold Innis has suggested in his study of empire and communications, even the choice of paper as the vehicle for communication indicated an emphasis on the necessity of covering spatial distance. Though he does not concentrate on the Spanish empire, he does discuss empires that similarly rely on paper—a medium that emphasizes space. "The growth of bureaucracy in the Roman empire had followed dependence on the papyrus roll, but stability assumed a fusion with religious organization based on the parchment codex. Bureaucracy in terms of the state implied an emphasis on space and a neglect of the problems of time and in terms of religion an emphasis on time and a neglect of the problems of space." Innis, *Empire and Communications.*, 167.

4. José Joaquín Real Díaz, *Estudio diplomático del documento indiano*, vol.

1st (Sevilla: Escuela de Estudios Hispanoamericanos, 1970), 25–26. Real Díaz points to distance directly as the reason for this measure. "Unas circunstancias, por completo ajenas al campo diplomático, determinan [la existencia de este grupo de originales múltiples]: la enorme distancia que separan los supremos organismos de gobierno en la península de los centros de gobierno delegados; un mar inmenso y peligroso—no sólo por los posible accidentes naturales que podrían producirse, sino por los muy frecuentes ataques de piratas y corsarios y armadas extranjeras en guerra—para los navíos que lo surcan, transportando en uno y otro sentido la documentación que relaciona la metrópoli con los súbditos americanos de la corona." (25) He also credits the distances between places in the empire as responsible for the other group of "originales múltiples," circulars sent to several places at once: "Uno de los grupos, que podíamos llamar *disposiciones generales o circulares*, nacen del concepto unitivo de la política indiana que dentro de la diversidad de territorios, separados geográficamente, a veces por enormes distancias, debe mantenerse." (23) Kenneth Banks discusses the parallel French system of writing multiple copies of each piece of correspondence in the eighteenth century. Banks, *Chasing Empire Across the Sea*, 50.

5. AGCA: Sig. A1, Leg. 16, Exp. 447; Leg. 1515, Folio 209; Leg. 1518, Folios 1v, 244; Leg. 1519, Folio 110; Leg. 1521, Folio 145; Leg. 1529, Folio 638; Leg. 1535, Folio 398; Leg. 1545, Folio 31; Leg. 1762, Folio 138 v.; Leg. 2577, Exp. 20781, Folio 28; Leg. 4575, Folio 115v. Sig. A3, Leg. 143, Exp. 2886; Leg. 144, Exp. 2896, Folio 6; Leg. 2558, Exp. 37546. After 1772, the treatment of correspondence of document "treasure" changes somewhat. Concerns for cost and weight overwhelm others, and orders are given to exchange the trunks for more practical, light-weight containers.

6. Kathryn Burns, *Into the Archive: Writing and Power in Colonial Peru* (Durham, N.C.: Duke University Press, 2010). Rama, *The Lettered City*, 33.

7. Real Díaz, *Estudio diplomático del documento indiano*. Vol. 1. Real Díaz's study, while in some sense entirely devoted to the question of document authenticity, also provides a careful formal examination of official documents composed both in the Americas and in Spain.

8. María Luisa Martínez de Salinas, *La implantación del impuesto del papel sellado en Indias* (Caracas: Academia Nacional de la Historia, 1986), 56–58.

9. Ibid., 58–59. The *papel sellado*, however, introduced its own difficulties relating to distance. In their deliberations, the Council of Indies lamented the mounting costs caused by the long-distance haul across the Atlantic. They worried that unless they doubled or even tripled the cost of the *papel sellado,* the costs would outweigh the benefits: "considering that the paper must be sent from here either already stamped or to be stamped, and that it consequently must be carried from one place to another, and that the distances extend to 5000 leagues, or 3000 leagues, or at the very minimum 1600 to 2000 leagues," ample opportunities arose for waste and loss. All things told, it seemed probable that once the proceeds of the *papel sellado* were collected, "the gains would be so minimal that they would not cover the costs." (Cited in Martínez de Salinas, *La implantación del impuesto del papel sellado en Indias*, 231. AGI, Indiferente General, Legajo 1739, Madrid 5 September 1637.) Though a plan was formulated to send the paper from Spain for the first

year and afterwards have it stamped in the Americas, in practice the paper was sent from Spain throughout the colonial period. (Martínez de Salinas, *La implantación del impuesto del papel sellado en Indias*, 111.)

10. AGCA, Sig. A3, Leg. 848, Exp. 15762, Folio 14. November 20, 1784. "Para poder dar curso sin confusión ni demora . . ."

11. Kenneth Banks writes of the "reliance on a clear hierarchy of command to communicate orders and receive reports" in the French Atlantic, which resulted in a similar process of duplication and a "use of written records and legal documents according to prescribed formulas." Banks, *Chasing Empire Across the Sea*, 4.

12. "Canutos de hoja de lata, en que siempre llegan maltratados e inservibles." AGCA, Sig. A3, Leg. 848, Exp. 15762, Folio 14. November 20, 1784.

13. In 1805, for example, Don Antonio Decano, the *Alcalde Ordinario* of the Villa de San Vicente, was accused of having opened and possibly stolen a document intended for a member of the *audiencia*. AGCA, Sig. A3, Leg. 147, Exp. 2940. In 1794, Don Francisco Galindo attempted to vindicate his honor after he was accused of having opened important documents not directed to him in Omoa. AGCA, Sig. A3, Leg. 142, Exp. 2858. And when an interim administrator of the mail service opened a letter destined for his superior in Guatemala in 1793, he was soundly censured by the main office in Spain. AGI, Correos 92A, June 2, 1793 correspondence.

14. AGCA, Sig. A1, Leg. 347, Exp. 7230, Folio 6. See Kathryn Burns for a detailed discussion of *escribano* fraud. Burns, *Into the Archive*.

15. AGCA, Sig. A1, Leg. 4502, Exp. 38311. "Noticia de las cosas mas apreciables que hay en este pueblo . . ."

16. "Este modo de discurrir no corresponde a los hombres idiotas . . ." Ibid.

17. María Portuondo's study of Spanish cosmography in the early colonial period examines the broader story of how this body of documents formed part of a changing science. Maria M. Portuondo, *Secret Science: Spanish Cosmography and the New World* (Chicago: University Of Chicago Press, 2009). For the later colonial period, see Daniela Bleichmar, "Visible Empire: Scientific Expeditions and Visual Culture in the Hispanic Enlightenment," *Postcolonial Studies* 12, no. 4 (2009): 441–466; Daniela Bleichmar et al., eds., *Science in the Spanish and Portuguese Empires, 1500–1800* (Stanford, Calif.: Stanford University Press, 2009).

18. Mundy, *The Mapping of New Spain: Indigenous Cartography and the Maps of the Relaciones Geográficas*, 8–9.

19. Matthew H. Edney, "Bringing India to Hand: Mapping an Empire, Denying Space," in *The Global Eighteenth Century*, ed. Felicity A. Nussbaum (Baltimore: The Johns Hopkins University Press, 2005), 65. See also Matthew H. Edney, *Mapping an Empire: The Geographical Construction of British India, 1765–1843* (Chicago: University Of Chicago Press, 1999).

20. Mundy, *The Mapping of New Spain: Indigenous Cartography and the Maps of the Relaciones Geográficas*, 9.

21. Rama, *The Lettered City*, 33.

22. See Daniela Bleichmar's chapter in Bleichmar et al., *Science in the Spanish and Portuguese Empires, 1500–1800*. There is no reason to think the valuing of images excluded the valuing of text. On the contrary, as the *relaciones geográficas* and

other questionnaires indicate, the two were thought to complement one another. My argument here is that text was also valued as a means to make the Americas visible.

23. For a more focused study of the Spanish cosmographers and the creation of these questionnaires, see Portuondo, *Secret Science*.

24. Francisco de Solano, Pilar Ponce Leiva, and Antonio Abellán García, *Cuestionarios para la formación de las relaciones geográficas de Indias: siglos XVI/XIX* (Madrid: Consejo Superior de Investigaciones Científicas Centro de Estudios Históricos Departamento de Historia de América, 1988), 3.

25. Ibid., 4.

26. These include a *real cédula* sent to the archbishop of Mexico from Valladolid on 27 November 1548, a *real cédula* to the archbishop of Mexico requesting "descripciones geográficas y eclesiásticas" sent from Madrid on 23 January, 1569, and a *real cédula* sent to the Audiencia of Quito from El Escorial on 16 August 1572.

27. "In the Ordenanzas," José Rabasa writes, "a brief version of the questionnaire structures the subject matter that the so-called *pacificadores* were to cover in their *relaciones*." José Rabasa, *Writing Violence on the Northern Frontier: The Historiography of Sixteenth Century New Mexico and Florida and the Legacy of Conquest* (Durham, N.C.: Duke University Press, 2000), 98. While the *ordenanzas* and the 1577 questionnaire were separate documents, many of the priorities overlapped. See also Portuondo, *Secret Science*, 115–125.

28. Solano, Ponce Leiva, and Abellán García, *Cuestionarios para la formación de las relaciones geográficas de Indias: siglos XVI/XIX*, 33.

29. Mundy, *The Mapping of New Spain: Indigenous Cartography and the Maps of the Relaciones Geográficas*, 13.

30. "Es necesario que se haga la Cosmografía . . . que dice el sitio y posición que las Indias y cada parte de ellas tienen respeto del universo, porque de esta manera las descripciones particulares que después se hicieren, serán más ciertas y se entenderán mejor." Solano, Ponce Leiva, and Abellán García, *Cuestionarios para la formación de las relaciones geográficas de Indias: siglos XVI/XIX*, 33–34.

31. Ibid., 34. Barbara Mundy and María Portuondo both discuss extensively the scientific background of Philip's cosmographers and the limited reach of their techniques among officials in the New World. A questionnaire on eclipses was sent to the Americas prior to the 1577 questionnaire, in an initial sweeping effort to establish longitudes. See Mundy, *The Mapping of New Spain: Indigenous Cartography and the Maps of the Relaciones Geográficas*; Portuondo, *Secret Science*.

32. Solano, Ponce Leiva, and Abellán García, *Cuestionarios para la formación de las relaciones geográficas de Indias: siglos XVI/XIX*, 38–40.

33. Rabasa, *Writing Violence on the Northern Frontier*, 97–98.

34. Solano, Ponce Leiva, and Abellán García, *Cuestionarios para la formación de las relaciones geográficas de Indias: siglos XVI/XIX*, 82.

35. Ibid., 83.

36. Ibid., 82.

37. Mundy, *The Mapping of New Spain: Indigenous Cartography and the Maps of the Relaciones Geográficas*, 11.

38. A questionnaire was sent to bishops of the Indies in 1581, and a 1603 questionnaire inquired into the "cities, towns, and other Spanish places and the

towns of the natives." A specific request for "maps and plans" was sent from Madrid in 1621, and in the seventeenth century more than one chronicler attempted to elicit sufficient material for a comprehensive account of the Indies. A 1635 *real cédula* requested "geographical and ecclesiastical descriptions to assist the chronicler of the Indies Don Tomás Tamayo," and a little over a decade later Don Gil González Dávila required similar information for his *Teatro eclesiástico de las Iglesias del Perú y Nueva España*. These questionnaires placed less emphasis on distances, in some cases asking only as a matter of course and in others asking for more general geographic information. Interestingly, the request for "maps and plans" seems less preoccupied with quantifications of space or distance. Concerned primarily with "where my *Audiencias* reside," it requests "plans and drawings of all the cities . . . with their ports, rivers and distances to the sea with all the qualities necessary so that each thing might be better understood." The main objective of these visual aids was "so that when it is desirable to see their disposition it will be possible to see them by ocular sight." Solano, Ponce Leiva, and Abellán García, *Cuestionarios para la formación de las relaciones geográficas de Indias: siglos XVI/XIX*, 111.

39. Mundy, *The Mapping of New Spain: Indigenous Cartography and the Maps of the Relaciones Geográficas*, 27.

40. The maps of the *relaciones geográficas* are beyond the scope of this study, but it is worth pointing out that many if not most prioritize both routes and central places.

41. The fairly brief and general inquiry circulated by the Guatemalan president departs from the minutely detailed questionnaire prepared in Madrid around 1730, which, with more than four hundred questions, would have required a far more precise reckoning from Guatemalan officials. Jorge Luján Muñoz, ed., *Relaciones geográficas e históricas del siglo XVIII del Reino de Guatemala*, 1st ed. (Guatemala: Universidad del Valle de Guatemala, 2006), xvi.

42. The practice of *reducción* or *congregación* is discussed further in Chapter 2. Solano, Ponce Leiva, and Abellán García, *Cuestionarios para la formación de las relaciones geográficas de Indias: siglos XVI/XIX*, 143–144.

43. "A la ciudad capital que es Santiago de Guatemala, hay cincuenta leguas." Luján Muñoz, *Relaciones geográficas e históricas del siglo XVIII del Reino de Guatemala*, 29.

44. "Dista de Guatemala tres leguas al rumbo Sur Sudeste." Ibid., 7.

45. "Dista de la capital de Guatemala cincuenta leguas." Ibid., 101.

46. Paul Carter, *The Road to Botany Bay: An Exploration of Landscape and History*, 1st American ed. (New York: Knopf, 1988), 69.

47. Luján Muñoz, *Relaciones geográficas e históricas del siglo XVIII del Reino de Guatemala*, 7.

48. Carter, *The Road to Botany Bay*, 76.

49. Luján Muñoz, *Relaciones geográficas e históricas del siglo XVIII del Reino de Guatemala*, 92.

50. Ibid., 92.

51. I am relying on the ideas of "cognitive distance" and "invisible landscapes" as elaborated by Peter Gould and Rodney R. White, *Mental Maps*, vol. 2 (Lon-

don: Routledge, 1986); Downs and Stea, *Maps in Minds: Reflections on Cognitive Mapping.*

52. Luján Muñoz, *Relaciones geográficas e históricas del siglo XVIII del Reino de Guatemala*, 167.

53. AGCA Sig. A1, Leg. 1508, Folio 35 (1742).

54. AGCA Sig. A1, Leg. 2335, Exp. 17508 (1744).

55. Ibid.

56. AGCA Sig. A1, Leg. 2019, Exp. 13999. "He resuelto a Consulta suya de cuarto de Junio próximo pasado . . ."

57. Ibid.

58. A *vara* (today about three feet) would measure roughly 70–90 centimeters; a *cuerda* contained 8.5 *varas*.

59. AGCA Sig. A1, Leg. 2445, Exp. 18753 (1776).

60. AGCA Sig. A1, Leg. 1530, Folio 480 (1774).

61. "Tan basta extension . . ." Ibid.

62. It is unclear in some cases whether the towns are considered sub-jurisdictions of others. AGCA Sig. A3, Leg. 246, Exp. 4670.

63. AGCA Sig. A3, Leg. 240, Exp. 4768.

64. These towns are not new: most of the places listed in the 1796 itinerary were mentioned in geographical report from 1740. Nor have the jurisdictional boundaries of the area changed. But the inclusion of the additional towns "lengthens" the distances of the region.

65. AGCA Sig. A3, Leg. 1936, Exp. 30113, Folio 412.

66. Solano, Ponce Leiva, and Abellán García, *Cuestionarios para la formación de las relaciones geográficas de Indias: siglos XVI/XIX.*, 177–178. Also found in AGI, Indiferente General, 1525, Doc. 33.

67. Ibid., 177–178.

68. Boundaries were to be marked with dotted lines and the political jurisdictions marked by different colors. A double line was to mark the principal thoroughfares, and the principal places along them were to be marked by circles. Single lines were to be used to mark lesser roads and byways. Other important elements of the landscape—mountains, forests, rivers, bridges, lakes, and so on—were to be included as well. The first line of inquiry thereby expanded and sharpened the expected contents of the "plano o carta," and while it placed a newer emphasis on boundaries and political territories, it continued to emphasize routes and particularly the lines of communication between places. Ibid., 205.

69. Ibid., 206.

70. Ibid., 207.

CHAPTER 2

1. Pedro Cortés y Larraz, Julio Martín Blasco, and Jesús M. García, *Descripción Geográfico-moral De La Diócesis De Goathemala* (Madrid: Consejo Superior de Investigaciones Científicas, 2001), 12. Remaining in his post until 1779, he returned afterward to Spain and concluded his career there.

2. Cortés y Larraz, Martín Blasco, and García, *Descripción geográfico-moral de la Diócesis de Goathemala.*

3. For discussion of a *visita*'s objectives and analysis of how one seventeenth-century *visita* unfolded, see Bravo Rubio, Berenise, and Marco Antonio Pérez Iturbe. "Tiempos y espacios religiosos novohispanos: la visita pastoral de Francisco Aguiar y Seijas (1683–1684)." In *Religión, poder y autoridad en la Nueva España*, 67–83. 1st ed. México D.F.: Universidad Nacional Autónoma de México, 2004, 67–83. Published Guatemalan *visitas* include Casaus y Torres, Ramón Francisco. *Carta del Illmo. Sr. Dr. D. Fr. Ramon Casaus y Torres, Obispo de Rosen, y Arzobispo Electo de Guatemala, á todos los Diocesanos de su iglesia Metropolitana.* Tapana, México, 1811; Jesús M. García, *Población y estado sociorreligioso de la Diócesis de Guatemala en el último tercio del siglo XVIII.* Guatemala, Centroamérica: Editorial Universitaria Universidad de San Carlos de Guatemala, 1987.

4. Neil Safier, *Measuring the New World: Enlightenment Science and South-America* (Chicago: University of Chicago Press, 2008), 59.

5. Julio Martín Blasco and Jesús María García Añoveros argue persuasively that Cortés y Larraz did not travel with a single guide, as other authors have claimed. They point to the rich knowledge of the terrain as evidence that the archbishop traveled with local guides, and they indicate that the identity of the painter is unknown. He may have been local as well. "El arzobispo habla en diversas ocasiones de '*mi familia*', de '*mis capellanes*', de '*mi secretario*'; seguramente les acompañarían también algún escribiente, varios criados o mozos de confianza (los cita en alguna ocasión), sin olvidar el dibujante, autor anónimo de los excelentes mapas en color de cada una de las parroquias. A este grupo se unirían de una parroquia a otra los guías (en una ocasión dice que se extraviaron), un grupo de indios encargados de trasportar las cargas . . . el cura, el alcalde . . . , y principales del pueblo. Son tantos los datos que aporta y los nombres de ríos montañas, haciendas, pueblos, etc. que cita en el camino de una parroquia a otra que es preciso suponer la presencia en el grupo de un buen conocedor del terreno que fuera facilitando la información." Cortés y Larraz, Martín Blasco, and García, *Descripción geográfico-moral de la Diócesis de Goathemala*, 16.

6. Ibid., 14.

7. Ibid., 15.

8. Ibid., 37. As discussed in Chapter 3, leagues were defined in particular ways in Guatemala. For a thorough discussion of league-measures throughout North America, see Roland Chardon, "The Linear League in North America," *Annals of the Association of American Geographers* 70, no. 2 (June 1980): 129–153.

9. Cortés y Larraz exemplifies what Bernhard Klein has described for the "writing of space" in early modern England and Ireland as three conceptual stages: space is measured, space is visualized, and space is narrated. Klein perceives these as a "cartographic transaction" which he studies in the Elizabethan and Jacobean periods, but the strategy of measuring, visualizing, and narrating clearly emerged beyond this region and period as well. Bernhard Klein, *Maps and the Writing of Space in Early Modern England and Ireland* (New York: St. Martin's Press, 2001), 3–5.

10. Cortés y Larraz, Martín Blasco, and García, *Descripción geográfico-moral de la Diócesis de Goathemala*, 67–68.

11. Ibid., 68–72.

12. "Una cuesta muy mala y violenta . . ." Ibid., 72.

13. Bruce Castleman confirms for Mexico what seems also to be true for Guatemala, stating that "the metropolitan government was primarily concerned with the lines of communication between Mexico City and port cities in Spain." This led to attempted improvements in the late Bourbon period: "The colonial government devoted a great deal of concern and effort to the improvement of overland transport during the late eighteenth century, but the problems posed by terrain and distance were immense." Bruce A Castleman, *Building the King's Highway: Labor, Society, and Family on Mexico's Caminos Reales, 1757–1804* (Tucson: University of Arizona Press, 2005), 7–8.

14. Stephen Daniels's study of the landscape architect Humphry Repton places particular emphasis on the aesthetic and functionality of roads in late eighteenth-century England. During a period (1750–1811) that saw the journey between London and other major cities in its environs cut by nearly two-thirds, roads were a rapidly transforming element of the landscape. Daniels points not only to the importance of roads and movement along them in Repton's landscape architecture, but also to the developing social mores to arise dictating forms of polite and proper travel. Improvements in travel permitted a markedly different sensibility as, for example, "walking along country lanes and by-roads acquired a serious moral purpose among those intent on observing the details of God's handiwork or the lives of the poor, which speeding carriage-folk overlooked." Stephen Daniels, *Humphry Repton: Landscape Gardening and the Geography of Georgian England* (New Haven: Published for the Paul Mellon Centre for Studies in the British Art [by] Yale University Press, 1999), 30.

15. I am relying here on ideas elaborated by Yi-Fu Tuan, in particular his notion of how the understanding of "good" in assessing the natural and man-made landscape incorporates a moral sensibility, as well as the comparative work by Mary W. Helms on cultural distance. Yi-fu Tuan, *Morality and Imagination: Paradoxes of Progress* (Madison: University of Wisconsin Press, 1989). Mary W. Helms, *Ulysses' Sail: An Ethnographic Odyssey of Power, Knowledge, and Geographical Distance* (Princeton, N.J.: Princeton University Press, 1988).

16. Cortés y Larraz, Martín Blasco, and García, *Descripción geográfico-moral de la Diócesis de Goathemala*, 467.

17. Ibid., 405.

18. Ibid., 105.

19. Ibid., 191.

20. Paul Carter discusses a parallel usafe of "plains" and bush" in the Australian context, where plains could be "visibly possessed" and "bush" came to mean the area "which lay beyond the bounds of settlement." Paul Carter, *The Road to Botany Bay: An Exploration of Landscape and History*, 1st American ed. (New York: Knopf, 1988), 148–149.

21. Cortés y Larraz, Martín Blasco, and García, *Descripción geográfico-moral de la Diócesis de Goathemala*, 420.

22. Ibid., 139.

23. Ibid., 374–375.

24. It would seem reasonable to expect that Cortés y Larraz traveled on a mule or even on a chair carried by one of his guides, but an occurrence in Santa María

Nevah (today Nebaj) gave him occasion to describe his travel circumstances in more detail, and he appears not to have been above walking. "Desde el pueblo de Santo Domingo Sacapulas al de Santa María Nevah hay ocho leguas, rumbo de sur a norte. El camino es el [más] pésimo que puede imaginarse. Los indios de Nevah acudieron al pueblo de Sacapulas con sillas de mano para toda la familia, diciendo: que no podía pasarse a su pueblo de otro modo. Las montañas que habían de pasarse estaban a cien pasos de Sacapulas, y me mostraban sus sendas para que viera que eran intransitables; con todo y por la grande repugnancia que siento a ir en silla, considerando que es ajena de mi estado, me obligó a perseverar en la determinación de ir en mula o a pie, no obstante que me decían que era imposible el ir en mula y más imposible a pie." Ibid., 313.

25. Ibid., 106.

26. Ibid., 261. Robert Patch, in his study of Maya and Spaniard in colonial Yucatán, identifies another impenetrable mountain in the southern reaches of Yucatán; while Spaniards called this region the Montaña, he points out the "strange choice of word, given the area's almost uniformly low terrain." In fact, he argues, "the Montaña, rather, was in the mind of the Spaniards. To people of Mediterranean culture, mountains were not exclusively topographic features. They were refuges, places difficult to control, and, in Fernand Braudel's words, regions of a 'separate religious geography.'" Robert Patch, *Maya and Spaniard in Yucatan, 1648–1812* (Stanford, Calif.: Stanford University Press, 1993), 46.

27. Cortés y Larraz, Martín Blasco, and García, *Descripción geográfico-moral de la Diócesis de Goathemala*, 111.

28. Ibid., 112.

29. Ibid., 106–107.

30. Patch, *Maya and Spaniard in Yucatan, 1648–1812*, 46.

31. Cortés y Larraz, Martín Blasco, and García, *Descripción geográfico-moral de la Diócesis de Goathemala*, 107.

32. Ibid., 112. By the time he reached Titiguapa, his tone was rather firmer: "This parish in its present situation cannot be governed, even if the *cura* had the assistance of two deacons, which the income for this parish cannot support. The only remedy is to gather the multitude of people spread throughout the towns in what are called *haciendas* but are not really *haciendas*—these are rather ranches erected here and there by the Indians and Ladinos according to whim, where they manage to live in complete freedom and without observing any laws whatsoever." Ibid., 188.

33. Ibid., 202–203.

34. Ibid.

35. Quoted in W. George Lovell, *Conquest and Survival in Colonial Guatemala: A Historical Geography of the Cuchumatan Highlands, 1500–1821*, 3rd ed. (Montreal: McGill-Queen's University Press, 2005), 76.

36. Ibid., 77.

37. Ibid., 83.

38. Patch, *Maya and Spaniard in Yucatan, 1648–1812*, 52.

39. Cortés y Larraz, Martín Blasco, and García, *Descripción geográfico-moral de la Diócesis de Goathemala*, 227.

40. Ibid., 250. John Lynch's analysis of Cortés y Larraz identifies a similarly stark prognosis that "the Indians of Guatemala were irredeemable. Lost to God and the Church. For the adults there was no remedy." John Lynch, *New Worlds: A Religious History of Latin America* (New Haven: Yale University Press, 2012), 90.

41. Cortés y Larraz, Martín Blasco, and García, *Descripción geográfico-moral de la Diócesis de Goathemala*, 183.

42. Ibid., 435.

43. Richard Kagan, *Urban Images of the Hispanic World, 1493–1793* (New Haven, Conn.: Yale University Press, 2000), 2.

44. Kagan identifies the following views: profile view, drawn at eye level; equestrian view, at an angle of ten degrees; oblique view, at an angle of thirty degrees; bird's eye view, at an angle of forty-five degrees; cartographic or perspective view, at an angle of sixty degrees; ichnographic or orthogonal view, at ninety degrees. Ibid., 5. The artist for the *visita* appears to have used the full spectrum of perspectives at different moments, but a majority of the paintings rely on views drawn from angles of thirty to sixty degrees.

45. Ibid., 64.

46. Cortés y Larraz, Martín Blasco, and García, *Descripción geográfico-moral de la Diócesis de Goathemala*, 88.

47. Ibid., 217.

48. Irisarri's account in many ways differs from the texts Mary Louise Pratt considers in her study of eighteenth and nineteenth century travel literature, but certain aspects of his account resonate with those which she examines as demonstrations of "creole self-fashioning." Irisarri was almost certainly not referencing Alexander von Humboldt in his fictionalized autobiography, yet the impulse to reimagine and celebrate the Americas runs through his text. Mary Louise Pratt, *Imperial Eyes: Travel Writing and Transculturation*, 2nd ed. (Routledge, 2007).

49. Antonio Irisarri, *El cristiano errante: novela que tiene mucho de historia*, 3 vols., Biblioteca Guatemala De Cultura Popular 31–33 (Guatemala, C.A.: Ministerio de Educación Pública, 1960).

50. Ibid., 181–183.

51. Ibid., 181–183.

52. Ibid., 181–183.

53. Ibid., 181–183.

54. Ibid., 126–127.

55. Ibid.

56. Ibid., 126–127.

57. Ibid., 128–129.

CHAPTER 3

1. AGI, Correos 90A, August 1, 1773 letter from Simón de Larrazábal.

2. The Maya kingdoms in the future *audiencia* of Guatemala relied on foot-messengers who needed to possess knowledge of the terrain, physical stamina, and an ability to retain and convey royal messages. Their rulers doubtlessly communicated with each other by messenger (as they did with rulers in Mexico), though their means of doing so is scarcely researched. The communications net-

work of the Aztecs has received more attention: Aztec messengers, who belonged to the military class and as such serviced only the empire, carried both written and oral messages, and their status approximated more what we think of today as dignitaries than mail carriers. The system of runners (*paynani*) was administrated by a *yciuhuatitlanti*, "one who goes quickly," and organized spatially around resting points set approximately six miles apart. By relaying messages from stop to stop, the *paynani* covered an estimated three hundred miles per day. Alicia G. de Backal, Laura Edith Bonilla, and Servicio Postal Mexicano, *Historia del correo en México* (México: Servicio Postal Mexicano: M.A. Porrúa Grupo Editorial, 2000). The continental Spanish communication system seems, in comparison, somewhat late to formalize. Its antecedents can be traced to the Roman system, but the considerable lapse between the dissolution of the Roman empire in Spain and the development of the Spanish imperial system left little for the early modern mail to build upon. In the thirteenth century, Spain and Europe more broadly developed a degree of reliance on official mail carriers. Alfonso X of Castile and León (1221–1284) termed the mail carriers "mandaderos" (messengers) and defined them as those who "bring messages in the form of letters, which like the feet of men, travel to bring messages without speaking." As early as 1293, there is evidence of mail carriers or "troters" organizing *cofradías* in Catalonia, and in the mid-fourteenth century the kings of Majorca and Aragon almost simultaneously developed legislation to establish official, royal mail services. From other related legislation the existence of a mail service for public use in Aragon can be confirmed as early as the fourteenth century, and the innovative use of horses to carry the mail in the ensuing century indicates an increasing prioritization of reliability and speed. In the fifteenth century the "leaders of the *correo* guilds" established more powerful *cofradías*, and legislation from the *Concelleres* in Barcelona testifies to their growing importance. Spain. Dirección General de Correos y Telégrafos., *Anales de las ordenanzas de correos de España* (Madrid: Imprenta Central a Cargo de Victor Saiz, 1879).

3. Ibid., XVIII. Postal systems in continental Europe emerged roughly contemporaneously. See Alvin F. Harlow, *Old Post Bags; the Story of the Sending of a Letter in Ancient and Modern Times* (New York: D. Appleton, 1928).

4. Backal, Bonilla, and Servicio Postal Mexicano, Historia Del Correo En México, 15.

5. Quoted in Ibid., 17. Transatlantic communication would prove similarly challenging for the French and English. See especially Kenneth J. Banks, *Chasing Empire Across the Sea: Communications and the State in the French Atlantic, 1713–1763* (Montreal: McGill-Queen's University Press, 2002); Howard Robinson, *Carrying British Mails Overseas* (London: G. Allen & Unwin, 1964).

6. Correspondence between Spain and the Americas flowed initially from Seville, by way of Cádiz and then the Canary Islands, to Santo Domingo in Hispaniola. Santo Domingo was soon discarded in favor of safer harbors in the Caribbean, and on the mainland the harbors in Veracruz (Mexico), Portobelo (Panama), and Cartagena (Colombia) were deemed the most suitable. Documents between Spain and Guatemala traveled initially through the port of Veracruz, and from Veracruz they were carried overland through Mexico to Guatemala and its provinces. How-

ever, this route proved cumbersome, and in the early seventeenth century an alternative was proposed that would funnel correspondence into Guatemala by way of the Yucatan. In practice, correspondence to and from Spain continued to travel mainly through Veracruz. In 1630, the crown acceded to the Guatemalan *audiencia's* request that the maritime correspondence be unloaded in Veracruz rather than Yucatan. (AGCA, Sig. A1, Leg. 1515, Folio 235.) Not until the later colonial period was the more convenient port of Omoa, in what is today Honduras, developed as a channel for communication between Guatemala and Spain. Routes through the Caribbean changed repeatedly in the colonial period in response to weather and piracy. See Ernst Schäfer's publication for a detailed discussion of how maritime routes changed over the colonial period and for descriptions of the maritime routes to destinations in what is today South America. Ernst Schäfer and John Pilaar, *Communications Between Spain and Her American Colonies and Inter-Colonial Communications* (Los Angeles, 1939). See also Secundino-José Gutiérrez Alvarez, *Las comunicaciones en América: de la senda primitiva al ferrocarril*, Colecciones MAPFRE 1492 (Madrid: Editorial MAPFRE, 1993).

7. Schäfer and Pilaar, *Communications Between Spain and Her American Colonies and Inter-Colonial Communications*, 5, 8. Despite efforts to avoid the tornado season, the fleet to New Spain that was intended to leave in April rarely left before June, and the fleet bound for Panama and Peru that was meant to leave in August or September usually left in November.

8. AGCA, Sig. A1, Leg. 1512.

9. AGCA, Sig. A1, Leg. 1513. Kenneth Banks has studied the travel of documents across the Atlantic through the French communication system. See especially his analysis of "response time." Banks, *Chasing Empire Across the Sea*, 54–55.

10. "Ya en 1529 la correspondencia oficial, la del comercio, la de los particulares y la de los empleados que circulaba entre las poblaciones del interior de la Nueva España y las del resto de las colonias se transportaba mediante conductos privados. Era el único medio de comunicación de que se disponía. Por lo general, esta correspondencia era interceptada y rara vez llegaba a su destino." Backal, Bonilla, and Servicio Postal Mexicano, *Historia del correo en México*, 16.

11. Pedro Froilán Barreda, *Geografía e historia de correos y telecomunicaciones de Guatemala: sus estudios* (Guatemala, 1961), 38.

12. Walter Björn Ludovico Bose, *Los orígenes del correo terrestre en Guatemala* (Santiago de Chile, 1930), 8.

13. Ibid., p. 22. Walter Bose's chronology details the circumstances of each *correo mayor's* tenure.

14. These reforms were mirrored by reforms elsewhere in Europe. For concurrent reforms in Canada and France, see Banks, *Chasing Empire Across the Sea*, 181. See also K. V Bazilevich, *The Russian Posts in the XIX Century* (Rossica Society of Russian Philately, 1987); Robinson, *Carrying British Mails Overseas*.

15. Backal, Bonilla, and Servicio Postal Mexicano, *Historia del correo en México*, 31.

16. Spain. Dirección General de Correos y Telégrafos., *Anales de las ordenanzas de correos de España*, 90–98.

17. AGCA, Sig. A1, Leg. 1508, folios 75, 86, 88. The mail was dispatched by

order of Don Thomas de Rivera and left for Mexico on no set date; in these instances it departed on the 25th, the 15th, and the 7th, respectively.

18. By the 1740s, the practice of sending a single protected fleet to and from Spain once a year had been abandoned. While the *navíos de registro*, registered ships that navigated their own routes independent of the fleets, had been sailing unofficially since the sixteenth century, these were officially recognized in 1720. In the 1740s licenses for the *navíos de registro* were increasingly easier to acquire. In this period the maritime routes to New Spain and Tierra Firme continued, but additional routes reaching Chile, Peru, and Buenos Aires were solidified. Schäfer and Pilaar, *Communications Between Spain and Her American Colonies and Inter-Colonial Communications*, 27.

19. The utility of the monthly mail service was hotly debated in Guatemala and in Spain. The *Fiscal* in Spain argued that an expense of more the five thousand *pesos* per year could not be considered egregious, as the six-year period had fallen during a time of war when the need for immediate and unexpected communication was inevitable. He concluded, however, that the monthly mail project should be attempted, setting as a condition that the Guatemala archbishop would report on the project's effectiveness. In Guatemala, the financial support the project received made clear that establishing a monthly mail service benefited local business as much as it did administrators who wished to communicate more frequently with Spain. "En Diciembre de 1748 quedaron establecidos los Correos Mensuales entre Guatemala y Nueva España (Oaxaca). Con este motivo el Gobernador comunicó el hecho a la Junta de Comercio y a la Compañía de Minas y Comercio, a fin de que contribuyan cada una con los 1,000 pesos que habían ofrecido para el establecimiento de los Correos. Al propio tiempo se dio aviso a los Oficiales Reales de Veracruz, para que no envíen con correos extraordinarios los cajones que traían los Navíos de Aviso, sino que lo hiciesen con el Correo ordinario semana hasta Oaxaca, donde se entregarían al correo mensual de Guatemala." Bose, *Los orígenes del correo terrestre en Guatemala*, 22–27.

20. AGCA, Sig. A1, Leg. 1509, Folios 27–30.

21. AGI, Correos 90B, October 1778 tables by Don Simón de Larrazábal.

22. AGCA, Sig. A1, Leg. 1508, Folio 254.

23. In 1765 the Guatemalan *correo* was officially incorporated by the crown. It took until 1767 for the change to take effect. Pedro Ortiz de Letona was compensated for the office and appointed *Regidor* of the mail system for the remainder of his lifetime. (AGI, Correos, 90B, Dec. 31, 1766.) This date coincided with broader policy initiatives in Spain. Charles III implemented the first free trade measures in 1765, and these were followed by similar measures in 1778. Gutiérrez Alvarez, *Las comunicaciones en América: de la senda primitiva al ferrocarril*, 25.

24. Other accounts date the mail service to the provinces back to 1749. In either case, the route was financed by a sales tax of four *reales* for every *tercio* of indigo. AGI, Correos 90B: 1773 draft of letter to Grimaldi.

25. AGI, Correos 90B: 1768 testimonio by Don Joseph de Garayalde.

26. AGCA, Signatura A3, Legajo 137, Expediente 2766. The *carta sencilla*, any letter weighing up to ½ ounce, would cost four *reales de vellón* in Spain and three *reales de plata fuerte* in the Indies. The *carta doble*, weighing between ½ and ¾

ounce, would cost nine *reales de vellón* in Spain and five *reales de plata fuerte* in the Indies. Letters weighing ¾ ounce would cost twelve *reales de vellón* in Spain and seven *reales de plata fuerte* in the Indies. For larger letter packets the cost would be twelve *reales de vellón* in Spain and ten *reales de plata fuerte* in the Indies. Mail sent among the Caribbean islands would be charged at a rate of ½ *real de plata fuerte* for the *sencilla*, one *real* for the *doble*, one and one-half *real* for the ¾ ounce, and 2 *reales* per ounce for packets. Letters from the Indies mainland to the islands would also be charged at this rate. Correspondence between New Spain and Tierra Firme would be charged double these rates.

27. AGI, Correos 90B, 1766 decree and 1768 testimonio by Garayalde.

28. This proclamation partially overturned the 1764 regulations sent from Spain, which still allowed for the sobre-porte.

29. AGI, Correos 90A, 1768 Bando by Don Pedro de Salazar Herrera. The fine was initially an exorbitant 500 pesos. In the late eighteenth century it was reduced to 50 pesos.

30. AGI, Correos 90B, 1770 Bando by Don Pedro de Salazar Herrera.

31. AGI, Correos 90A, 1768 Correspondence by Don Joseph de Garayalde.

32. AGI, Correos 90A, 1768 Correspondence by Don Joseph de Garayalde.

33. AGI, Correos 90A, 1769 Correspondence by Don Joseph Melchor de Ugalde.

34. AGI, Correos 90A, April 1, 1770 Correspondence from Don Joseph Melchor de Ugalde.

35. ". . . Por su comercio, y abundancia de gente Española, y Ladina." AGI, Correos 90A, January 1, 1770 Correspondence from Don Joseph Melchor de Ugalde.

36. AGCA, Sig. A3, Leg. 2885, Exp. 42102: 1772.

37. AGI, Correos, 90A, September 16, 1773 letters by Don Simón de Larrazábal.

38. The system was still rough at the edges. In 1777, a lengthy correspondence ensued between Larrazábal, administrators in Spain, and the governor in Cartago, Costa Rica, who protested of infrequent communication with the rest of Guatemala. Larrazábal, after weighing several options, decided the scant correspondence and the great expense of the journey made relying on travelers to carry occasional letters the most favorable alternative. (AGI, Correos 90B, 1777 Larrazábal correspondence.)

39. AGI, Correos 91A, 1778 bando by Don Martín de Mayorga.

40. The correo on horseback, who paid for his own expenses, cost 1,360 reales; the "indio correo" who carried the mail on foot between Totonicapan and Quesaltenango cost 6 *reales*; and the two Indians who carried the mail between Ciudad Real and Tuxtla cost 32 *reales*. AGI, Correos 91B, 1778 Report by Don Simón de Larrazábal.

41. Adapted from tables in AGI, Correos 90B, 1778 Report by Don Simón de Larrazábal.

42. AGI, Correos 91A, July 16, 1781 letter from Don Juan Miguel de Yzaguirre.

43. See, for example, the 1787 debate that resulted in switching the departure date from the fifteenth to the second of the month. (AGI, Correos 91A, 1787 bando.)

44. AGI, Correos 92B, November 2, 1795 correspondence by Don Miguel de Ateaga.

45. AGCA, Signatura A1, Legajo 2603, Expediente 21389.

46. AGI, Correos 102B, 1772 Chart.

47. This chart bears a striking similarity to a general "mapa y tabla de leguas comunes" found at the John Carter Brown Library and showing distances in Spanish North America. The table showing distances is accompanied by a map and illustrations. Joseph Nava, "Mapa y Tabla Geográfica de Leguas Comunes, que ai de unos á otros Lugares, y Ciudades principales de la America septentrional." (Puebla de los Angeles, 1755), Record number 28987, John Carter Brown Library.

48. AGI, MP—Buenos Aires 253; 25-02-1804.

49. AGI, Correos 110A, 1806 Report.

50. See, for example, a 1766 list of place-names from Yucatan (AGI Correos 142C) and an 1814 list from Peru (AGI Correos 113B). One notable precedent from Spain is Fernández de Mesa's 1755 account of continental roads, inns, and postal routes. Fernández's appendix on "postal routes, established in Spain, and the distance in Leagues between one place and another" represents the postal routes in two ways: as short links of consecutive *leguas* from one place to another, or itinerary tables identical to Ateaga's, and as longer distances radiating out from a central city or place, identical to Ateaga's table of distances from Guatemala. Tomás Manuel Fernández de Mesa y Moreno, *Tratado legal, y politico de caminos publicos, y possadas. Dividido en dos partes. La una, en que se hable de los caminos; y la otra, de las possadas: y como anexo, de los correos, y postas, assi publicas, como privadas: donde se incluye el Reglamento general de aquellas, expedido en 23. de abril de 1720* (Valencia: J. T. Lucas, 1755), 182.

51. ". . . Mapa Topográfico comprehensivo de las Estafetas agregadas a esta Pral, las distancias de unas a otras, su situación local, paradas de Postas, y ramales de division." AGI, Correos 92B, April 2, 1795 letter by Don Miguel de Ateaga. Ateaga's tables thus intended to record and describe the extent of the postal service rather than to provide *correos* or even other officials with a practical guide.

52. Maria M. Portuondo, *Secret Science: Spanish Cosmography and the New World* (Chicago: University Of Chicago Press, 2009); Alison Sandman, "Controlling Knowledge: Navigation, Cartography, and Secrecy in the Early Modern Spanish Atlantic," in *Science and Empire in the Atlantic World*, ed. James Delbourgo and Nicholas Dew (New York: Routledge, 2008). For a more general history of how cartographic forms evolved, see John R. Short, *Making Space: Revisioning the World, 1475–1600* (Syracuse, N.Y.: Syracuse University Press, 2004); J. B. Harley and David Woodward, *The History of Cartography* (Chicago: University of Chicago Press, 1987); Leo Bagrow and R. A. Skelton, *History of Cartography* (Chicago: Precedent Pub., 1985).

53. Ricardo Padrón makes much of the Hapsburg's prohibiting their maps from appearing in print. He observes that the Spanish Bourbons corrected what was perceived as a consequent cartographic backwardness by importing cartographic techniques from France. It seems likely, however, that these techniques had not yet been systematically applied to the creation of detailed maps in Guatemala. Ricardo Padrón, *The Spacious Word: Cartography, Literature, and Empire in Early Modern*

Spain (Chicago: University of Chicago Press, 2004). Recent studies suggest that while the crown may have succeeded only unevenly in preserving maps as state secrets, it certainly succeeded in stifling the production of state-of-the-art maps. This would explain the relative absence of not only maps but of cartographic production in Guatemala. Portuondo, *Secret Science*; Sandman, "Controlling Knowledge: Navigation, Cartography, and Secrecy in the Early Modern Spanish Atlantic."

54. Kit S. Kapp, *The Printed Maps of Central America up to 1860* (London: Map Collectors' Circle, 1974). See also the following recent collection: Jens P Bornholt et al., *Cuatro siglos de expresiones geográficas del istmo centroamericano, 1500–1900* (Guatemala: Universidad Francisco Morroquín, 2007).

55. "En este Reyno no hay mapa general de ellas, como a esta subdelegación y superior gobierno he hecho presente." AGI, Correos 90B, October 20, 1778 letter from Don Simón de Larrazábal.

56. "La situación local de las Estafetas, que no puede expresarse por carecer el Reino de Mapas formales, y no ser las noticias que han comunicado los Admin. capaces de instruir en la material." AGI, Correos 92B, October and November 1795 letters by Don Miguel de Ateaga.

57. Padrón, *The Spacious Word: Cartography, Literature, and Empire in Early Modern Spain*, 71.

58. Ibid., 47. "Mapa: La descripción geográfica de la tierra, que regularmente se hace en papel o lienzo, en que se ponen los lugares, mares, ríos, montañas, y otras cosas notables, con las distancias proporcionadas, según el pitipié que se elige, señalando los grados de longitud y latitud que ocupa el País que se describe, para conocimiento del parage o lugar que cada cosa destas ocupada en la tierra." Real Academia Española., *Diccionario de autoridades*, vol. ed. facsímil. (Madrid: Editorial Gredos, 1964).

59. Padrón, *The Spacious Word: Cartography, Literature, and Empire in Early Modern Spain*, 47. "Mapa—llamamos la tabla, lienço o papel donde se descrive la tierra universal o particularmente y puede venir de mappa, que quiere decir lienço o toalla." Sebastián de Covarrubias Horozco, *Tesoro de la lengua castellana o española según la impresión de 1611*, ed. Benito Remigio Noydens and Martín de Riquer (Barcelona: S. A. Horta, 1943).

60. See Denis E. Cosgrove, *Apollo's Eye: A Cartographic Genealogy of the Earth in the Western Imagination* (Baltimore: Johns Hopkins University Press, 2001); Bagrow and Skelton, *History of Cartography*; Harley and Woodward, *The History of Cartography*; Short, *Making Space: Revisioning the World, 1475–1600*.

61. Padrón, *The Spacious Word: Cartography, Literature, and Empire in Early Modern Spain*, 79–82.

62. "Espacio—del nombre latino *spatium, capedo, intervallum*; vale lugar. Mucho espacio, poco espacio. También sinifica el intervalo del tiempo, y dezimos por espacio de tiempo de tantas horas, etc. . . . ." Covarrubias Horozco, *Tesoro de la lengua castellana o española según la impresión de 1611*, 48.

63. Padrón, *The Spacious Word: Cartography, Literature, and Empire in Early Modern Spain*, 47. "Espacio: capacidad, anchura, longitud, a latitud de terreno, lugar, sitio, u campo. Es tomado del Latin Spatium que significa esto mismo." Real Academia Española., *Diccionario de autoridades*.

64. Real Academia Española., *Diccionario de autoridades.*

65. "Lugar se dize todo aquello que contiene en sí otra cosa . . . Lugar sinifica muchas vezes ciudad o villa o aldea, y assí dezimos: En mi lugar, en el pueblo donde nací . . . Hacer lugar, desembaraçar y dar passo. No tener lugar, no tener tiempo." Covarrubias Horozco, *Tesoro de la lengua castellana o española según la impresión de 1611.*

66. "Tener tiempo, tener lugar . . . Dar tiempo al tiempo, dar lugar." Ibid.

67. "Lugar: El espacio que contiene en sí otra cosa. Sale del Latín *locus*, que significa lo mismo; lugar2: significa también sitio u parage; lugar3: vale también Ciudad, villa, o aldea; . . . lugar6: significa también tiempo, espacio, oportunidad u ocasión." Real Academia Española., *Diccionario de autoridades.*

68. "La duración successiva de las cosas." Ibid.

69. "El espacio o intervalo de lugar u tiempo, con que las cosas o los sucessos están apartados unos de otros." Ibid.

70. Roland Chardon, "The Linear League in North America," *Annals of the Association of American Geographers* 70, no. 2 (June 1980): 131.

71. Ibid., 130.

72. "Espacio de camino, que contiene en sí tres millas." Covarrubias Horozco, *Tesoro de la lengua castellana o española según la impresión de 1611.* This suggests that he relied on the *legua legal* for his definition. For a discussion of the *legua legal*, see Chardon, 1980.

73. "Medida de tierra, cuya magnitud es mui varia entre las Naciones. De las leguas Españolas entran diez y siete y media en un grado de circulo maximo de la tierra, y cada una es lo que regularmente se anda en una hora." Real Academia Española., *Diccionario de autoridades.*

74. "Roughly, the distance that can be traveled on horseback in an hour, varying with the terrain." Lillian Ramos Wold and Ophelia Márquez, *Compilation of Colonial Spanish Terms and Document Related Phrases*, vol. 2nd (Midway City, Calif.: SHAAR Press, 1998). Other definitions include the following: "legua—la del país mide en longitud terrestre 5,000 baras o 4,190 metros lo mismo en Cuba, Puerto Rico y Guatemala." Francisco Javier Santamaría and Joaquín García Icazbalceta, *Diccionario de mejicanismos: razonado, comprobado con citas de autoridades, comparado con el de americanismos y con los vocabularios provinciales de los más distinguidos diccionaristas hispanoamericanos* (Méjico: Editorial Porrúa, 1992). Also "Legua—Medida lineal de dimensión variada. De las leguas españolas, 17 y media en un grado de círculo máximo de la tierra y cada una era la medida de lo que regularmente se camina en una hora." Stella María González Cicero and Delia Pezzat A., *Guía para la interpretación de vocablos en documentos novohispanos: siglos XVI a XVIII. Presentación de Stella María González Cicero; introducción de Delia Pezzat Arzave*, vol. 1a (México, D.F.: Secretaría de Gobernación: Archivo General de la Nación-México, 2001).

75. In any case, all of the dozen or more Spanish American leagues are roughly 4.2 kilometers or 2.6 miles in modern equivalences. Chardon, "The Linear League in North America," 150.

76. Ibid., 150, 134.

77. AGI, Correos 90B, 1778 Report by Don Simón de Larrazábal; "Estado

o Razon de las distancias que hay desde esta Capital a las demas Ciudades de este Reyno y Cabezeras de Partidos" seems to utilize three descriptive approaches. AGCA, Sig. A1, Leg. 2603, Exp. 21389. As stated above, this representation is nearly identical to the 1795 table housed at the AGI. Henri Lefebvre, *The Production of Space* (Cambridge, Mass.: Blackwell, 1991), 151.

78. "Nota de estas Ciudades, Valles, Provincias, Pueblos, Poblaciones, Haziendas, y demas Lugares, de las Administraciones agregadas a esta Principal." AGCA, Sig. A3, Leg. 2885, Exp. 42102.

79. This depiction echoes Lauren Benton's conception of colonial spaces as "encased in irregular, porous, and sometimes undefined borders. Although empires did lay claim to vast stretches of territory, the nature of such claims was tempered by control that was exercised mainly over narrow bands, or corridors, and over enclaves and irregular zones around them." Lauren Benton, *A Search for Sovereignty: Law and Geography in European Empires, 1400–1900*, 1st ed. (Cambridge: Cambridge University Press, 2009), 2.

80. The tables also include, in some sections, specific references to "correo de a pie." It seems likely that in these cases *"legua"* signifies distance covered on foot in an hour.

CHAPTER 4

1. "Blas Cabrera, correo de su majestad, en la mejor forma que haya lugar . . ." AGI Correos 90B, "Don Simón de Larrazábal, Administrador Principal, por su Magestad . . ." 1772.

2. A document from Honduras indicates that the Indians of Comayagua were obliged to provide *correo* services on demand. AGCA Sig. A3, Leg. 1566, Exp. 10210, Folio 58: 1681 Reglamento. For mention of Indian *correos* as much as a century earlier, see Barreda, *Geografía e historia de correos y telecomunicaciones de Guatemala: sus estudios*, 38.

3. AGCA Sig. A3, Leg. 137, Exp. 2767: 1770 letter by Melchor de Ugalde.

4. The routes to Omoa and to the coast seem to have allowed for this relay method more than other routes. The routes to Oaxaca and the provinces were more often walked by solitary *indios correos*. A representative case is that of Marcelo Moya, an *indio correo* who was paid 100 pesos to carry certain books from Guatemala to Granada. (AGCA Sig. A3, Leg. 265, Exp. 5790.)

5. See legal cases against *correos*: AGCA Sig. A3, Leg. 146, Exp. 2927; 1803 case against José Andrade, a 22-year-old Spanish carpenter; AGCA Sig. A3, Leg. 146, Exp. 2935: 1804 case against José Romero, a 35-year-old Spaniard; AGCA Sig. A3, Leg. 147, Exp. 2941: 1805 case against Francisco Anzueto, a 24-year-old *mestizo* weaver; AGCA Sig. A3, Leg. 147, Exp. 2947: 1805 case against José Rivera, in his seventies; AGCA Sig. A3, Leg. 149, Exp. 2983: 1819 case against José María Custodio and José Maria Crujente, 25 and 32 years old, respectively, and both tailors.

6. AGI, Correos 90B, "Don Simon de Larrazabal, Administrador Principal . . ." 1772.

7. The textiles from China would not have been considered contraband; rather, their transportation by the correo broke taxation laws and the specific *encomienda* laws. In fact, contraband trade was a much larger problem for city officials in Gua-

temala at this time, in light of which the transgressions by Larrazábal seem relatively minor. See Gustavo Palma Murga's chapter in Jordana Dym and Christophe Belaubre, *Politics, Economy, and Society in Bourbon Central America, 1759–1821* (Boulder: University Press of Colorado, 2007). Whether or not they were carried as *encomiendas* by *correos*, goods from China were in great demand in Guatemala. "It was estimated in 1746 that 150,000 to 175,000 pesos of Asian goods entered Guatemala City annually, 'the principal commodity of the goods that are purchased in Mexico.' Trade expanded with Campeche and Havana from Honduras. Small vessels sailed between Cartagena, Portobelo, and Granada via the Río San Juan. The mule trains from Costa Rica to Panama became larger and more frequent." Wortman, *Government and Society in Central America, 1680–1840*, 117. Imports from China, specifically, continued to form the greater proportion of imports to Guatemala. Except for during wartime, textile imports from China exceeded even trade with Mexico. Miles Wortman, "Bourbon Reforms in Central America: 1750–1786," *The Americas* 32, no. 2 (1975): 222–238.

8. Though the categories seem to overlap, in practice *correos* and *arrieros* were clearly distinct and were treated as such by administrators. Muleteers not infrequently traveled with a dozen or more mules, and they are sometimes described as "merchants" in documentation. Both scale and the decidedly commercial bent of their work set muleteers apart.

9. AGI Correos 90B, "Muy señores mios: la adjunta copia del respectivo expediente . . ." 1777.

10. Wortman, *Government and Society in Central America, 1680–1840*; Troy S. Floyd, "The Guatemalan Merchants, the Government, and the Provincianos, 1750–1800," *The Hispanic American Historical Review* 41, no. 1 (1961): 90–110.

11. AGCA Sig. A3, Leg. 146, Exp. 2938.

12. AGI Correos 90B, "Muy señores mios. Adjunto a VSS un plan extractado . . ." 1778. The mail system calculated its expenses in both *reales* and *pesos*. The *real de plata fuerte*—silver *real*—was the standard for much of the eighteenth century; a *peso* was worth eight *reales*.

13. See, for example, AGCA Sig. A3, Leg. 137, Exp. 2747 (1725); Leg. 140, Exp. 2813 (1791); Leg. 142, Exp. 2849 (1794) and Exp. 2864 (1793); Leg. 146, Exp. 2928 (1805).

14. AGI Correos 90B, "Muy señores mios: Para mejor inteligencia de lo que tengo informado . . ." 1784.

15. "Hasta la presente se nos dan y han dado a nuestros antecesores quince pesos . . ." AGI, Correos 91A, #13, 1787 letter by correos.

16. AGI, Correos 90B, #25, August 1773 letter to Grimaldi.

17. "Siempre se toleró que los correos llevasen, y trajesen encomiendas permitidas." AGI, Correos 90B, #25, July 1773 letter from Larrazábal.

18. AGCA Sig. A3, Leg. 137, Exp. 2754.

19. AGI Correos, 90B, #21, 1773 letter from Juan González Bustillo puts the weight of the cloth at 3 *arrobas*, 6 pounds.

20. AGCA Sig. A3, Leg. 146, Exp. 2938.

21. "José Ribera llegó a esta ciudad ayer . . ." AGCA, Sig. A3, Leg. 147, Exp. 2947.

22. In his complaint he solicited support from none other than the viceroy of Mexico. The dispute among these high-ranking officials continued for years, finding a tentative resolution only in 1777. The final decision from Spain to continue permitting *small* encomiendas, as long as they did not retard the correo's journey, effectively condoned the former practice of turning a blind eye. This decision allowed the debate over encomiendas to continue for decades, so that in the early nineteenth century it remained a problem. (AGI Correos 90B, #25 1773–1777 correspondence.)

23. The *correo* generally paid for at least three animals, however: a mount for himself, a mule for the mail trunks, and a mule for the *tayacan*. The total cost might be 1.5 or 2 reales per league, depending on the number of trunks.

24. AGI Correos, 90B, #21, 1773 letter by Juan González Bustillo.

25. Disputes over *arancel* rates and the payment of fees went beyond the mail system. William B. Taylor's discussion of disputes among parish priests over *aranceles*, for example, points to a similar delicate balance. The fee schedules might have, theoretically, prevented exploitation on either side. In practice, the *arancel* could be either rigid or flexible as the parties involved allowed. William B Taylor, *Magistrates of the Sacred: Priests and Parishioners in Eighteenth-Century Mexico* (Stanford, Calif.: Stanford University Press, 1996), 435–438.

26. AGI Correos 90B, #23: "Goathemala a 1 de Octubre de 1772 . . ."

27. AGCA Sig. A3, Leg. 137, Exp. 2752: 1764 maritime mail regulations.

28. AGCA Sig. A3, Leg. 137, Exp. 2774: 1773 Complaint by the *naturales* of Acala. This case resolves itself in a revealing manner. Simón de Larrazábal and other officials in the capital consider rerouting the *correo* to avoid Acala, but they determine that the fourteen-league detour would be to great. Instead, Larrazábal suggests preserving the existing route but demanding that *ladinos*, rather than *indios* in Acala provide the supplies.

29. The town of Chinautla had the misfortune of finding itself directly on the outgoing route for both Oaxaca and the provinces after the relocation of Guatemala City following the 1773 earthquake. For eighteen years, they provided supplies to every *correo* who left the city, but in 1793 they finally complained, stating that they spent three days accompanying each outgoing *correo* to Petén and Omoa and their animals simply could not shoulder the burden. AGCA Sig. A3, Leg. 141, Exp. 2837.

30. AGI Correos 91B, #5: "Testimonio de las providencias de este Superior Govierno para el mas pronto curzo de los correos . . ." 1786.

31. In discussing how a route to Petapa might be detoured, officials noted that the route, "which was previously part of the King's highway and was therefore traveled by mail carriers, muleteers, and travelers" had fallen into disuse after the earthquake that ruined Guatemala City. People were traveling instead to and from the provinces "by the route called Canales, and since the former route has consequently become impassable, the old route to Petapa has been closed." AGCA Sig. A3, Leg. 141, Exp. 2837.

32. "Me han asegurado ambos que hay vereda conocida por los Indios . . ." AGCA Sig. A1, Leg. 193, Exp. 3934.

33. "Pero los Indios que lo conducían, lo extraviaron . . ." AGCA Sig. A1, Leg. 193, Exp. 3934.

34. "El motivo que tuvieron los Indios para haberlo ocultado . . ." AGCA Sig. A1, Leg. 193, Exp. 3934.

35. AGI, Correos 90B, #20: "En 13 de Agosto ultimo mando verificar este cavallero Presidente . . ." 1804.

36. AGI Correos 92A, # 21, 24: "Estado del corte general de Caja hecho . . ." 1793, 1794.

37. AGI Correos 93B, #24. The administrator, however, suggested more than doubling these costs to expand the office and compensate the employees more fairly.

38. AGI Correos 92A, # 21, 24: "Estado del corte general de Caja hecho . . ." 1793, 1794.

39. AGCA Sig. A3, Leg. 139, Exp. 2799

40. See AGCA Sig. A3, Leg. 144, Exp. 2905; AGCA Sig. A3, Leg. 146, Exp. 2930; AGCA Sig. A3, Leg. 151, Exp. 5562 and 5563. And see the inventory of clandestine mail cases created by Faustino Capetillo in AGCA Sig. A3, Leg. 147, Exp. 2944.

41. "De solo los pueblos inmediatos a esta Ciudad salen casi diariamente correos propios." AGCA Sig. A3, Leg. 147, Exp. 2939.

42. "Desde el año pasado de 1780 en que tome posesión de mi empleo . . ." AGCA Sig. A3, Leg. 147, Exp. 2944.

43. AGI Correos 90B, #27: "Don Simón de Larrazábal, Administrador Principal, por su Majestad . . ." 1772.

44. After 1777, there is roughly one criminal case per year against a *correo* until 1812. See AGCA Sig. A3, Leg. 139–150. Logbooks from the end of the eighteenth century indicate that in any one year there were roughly twenty *correos* operating the routes. AGCA Sig. A1, Leg. 6086, Exp. 55056: 1898.

45. AGI Correos 91A, #13: 1787 document.

46. "Su marcha la verificó con buena salud . . ." AGI Correos 92A, #19: 1794 case.

47. "Este conductor ha sido uno de los de mayor aprobación y cumplimiento en la Renta, con cuyo inmenso trabajo mantenía a su mujer y cuatro hijos." Ibid.

48. AGCA Sig. A3, Leg. 139, Exp. 2790: 1778 documents.

49. AGCA Sig. A3, Leg. 146, Exp. 2935: 1804 case on José Romero.

50. *Aguardiente*—burning water—is the generic term for liquor with a high alcohol content. AGCA Sig. A3, Leg. 140, Exp. 2810: 1791 case against Miguel Custodio.

51. AGI Correos 91B, #5: 1786 complaint that mentions Miguel Custodio.

52. AGCA Sig. A3, Leg. 146, Exp. 2927: 1803 case against José Andrade. In these cases, the use of alcohol coincided with violent behavior, but as other cases involving violent correos demonstrate, the two were not necessarily linked. Furthermore, correos and officials did not *use* alcohol as an explanation for violence. If anything, alcohol use was posited as an explanation (or excuse) for sickness or confusion resulting in poor work performance. William B. Taylor, *Drinking, Homicide and Rebellion in Colonial Mexican Villages* (Stanford, Calif.: Stanford University Press, 1979).

53. See AGCA Sig. A3, Leg. 137, Exp. 2752 for the 1764 regulations that es-

tablish the *fuero*. Ana Margarita Gómez discusses the social and legal dimensions of the comparable *fuero* for members of the Bourbon military. Gómez suggests that the *fuero* allowed soldiers (often of low social standing and mixed race) a rare social distinction. Ana Margarita Gómez, "The Evolution of Military Justice in Late Colonial Guatemala, 1762–1821," *A Contracorriente* 4, no. 2 (2007): 31–53.

54. AGCA Sig. A3, Leg. 139, Exp. 2793: 1779 documents allowing banned weapons. The first Bourbon prohibitions on carrying arms in Guatemala date to 1759. These prohibitions carried with them different penalties for *españoles, indios,* and *castas*. A 1779 *acuerdo* reinforced the prohibition and amplified the penalties associated with it. Ana Margarita Gómez and Sajid Alfredo Herrera Mena, *Los rostros de la violencia: Guatemala y El Salvador, siglos XVIII y XIX*, vol. 1. (San Salvador, El Salvador: UCA Editores, 2007). pp. 123–132.

55. Ibid., 1.:123–158.

56. AGCA Sig. A3, Leg. 139, Exp. 2786.

57. ". . . Un Alcalde de mierda, un papo, un carajo, y otras expresiones de igual naturaleza." Ibid.

58. ". . . Que se cagaba en ellos, en [sus] cadenitas de divisa." Ibid.

59. "Una larga experiencia me ha hecho conocer que de los correos, pocas ocasiones aparece de su conferencia y convencimiento la verdad, y que por lo común quedan largos . . . resentimientos entre aquellos testigos que se disponen." AGCA Sig. A3, Leg. 149, Exp. 2983: 1819 case against José Maria Custodio and José Maria Crujente.

60. ". . . [Una] espada derecha de hoja angosta con dos filos." AGCA Sig. A3, Leg. 147, Exp. 2941: 1805 case against Francisco Anzueto.

61. For cases of assaults against men, see for example AGCA Sig. A3, Leg. 145, Exp. 2919; AGCA Sig. A3, Leg. 149, Exp. 2968; AGCA Sig. A3, Leg. 149, Exp. 2970; AGCA Sig. A3, Leg. 149, Exp. 2977; AGCA Sig. A3, Leg. 154, Exp. 5588. A thorough study of social violence in late colonial Guatemala would permit a more contextualized consideration of these cases. The cases of domestic violence, for example, clearly extend beyond the correo population. Faustino Capetillo, the interim mail administrator in Guatemala City at the turn of the century, was brought up on charges of domestic abuse brought by his wife in 1803. (AGCA, Sig. A3, Leg. 145, Exp. 2922.)

62. "El Tayacán como era Indio (por lo común tímido) huyó a esconderse a un montecito para libertarse de que lo maltrataran, hasta que las lamentaciones y voces que daba el correo lo trajeron." AGI Correos 92A, #8: 1790 correspondence.

63. AGI Correos 92A, #7: 1790 correspondence.

64. For an example of changes to the route designed to avoid assaults, see AGCA Sig. A3, Leg. 142, 2859.

65. Wortman, *Government and Society in Central America, 1680–1840*, 254.

66. Service to "New Spain" (meaning Mexico) and Petén would continue to leave Guatemala on the third and eighteenth of the month, as would the mail for Gualán. The mail to the provinces would leave for León on the seventh and twenty-second of each month, returning on the first and seventeenth. Established by decree of January 25, 1821. (AGCA Sig. B, Leg. 4125, Exp. 92802, Folio 17v.)

67. AGCA, Sig. B, Leg. 1300, Exp. 31477.

68. AGCA Sig. B, Leg. 72, Exp. 2037, Folio 74.

69. "Las salidas de dos correos montados, mensualmente, a Oaxaca, tres de igual clase para las Provincias Orientales, dos veraderos de a pie para la provincia de Chiquimula, Zacapa, y Gualán, dos para la de Verapaz y Petén, y dos para la Antigua Guatemala." AGCA, Sig. B, Leg. 95, Exp. 2620.

70. AGCA, Sig. B, Leg. 94, Exp. 2570.

71. AGCA, Sig. B, Leg. 1198, Exp. 29367, Folio 5v. As of 1824, the *Renta de Correos* became the responsibility of the *Ministerio de Hacienda*. This remained the case into the 1830s. AGCA Sig. B, Leg. 140, Exp. 3175, Folio 4.

72. AGCA, Sig. B, Leg. 3483, Exp. 79641, Folio 534.

73. AGCA, Sig. B, Leg. 1937, Exp. 44583; AGCA Sig. B, Leg. 1939, Exp. 44629. The fact that these proposals were in some cases made repeatedly over a period of several years indicates that "established" service sometimes failed to take hold immediately. Another proposal was made in 1834 for a weekly service between Guatemala and Quetzaltenango. AGCA, Sig. B, Leg. 1940, Exp. 44708.

74. AGCA, Sig. B, Leg. 176, Exp. 3757.

75. AGCA, Sig. B, Leg. 1301, Exp. 31585; Exp. 31586; Exp. 31589; AGCA, Sig. B, Leg. 1940, Exp. 44711;

76. AGCA, Sig. B, Leg. 1301, Exp. 31595; Exp. 31601.

77. Wortman, *Government and Society in Central America, 1680–1840,* 262.

78. Wortman, *Government and Society in Central America, 1680–1840;* Douglass Sullivan-González, *Piety, Power, and Politics: Religion and Nation Formation in Guatemala, 1821–1871* (Pittsburgh: University of Pittsburgh Press, 1998). For more in-depth discussion of the transformations occurring in this period, see also Lowell Gudmundson and Héctor Lindo-Fuentes, *Central America, 1821–1871: Liberalism Before Liberal Reform* (Tuscaloosa: University of Alabama Press, 1995); Arturo Taracena Arriola, *Invención criolla, sueño ladino, pesadilla indígena: Los Altos de Guatemala: de región a Estado, 1740–1850, 1740–1850* (Antigua, Guatemala; San José, Costa Rica: Centro de Investigaciones Regionales de Mesoamérica; Porvenir, 1997); Ralph Lee Woodward, *Central America: A Nation Divided,* vol. 3, Latin American Histories (New York: Oxford University Press, 1999).

79. AGCA, Sig. B, Leg. 3610, Exp. 84169.

80. AGCA, Sig. B, Leg. 1301, Exp. 31590.

81. AGCA, Sig. B, Leg. 1301, Exp. 31631; AGCA Sig. B., Leg. 1301, Exp. 31658; Exp. 31649. These assaults seem to have been an almost regular occurrence on the route during this period. In a single month, three of the weekly mails from El Salvador were assaulted in 1840. AGCA, Sig. B, Leg. 3610, Exp. 84160.

82. AGCA, Sig. B, Leg. 1301, Exp. 31652; Exp. 31703; Exp. 31705.

83. AGCA, Sig. B, Leg. 3610, Exp. 84221.

84. AGCA Sig. B, Leg. 3610, Exp. 84179; AGCA, Sig. B, Leg. 1301, Exp. 31702. Nor was there frequently correspondence from other regions: AGCA Sig. B, Leg. 3610, Exp. 84173.

85. AGCA, Sig. B, Leg. 1301, Exp. 31618; AGCA, Sig. B, Leg. 3610, Exp. 84138.

86. Table prepared from AGCA, Sig. B, Leg. 3610, Exp. 84165. The state of Los Altos, formed by the Guatemalan departamentos of Sololá, Totonicapán, and Quesaltenango, enjoyed a brief independence during this period.

87. "Que necesarios y productivos solo considero los del Departamento de Chiquimula, por que girando por medio de ellos las correspondencias del Puerto de Yzaval y ultramar, son interesantes al comercio." AGCA, Sig. B, Leg. 1301, Exp. 31675.

88. "Esto demuestra que son innecesarios, puesto que no hay sino muy pocas personas que escriban por ellos." Ibid.

89. AGCA Sig. A3, Leg. 137, Exp. 2767.

90. Ibid.; AGI Correos 90A, April 1, 1770.

91. AGCA Sig. A1, Leg. 2791, Exp. 24477.

92. See, for example, AGCA Sig. B, Leg. 1300, Exp. 31475; Exp. 31476; Exp. 31479; Exp. 31480; Leg. 2508, Exp. 56322; Exp. 56324; Leg. 3610, Exp. 84112; Exp. 84113; Exp. 84115.

93. Taracena Arriola, *Invención criolla, sueño ladino, pesadilla indígena: Los Altos de Guatemala: de región a Estado, 1740–1850, 1740–1850.*

94. Robert H. Claxton, "Miguel Rivera Maestre: Guatemalan Scientist-Engineer," *Technology and Culture* 14, no. 3 (1973): 391.

95. Rivera Maestre had unusual training for this project. With formal school in neither engineering nor architecture, he was first distinguished as an artist of particular talent. He studied drawing at the Guatemalan Economic Society's School of Drawing, and he was either apprenticed to a surveyor or taught himself. After the 1823 split with Mexico, Rivera Maestre accepted a government position advising the new state on how to develop its economy, though he turned down many other government posts in the post-independence period. As Robert Claxton's study of Rivera Maestre sums up, "While Rivera Maestre may have been a most reluctant politician, he was a more willing scientist and public works administrator." Ibid., 389.

96. Raymond B. Craib, *Cartographic Mexico: A History of State Fixations and Fugitive Landscapes* (Durham, N.C.: Duke University Press, 2004), 24.

97. Miguel Rivera Maestre, *Atlas Guatemalteco: Año De 1832* (Guatemala: Ministerio de Relaciones Exteriores, 2001).

98. AGCA Sig. B, Leg. 2488, Exp. 54973–54981: 1826.

99. Ibid., undated.

100. Ibid., "La larga y dificilísima comunicación en que está este distrito con los demás puntos de la frontera no permite que un solo jefe pueda atender a la defensa de toda ella: es pues indispensable que la de esta parte esté confiada esclusivamente a uno."

101. Ibid., "No podrá ser grande a causa de la mucha distancia . . ."

102. Ibid., 1826.

103. Ibid., 1826.

104. Ibid., July, 1826. The total population was 4,100: 150 *blancos*; 600 *pardos libres*; 500 *negros libres*; 2000 *esclavos*; 850 soldiers.

CHAPTER 5

1. AGCA Sig. A1, Leg. 1523, Folio 758: June 25, 1597 Real Cédula.

2. "Clerk" may come closest to encapsulating the *escribano*'s position. For a detailed discussion of the history and function of *escribanos* in Guatemala, see Jorge Luján Muñoz and Instituto Guatemalteca de Derecho Notarial, *Los escribanos en*

las Indias Occidentales y en particular en el reino de Guatemala, vol. 2 (Guatemala: Instituto Guatemalteca de Derecho Notarial, 1977). Kathryn Burns considers the *escribano* and notary as writers of official "truth." Kathryn Burns, "Notaries, Truth, and Consequences," *The American Historical Review* 110, no. 2 (April 2005): 43–68. For a history of *escribanos* in colonial Quito that places an emphasis on the *escribano*'s role as archivist, see Tamar Herzog, *Mediación, archivos y ejercicio: los escribanos de Quito (siglo XVII)*, Ius Commune. Sonderhefte; 82 (Frankfurt am Main: Klostermann, 1996). Research by Pilar Ostos Salcedo and María Luisa Pardo Rodríguez on the *escribanos* of Sevilla in the medieval period looks closely at document production and suggests that many of the processes evident in late colonial Guatemala (and Spanish America as a whole) have their origins in early practices. Pilar Ostos Salcedo and María Luisa Pardo Rodríguez, *Documentos y notarios de Sevilla en el siglo XIII* (Madrid: Fundación Matritense del Notariado, 1989); Pilar Ostos Salcedo and María Luisa Pardo Rodríguez, *Documentos y notarios de Sevilla en el siglo XIV (1301–1350)* (Sevilla: Universidad de Sevilla, 2003).

3. As Kathyrn Burns writes, "Their truth was recognizable not by its singularity but by its very regularity. It was truth by template—*la verdad hecha de molde.*" Burns, "Notaries, Truth, and Consequences."

4. Rama, *The Lettered City*, 8–9.

5. Burns, "Notaries, Truth, and Consequences," 3.

6. Burns, *Into the Archive*, 93–94.

7. Luján Muñoz and Instituto Guatemalteca de Derecho Notarial, *Los escribanos en las Indias Occidentales y en particular en el reino de Guatemala*, 82. AGCA, Sig. A1, Leg. 4575, Folio 43v.: April 12, 1535. A similar request for a report on existing *escribanos* was made in 1540. AGCA, Sig. A1, Leg. 4575, Folio 49v.: November 5, 1540.

8. Burns, "Notaries, Truth, and Consequences."

9. AGCA Sig. A1, Leg. 1514, Folio 46: November 15, 1576; AGCA Sig. A1, Leg. 4578, Folio 26v: August 16, 1622. Although restrictions on *escribano* assignments were also intended to minimize potential abuses from other directions as well. A 1603 *cédula* prohibited any of the president's, *oidores'*, or *fiscal's* relatives from serving in the post of *escribano de cámara y gobierno.* AGCA Sig. A1, Leg. 1514, Folio 49: December 31, 1603.

10. AGCA Sig. A1, Leg. 1515, Folio 40: October 19, 1619.

11. Herzog, *Mediación, archivos y ejercicio: los escribanos de Quito (siglo XVII)*; Luján Muñoz and Instituto Guatemalteca de Derecho Notarial, *Los escribanos en las Indias Occidentales y en particular en el reino de Guatemala*, 2:.

12. AGCA Sig. A1, Leg. 4575, Folio 403: May 24, 1582; Sig. A1, Leg. 1513, Folio 608: May 27, 1582; Sig. A1, Leg. 1514, Folio 64: May 11, 1605. The eventual reply from Spain indicated that the post of *escribano* had never been intended for Indian towns, but only for the towns with a Spanish population. AGCA Sig. A1, Leg. 1517, Folio 184: May 27, 1640.

13. AGCA Sig. A1, Leg. 5405, Exp. 46049: October 28, 1638. Tamar Herzog writes that in seventeenth-century Quito, the category distinctions among *escribanos* may have existed more in theory than in practice. In Quito, at least, they were not easily classifiable as either "notary" or "secretary." It seems likely that in Gua-

temala, where the number of *escribanos* remained (comparatively) small throughout the colonial period, a similar blurring of lines existed. Herzog, *Mediación, archivos y ejercicio: los escribanos de Quito (siglo XVII)*, 13.

14. AGCA Sig. A1, Leg. 2195, Exp. 15749, Folio 217v.: October 6, 1525.

15. AGCA Sig. A1, Leg. 2195, Exp. 15749, Folio 116: May 19, 1536.

16. AGCA Sig. A1, Leg. 2195, Exp. 15749, Folio 79: December 18, 1566.

17. Luján Muñoz notes that *escribanos* beyond the city in smaller towns of the *audiencia* were also relied upon to manage and respond to official documents, logging incoming judicial correspondence and writing replies. Luján Muñoz and Instituto Guatemalteca de Derecho Notarial, *Los escribanos en las Indias Occidentales y en particular en el reino de Guatemala*, 2:40.

18. "Presidente y oidores de mi Real Audiencia que reside en la ciudad de Santiago . . ." AGCA Sig. A1, Leg. 1513, Folio 758, 1596 *real cédula*. Later *cédulas* echo the import of the 1596 *cédula*: AGCA Sig. A1, Leg. 1514, Folio 002.bis: May 31, 1600; AGCA Sig. A1, Leg. 1514, Folio 57: February 13, 1604; AGCA Sig. A1, Leg. 1516, Folio 81: October 8, 1635.

19. AGCA Sig. A1, Leg. 2195, Folio 61: July 13, 1587. "Para tomar la hizo sacar del archivo . . ." A similar case resulted in the same order being repeated one year later. AGCA Sig. A1, Leg. 2195, Folio 63: May 1, 1588.

20. AGCA, Sig. A1, Leg. 4576, Folio 65: June 7, 1621.

21. AGCA Sig. A1, Leg. 4576, Folio 109v: October 16, 1624. "Por el peligro que tienen de perderse y desminuirse . . ."

22. AGCA, Sig. A1, Leg. 3089, Exp. 29520, 1626.

23. AGCA Sig. A1, Leg. 1517, Folio 39: May 4, 1643.

24. AGCA Sig. A1, Leg. 1523, Folio 80: October 13, 1692. The *Fiscal*, as an attorney for the Crown, likely required the documents for a case he was pursuing.

25. "La Audiencia de Guatemala, por su parte, por auto acordado de 29 de abril de 1699 . . ." (Citing José Joaquín Pardo, *Efemérides de la Antigua Guatemala, 1541–1779*. Guatemala: Unión Tipografía, 1944, p. 97.) Luján Muñoz and Instituto Guatemalteca de Derecho Notarial, *Los escribanos en las Indias Occidentales y en particular en el reino de Guatemala*, 2.:57. For further mandates on providing *traslados* or copies, see AGCA Sig. A1, Leg. 1525, Folio 11: May 30, 1708; Folio 21: October 13, 1708; AGCA Sig. A1, Leg. 2026, Expediente 14049, Folio 71: October 7, 1764.

26. This may be due to the absence of an *escribano* training facility in Guatemala. Luján Muñoz notes that Guatemala never boasted a training facility for *escribanos*, while Mexico and other places in Spanish America did. "En Guatemala nunca existió una institución en la cual se diera, a los futuros escribanos, una preparación especial. En México, con la fundación del Real Colegio de Escribanos, establecido por Real Cédula de 29 de junio de 1792, se abrió una academia dependiente del Colegio, la cual tenía a su cargo la formación de los escribanos. A esta Academia debía asistir el futuro escribano por un período de seis meses." Ibid., 2.:66–67. While *escribano* practices across Spain and Spanish America in the eighteenth-century bear certain similarities, the absence of a school for *escribanos* does set Guatemala apart. Differences with Mexico and, even more so, places in Spain become more marked in the eighteenth century. See, for example, Raimundo

Noguera de Guzmán, *Los notarios de Barcelona en el siglo XVIII* (Barcelona: Colegio Notarial de Barcelona, 1978).

27. AGCA Sig. A3, Leg. 503, Exp. 10350, Folio 1: July 21, 1721.

28. See, for example, AGCA Sig. A1, Leg. 3089, Exp. 29528.

29. AGCA Sig. A1, Leg. 2820, Exp. 24962, 1710–1727 correspondence.

30. AGCA Sig. A1, Leg. 4622, Folio 134.

31. Ibid.

32. Herzog indicates that keeping track of documents was a challenge for *escribanos* elsewhere, as well. "El flujo de papeles que salían y volvían a los archivos debía controlarse mediante un registro llamado 'libro de reconocimientos'. En él, el escribano debía anotar los datos de los documentos (la identidad de las partes interesadas y su naturaleza jurídica) y el nombre de la persona que los sacaba. Esta última tenía que mostrar su conformidad con esta información firmando la razón insertada en el libro. El escribano tenía la obligación de velar por la devolución de los papeles y asegurarse de que la nota correspondiente en el libro fuera tachada a medida que iban regresando los documentos. Pero, según se desprende de los mismos libros de reconocimiento . . . así como de las visitas a escribanos, la mala gestión de la salida y entrada de documentos en los archivos era un fenómeno muy común." Herzog, *Mediación, archivos y ejercicio: los escribanos de Quito (siglo XVII)*, 25.

33. See, for example, AGCA Sig. A1, Leg. 347, Exp. 7229, 1734–1738; Exp. 7232, 1739–1752; Exp. 7233, 1754–1758; Exp. 7234, 1748–1760; Leg. 4504, Exp. 3830, 1745; Leg. 4505, Exp. 38359, 1766; Exp. 38360, 1766; Leg. 4506, Exp. 38367, 1768; Exp. 38369, 1768; Leg. 4508, Exp. 38389, 1774–1778; Exp. 38394, 1776; Leg. 4509, Exp. 383400, 1777; Exp. 38401, 1777–1794.

34. AGCA Sig. A3, Leg. 2169, Exp. 32567, 1771. Similarly, a 1768 volume indexed correspondence with León and San Salvador (AGCA Sig. A3, Leg. 1366, Exp. 22855) and a volume from the same year indexed correspondence with Tuxtla and Tegucigalpa (AGCA Sig. A3, Leg. 1366, Exp. 22858).

35. AGCA Sig. A1, Leg. 4521, Exp. 38521. Document is undated, but the reference to "Vieja Guatemala" suggests the late eighteenth or early nineteenth century.

36. AGCA Sig. A3, Leg. 1365, Exp. 22851, 1767.

37. AGCA Sig. A1, Leg. 349, Exp. 7253, 1753–1792.

38. Burns, *Into the Archive*, 68.

39. "Será obligación de los Escribanos de Ayuntamiento de las Cabezas de Partido . . ." AGCA Sig. A1, Leg. 1531, Folio 355: January 31, 1768.

40. "El Instrumento que se há de exhibir en el Oficio de hipotecas . . ." Ibid.

41. "Para facilitar el hallazgo de las cargas y liberaciones . . ." Ibid.

42. "Como la conservación de los documentos públicos importa tanto al Estado . . ." Ibid.

43. AGI, MP-LIBROS MANUSCRITOS, 59/ 1726, "Representación sobre el desperdicio y perdida de los Papeles Políticos de España y remedios que deben practicarse para su conservación," Folios 9v–10, 15.

44. Ibid., folio 23v. "En el año de 1718 . . ."

45. Ibid., 93v.

46. Ibid., 103–103v. "Se han tratado con tal abandono . . ."

47. Ibid., 158v–159. ". . . Lleva el Consejo de Inquisición a los demás la gran ventaja . . ."

48. Ibid., 163.

49. Ibid., 118. "La forma en que se manejan sus Papeles . . ."

50. Ibid., 132–133. "Sería muy importante se hiciese un Índice de estos papeles . . ."

51. Herzog, *Mediación, archivos y ejercicio: los escribanos de Quito (siglo XVII)*, 18. "Durante el siglo XVII se crearon y ordenaron los archivos centrales de la Monarquía Hispana en Simancas y Roma y se insistió en la posibilidad de formar archivos locales, tanto de documentación gubernativa como de carácter particular. Se concibió así la posibilidad, nunca plasmada en la realidad, de acabar por esta vía con el monopolio de los escribanos sobre los archivos que contenían documentación producida por ellos mismos." It seems questionable that these two tendencies—the divesting of *escribano* power and the consolidation of archives—were causally related in such a clear-cut way. For one thing, Simancas was created in the sixteenth century, when the intention of minimizing *escribano* control was not even contemplated, so the creation of archives (like Simancas) cannot necessarily be taken as evidence of a desire to minimize *escribano* control. Furthermore, as Riol and the *escribano* disputes in Guatemala (discussed below) suggest, document access was only as important—and perhaps less important—than preservation. As a result, in Guatemala—and likely elsewhere—there appears to have been far more enduring ambivalence throughout the eighteenth century over the question of whether or not archives belonged to *escribanos*.

52. Luján Muñoz and Instituto Guatemalteca de Derecho Notarial, *Los escribanos en las Indias Occidentales y en particular en el reino de Guatemala*, 2:57. "La Audiencia de Guatemala, por su parte, por auto acordado de 29 de abril de 1699 mandó establecer el archivo de escribanos públicos y reales, adscrito al Ayuntamiento de la ciudad de Santiago. En este archivo se debían depositar los registros de los escribanos fallecidos ". . . y de los que de aquí en adelante fallecieren . . ." (Citing José Joaquín Pardo, *Efemérides de la Antigua Guatemala, 1541–1779*. Guatemala: Unión Tipografía, 1944, p. 97.)

53. Ibid.

54. AGCA Sig. A1., Leg. 3089, Exp. 29550: August 26, 1755.

55. AGCA Sig. A1, Leg. 4004, Exp. 30381: 1769. "El sindico Procurador general de VS dice . . ." Coincidentally, Pedro Ortiz de Letona was also the royal mail administrator prior to the mail service's incorporation by the crown.

56. "El sindico Procurador General de este N.A. hace presente . . ." AGCA Sig. A1, Leg. 3089, Exp. 29564: 1778.

57. "Por quanto, aviendome representado los Oficiales de mi Real Hacienda de las Islas Philipinas . . ." AGCA Sig. A1, Leg. 2026, Exp. 14049, Folio 71: October 7, 1764.

58. AGCA Sig. A1, Leg. 1586, Expediente 10230, Folio 64. ". . . Y mandarse restituya luego y sin dilaciones alguna . . ."

59. Burns observes the same about *escribanos* keeping their offices at home in Peru. Burns, *Into the Archive*, 70.

60. Ibid., "Para que los alcaldes ordinarios de la villa de Sonsonate . . ."

61. It is possible that the "su" refers to Sonsonate, but it is much more likely that it refers to the *escribano*.

62. AGCA Sig. A1, Leg. 2791, Exp. 24477. "El escribano de estas dichas provincias . . ."

63. Ibid. Unfortunately, a severely damaged page makes this passage somewhat difficult to decipher. "[. . .] escribanos que. [. . .] en este juzgado hayan tenido [. . .] casas dicho Archivo: si no es que siempre sea mantenido como va dicho en la casa Real . . ."

64. Ibid. "Me presenté a fin de que se me entregase el Archivo correspondiente a este Juzgado . . ."

65. Born in Cuzco in 1751, he held various posts, including *alguacil mayor* for the Inquisition, the *alcalde mayor* for Suchitepequez, and *juez subdelegado de tierras*. For information on Mollinedo y Villavicencio, see the entry in "AFEHC: Diccionario: MOLLINEDO Y VILLAVICENCIO Tomas: MOLLINEDO Y VILLAVICENCIO Tomas," n.d., http://afehc.apinc.org/index.php?action=fi_aff&id=630.

66. AGCA Sig. A1, Leg. 2791, Exp. 24477. "El Fiscal dice: que por que el archivo esté en la casa del corregidor no dejar de ser el cargo del escribano."

67. Ibid. "Se declara que el archivo debe existir en la pieza destinada para él . . ."

68. Ibid. ". . . Que a mi me corresponde tener dicho Archivo."

69. Ibid. "No es esto Señor lo mas, cuanto que en la Pieza en donde existe . . ."

70. Ibid.

71. AGCA Sig. A3, Leg. 138, Exp. 2776: 1774.

72. Ibid.

73. Ibid. "Con lo cual se expresó no haber ya más Papeles, Cartas, ni Muebles pertenecientes a la Administración."

74. AGI, Correos 90A: November 1, 1770 letter by Don Simón de Larrazábal gives notice of Melchor de Ugalde's death on October 18, 1770.

CHAPTER 6

1. AGCA B, Leg. 2406, Exp. 50422: June 30, 1836. "Sin embargo de mi achacosa salud . . ."

2. In 1812, for example, the position of *escribano* for the Guatemalan *ayuntamiento* was dissolved and replaced by a secretary. AGCA Sig. B1, Leg. 7, Exp. 282: July 10, 1812; Sig. A1, Leg. 2595, Folio 333: August 22, 1812. At the same time, the sale of office for *escribanos* was abolished.

3. Oscar A. Salas M., *Derecho notarial de Centroamérica y Panamá* (San José, Costa Rica: Editorial Costa Rica, 1973), 29–30.

4. AGCA Sig. A1, Leg. 4795, Folio 146v.: July 8, 1777.

5. The exact date of his death is unknown, but a document from 1815 disposes of his archive after his death. AGCA Sig. A3, Leg. 207, Exp. 3736, Folio 38: May 10, 1815.

6. AGCA Sig. A1, Leg. 349, Exp. 7250: 1600–1782.

7. Ibid., 1–7.

8. AGCA Sig. A1, Leg. 4509, Exp. 38400: 1777; Exp. 38401: 1777–1794; Exp. 38405: 1778–1781; Leg. 4510, Exp. 38406: 1779–1789; Exp. 38407: 1778–

1780; Exp. 38408: 1778–1780; Leg. 4511, Exp. 38411: 1779–1793; Exp. 38415: 1779–1785; Exp. 38417: 1779–1795; Exp. 38419: 1780; Exp. 38423: 1781–1782; Exp. 38430: 1782; Leg. 4513, Exp. 38433: 1784; Exp. 38436: 1778–1793; Leg. 4514, Exp. 38441: 1768–1789; Exp. 38422: 1780–1792; Leg. 1977, Exp. 13483: 1806; Leg. 2565, Exp. 20684: 1800; Exp. 20686: 1802–1815; Exp. 20687: 1802.

9. AGCA Sig. A1, Leg. 4513, Exp. 38436: 1778–1793. A similar logbook for the 1808 to 1813 period kept track of the documents provided to *procuradores.* AGCA Sig. A1, Leg. 2569, Exp. 20706: 1808–1813.

10. AGCA Sig. A1, Leg. 4512, Exp. 38422: 1781.

11. AGCA Sig. A1, Leg. 2564, Exp. 20675: 1793–1804.

12. See, for example, AGCA Sig. A1, Leg. 2565, Exp. 20687: 1802.

13. AGCA Sig. A1, Leg. 349, Exp. 7250: 1600–1782. See Chapter 3 in particular in Burns, *Into the Archive.*

14. Ibid.

15. AGCA Sig. A1, Leg. 2821, Exp. 24991: September 28, 1780. "Respecto a que aun se halla en la arruinada Guatemala el archivo secreto de cabildo . . ."

16. AGCA Sig. A1, Leg. 2214, Exp. 15849: September 27, 1780.

17. Ibid: May 25, 1781.

18. Ibid. "Quisiera que Vm se pusiera a considerar lo mucho que se ha trabajado con los papeles que vinieron de Guatemala del archivo de cabildo . . ."

19. Ibid: December 10, 1781. "Contra la terminante disposición de la ley . . ."

20. Ibid: December 22, 1781.

21. Ibid: February 22, 1798.

22. AGCA Sig. A3, Leg. 1943: August 5, 1802 (Madrid).

23. AGCA Sig. A1, Leg. 1595, Folio 333: August 22, 1812. Nor was it necessary to be licensed as an *escribano* to be appointed secretary of the *ayuntamiento.* AGCA Sig. B1, Leg. 7, Exp. 282, Folio 1: July 10, 1812.

24. AGCA Sig. A1, Leg. 1538, Folio 65: August 22, 1812; Folio 121: October 9, 1812.

25. AGCA Sig. A1, Leg. 1538, Folio 276: April 23, 1813. "Las Cortes generales y extraordinarias, deseando que se cumpla puntualmente su Soberana resolución de 12 de Marzo de 1811 . . ."

26. AGCA Sig. A3, Leg. 207, Exp. 3736, Folio 38: May 10, 1815.

27. AGCA Sig. B85, Leg. 1146, Exp. 26217: 1825.

28. AGCA Sig. A4, Leg. 1, Exp. 43: 1823. Grijalva was temporarily substituted by Manuel Beteta in the early 1820s.

29. AGCA Sig. B117, Leg. 2406, Exp. 50407: August 13, 1823.

30. AGCA Sig. B108, Leg. 1933, Exp. 44324: August 19, 1823.

31. AGCA Sig. B80, Leg. 1074, Exp. 22588: September 29, 1832. Similarly, documents were requested from Bernardo Martínez, who was thought to have documents relevant to the region's history. AGCA Sig. B83, Sig. 3591, Exp. Exp. 82364: Sept. 21, 1832.

32. This was done as a matter of course, so little documentation exists other than for those cases that presented obstacles for the archivist, such as the recovery of the documents by *escribano* Francisco Quiroz. AGCA Sig. B, Leg. 2418, Exp. 50765.

33. AGCA Sig. B92, Leg. 1391, Exp. 32137: 1835.

34. AGCA Sig. B117, Leg. 2414, Exp. 50698: 1830 (?). The document is un-dated, but Los Altos was dissolved in 1829.

35. AGCA Sig. B, Leg. 2519, Exp. 56835: April 18, 1834. "Don Manuel Toledo vecino de Zacapa . . ."

36. A clear representation of these changing centers and boundaries can be found in Hall, Pérez Brignoli, and Cotter, *Historical Atlas of Central America*, 172–175.

37. AGCA Sig. B6, Leg. 98, Exp. 2711: March 9, 1824. "Habiéndose ya insta-lado el Congreso constituyente de este Estado . . ."

38. Hall, Pérez Brignoli, and Cotter, *Historical Atlas of Central America*, 174.

39. AGCA Sig. B10, Leg. 178, Exp. 3819: August 6, 1835. " . . . Es de pedirse al Gefe del Estado de Guatemala el archivo del referido Consulado por pertenecer a la federación . . ."

40. Though it is impossible to say for certain, it seems likely that the Miguel Talavera assigned to attend to the *consulado* archive's organization and transfer was the same person designated in 1802 among the "archivero" appointments in the office of the president. Miguel Talavera's reference in 1836 to his "cuarenta y siete años de una larga carrera por la senda del honor" make it likely that he was, in fact, employed in 1802.

41. AGCA Sig. B117, Leg. 2406, Exp. 50422, Folio 1: May 13, 1836. "Puse en conocimiento del Ejecutivo nacional la comunicación de U. de 5 del corriente . . ."

42. Ibid., May 26, 1836.

43. Ibid., June 3, 1836.

44. Ibid., June 10, 1836. "En cuanto logre mejorarme de mi actual enfermedad . . ."

45. Ibid., June 30, 1836. "Este voluminoso archivo . . ."

46. Ibid., August 8, 1836.

47. Ibid., August 8, 1836.

48. AGCA Sig. A1, Leg. 349, Exp. 7250: 1600–1782. Guerra y Marchán's re-gional subdivisions are: Leon, Subtiba, Matagalpa, Sonsonate, Chiquimula, Sacate-pequez, Quetzaltenango, Suchitepequez, Ciudad Real, Tuxtla, Soconusco, Omoa.

49. AGCA Sig. B117, Leg. 2406, Exp. 50422: September 4, 1836. "De aquellos que se ha verificado aparece en ellos muchos picados e incompletos, y por lo tanto inútiles los cuales ascienden incluso los rompimos y sucios . . ." At this point, Talavera continued with his efforts to erect the new shelving and store the archive in the *aduana*.

50. Ibid., November 4, 1836; November 24, 1836. Talavera's budget from No-vember 24 provides a remarkable snapshot of the material aspect of the archive's reorganization. He carefully itemized the cost for each item, including also a ruler, string, and needles (to bind loose documents). The total budget came to eleven *pesos* and three *reales*.

51. Ibid., December 21, 1836.

52. Ibid., January 6, 1837.

53. AGCA Sig. B177, Leg. 2415, Exp. 50720: 1838.

54. AGCA Sig. B117, Leg. 2406, Exp. 50426: May 29, 1840; Sig. B118,

Leg. 2438, Exp. 52239, Folio 56: June 4, 1840; Sig. B92, Leg. 1392, Exp. 32181: 1841.

55. AGCA Sig. B117, Leg. 2406, Exp. 50429: December 29, 1841. ". . . Pues corresponde a toda la nación."

56. Ibid.

57. Ibid.

58. AGCA Sig. B117, Leg. 2416, Exp. 50727: December 10, 1847. Additional inventories were composed in this same period for the transfer of documents back to Guatemala. AGCA Sig. B117, Leg. 2416, Exp. 50728: July 10, 1847; Exp. 50726: December 28, 1847.

59. AGCA Sig. B117, Leg. 2406, Exp. 50432: July 3, 1843.

60. AGCA Sig. B117, Leg. 2406, Exp. 50439: November 6, 1844; Exp. 50449: May 29, 1848; Exp. 50450: November 9, 1848.

61. AGCA Sig. B117, Leg. 2406, Exp. 50438: June 19, 1844; Exp. 50436: December 31, 1844.

62. AGCA Sig. B117, Leg. 2406, Exp. 50441: July, 1945. "El archivo general del Gobierno se halla en un estado de trastorno tal que dificulta y retarda el despacho con grave perdida de tiempo, y recargo de trabajo no solo para el archivero sino para esta Secretaría."

63. Ibid., July 10, 1845.

64. AGCA Sig. B78, Leg. 864, Exp. 21213: May 4, 1821.

65. AGCA Sig. B78, Leg. 859, Exp. 20749: October 25, 1853; Leg. 860, Exp. 20864: December 19, 1872.

66. AGCA Sig. B78, Leg. 755; Exp. 17921; Exp. 17892; Leg. 862, Exp. 21040; Exp. 21041; Exp. 21072; Leg. 887, Exp. 21592; Sig. B107, Leg. 1856, Exp. 43061.

67. AGCA Sig. B78, Leg. 860, Exp. 20902: July 6, 1875.

68. The following are examples of numerous inventories or requests for inventories made over the period. In 1855, it was once again necessary to recover and inventory the documents from the colonial government archive. (AGCA Sig. B117, Leg. 2416, Exp. 50734: 1855). In 1866, the *síndico* of Guatemala noted that the archive was in disarray and that it had to be inventoried. (AGCA Sig. B78, Leg. 655, Exp. 13718: April 27, 1866.) In 1873, *escribano nacional* Francisco Solares offered his services for the formation of an inventory of the archive. (AGCA Sig. B78, Leg. 655, Exp. 13720: July 1, 1873.) An inventory commenced in 1880 took stock of the archive of in the capital. (AGCA, Sig. B117, Leg. 2426, Exp. 50801: 1880.) A similar inventory was created in 1891. (AGCA Sig. B117, Leg. 2423, Exp. 50790: October 12, 1891.)

69. Another notebook is signed "Victor González." AGCA Sig. B177, Leg. 2419, Exp. 50773, 50775.

70. AGCA Sig. B177, Leg. 2422, Exp. 50777.

71. AGCA Sig. B177, Leg. 2406, Exp. 50457: October 15, 1892.

72. AGCA Sig. B, Leg. 2414, Exp. 50677: January 15, 1902.

EPILOGUE

1. AGCA Sig. A, Leg. 2335, Exp. 17508: 1744, Folio 4v, 5.

2. Carlo Ginzburg, Martin H. Ryle, and Kate Soper, *Wooden Eyes: Nine Reflections on Distance* (New York: Columbia University Press, 2001).

3. Greg Grandin and René Reeves discuss one example in the western Guatemalan highlands. While the AGCA in Guatemala City does have a sizable nineteenth-century collection, the Los Altos region has significant holdings for the nineteenth century. Greg Grandin and Rene Reeves, "Archives in the Guatemalan Western Highlands," *Latin American Research Review* 31, no. 1 (1996): 105–112.

Bibliography

Acuña, René, ed. *Relaciones geográficas del siglo XVI: Guatemala*. México: UNAM, 1982.

Akerman, James R. *The Imperial Map: Cartography and the Mastery of Empire*. Chicago: University of Chicago Press, 2009.

Altman, Ida. "Reconsidering the Center: Puebla and Mexico City, 1550–1650." In *Negotiated Empires: Centers and Peripheries in the Americas, 1500–1820*, 43–58. New York: Routledge, 2002.

Archival Science special issue: "In and Out of Archives" (2010) 10:195–200.

Archives of the Scientific Revolution: The Formation and Exchange of Ideas in Seventeenth-Century Europe. Woodbridge, UK: Boydell Press, 1998.

Archivo General de Simancas. *Guía del Archivo General de Simancas*. Madrid: Dirección General de Archivos y Bibliotecas, 1958.

Arnold, Linda. *Bureaucracy and Bureaucrats in Mexico City, 1742–1835*. Tucson: University of Arizona Press, 1988.

Ayala, Manuel José de, and Laudelino Moreno. *Diccionario de gobierno y legislación de Indias*. Madrid: Compañía Ibero-Americana de Publicaciones, 1929.

Backal, Alicia G. de, Laura Edith Bonilla, and Servicio Postal Mexicano. *Historia del correo en México*. México: Servicio Postal Mexicano: M.A. Porrúa Grupo Editorial, 2000.

Bagrow, Leo, and R. A. Skelton. *History of Cartography*. Chicago: Precedent Pub., 1985.

Banks, Kenneth J. *Chasing Empire Across the Sea: Communications and the State in the French Atlantic, 1713–1763*. Montreal: McGill-Queen's University Press, 2002.

Bannet, Eve Tavor. *Empire of Letters: Letter Manuals and Transatlantic Correspondence, 1688–1820*. Cambridge: Cambridge University Press, 2005.

Barreda, Pedro Froilán. *Geografía e historia de correos y telecomunicaciones de Guatemala: sus estudios*. Guatemala, 1961.

Barrera-Osorio, Antonio. *Experiencing Nature: The Spanish American Empire and the Early Scientific Revolution*. 1st ed. Austin: University of Texas Press, 2006.

Bayly, C. A. *Empire and Information: Intelligence Gathering and Social Communication in India, 1780–1870*. Cambridge: Cambridge University Press, 1996.

Bazilevich, K. V. *The Russian Posts in the XIX Century*. Rossica Society of Russian Philately, 1987.

Bell, Michael. *Childerley: Nature and Morality in a Country Village*. Chicago: University of Chicago Press, 1994.

Benton, Lauren. *A Search for Sovereignty: Law and Geography in European Empires, 1400–1900*. 1st ed. Cambridge: Cambridge University Press, 2009.

———. "Legal Spaces of Empire: Piracy and the Origins of Ocean Regionalism." *Comparative Studies in Society and History* 47, no. 4 (October 2005): 700–724.

———. "Spatial Histories of Empire." *Itinerario* 30, no. 3 (2006): 19–34.

Blainey, Geoffrey. *The Tyranny of Distance: How Distance Shaped Australia's History*. Melbourne: Sun Books, 1966.

Blasco, Julio Martín, and Jesús M. García. *El arzobispo de Guatemala Don Pedro Cortés y Larraz (Belchite 1712, Zaragoza 1786); defensor del la justicia y de la verdad*. Badajoz: Excmo. Ayuntamiento de Belchite (Zaragoza), 1992.

Bleichmar, Daniela, Paula De Vos, Kristin Huffine, and Kevin Sheehan, eds. *Science in the Spanish and Portuguese Empires, 1500–1800*. Stanford, Calif.: Stanford University Press, 2009.

Bleichmar, D. "Visible Empire: Scientific Expeditions and Visual Culture in the Hispanic Enlightenment." *Postcolonial Studies* 12, no. 4 (2009): 441–466.

Bornholt, Jens P, William H Hempstead, Philippe Vandermaelen, and Juan de la Cruz Cano y Olmedilla. *Cuatro siglos de expresiones geográficas del istmo centroamericano, 1500–1900*. Guatemala: Universidad Francisco Morroquín, 2007.

Bose, Walter Björn Ludovico. *El correo en la constitución nacional de 1853; antecedentes sobre la nacionalización del correo Argentino*. Buenos Aires: Imp. Amoretti, 1943.

———. *Historia del correo de España e Hispanoamérica. 1500–1820*. Buenos Aires, 1951.

———. *La organización de los correos nacionales en la Confederación Argentina (1852–1862)*. Buenos Aires: Talleres gráficos "Tomas Palumbo," 1938.

———. *Los orígenes del correo terrestre en Chile*. Santiago de Chile: Imprenta Universitaria, 1936.

———. *Los orígenes del correo terrestre en Cuba, 1754–1769*. Buenos Aires: Casa Jacobo Pueser, 1941.

———. *Los orígenes del correo terrestre en Guatemala*. Santiago de Chile, 1930.

———. *Los orígenes del correo en el Paraguay, 1769–1811*. Buenos Aires: s.n., 1940.

———. *Signos postales del Río de la Plata*. Buenos Aires: La Facultad, 1938.

Bose, Walter Björn Ludovico, and Julio C. Sáenz. *Correo argentino: una historia con futuro = Correo argentino: history with future*. Buenos Aires: Manrique Zago Ediciones, 1994.

Bouza Álvarez, Fernando J. *Communication, Knowledge, and Memory in Early Modern Spain*. Philadelphia: University of Pennsylvania Press, 2004.

Bravo Rubio, Berenise, and Marco Antonio Pérez Iturbe. "Tiempos y espacios religiosos novohispanos: la visita pastoral de Francisco Aguiar y Seijas (1683–1684)." In *Religión, poder y autoridad en la Nueva España*, 67–83. 1st ed. México D.F.: Universidad Nacional Autónoma de México, 2004.

Brotton, Jerry. *A History of the World in Twelve Maps*. London: Allen Lane, 2012.

Brown, Richard D. *Knowledge is Power: The Diffusion of Information in Early America, 1700–1865*. New York: Oxford University Press, 1989.

Burke, Peter. *A Social History of Knowledge: From Gutenberg to Diderot*. Cambridge: Polity, 2000.

Burnett, D. Graham. *Masters of All They Surveyed: Exploration, Geography, and a British El Dorado*. Chicago: University of Chicago Press, 2000.

Burns, Kathryn. *Into the Archive: Writing and Power in Colonial Peru*. Durham, N.C.: Duke University Press, 2010.

———. "Notaries, Truth, and Consequences." *The American Historical Review* 110, no. 2 (April 2005): 43–68.

Bushnell, Amy Turner. "Gates, Patterns, and Peripheries: The Field of Frontier Latin America." In *Negotiated Empires: Centers and Peripheries in the Americas, 1500–1820*, 15–28. New York: Routledge, 2002.

Cañizares-Esguerra, Jorge. *How to Write the History of the New World: Histories, Epistemologies, and Identities in the Eighteenth-Century Atlantic World*. Cultural sitings. Stanford, Calif.: Stanford University Press, 2001.

Carter, Paul. *The Road to Botany Bay: An Exploration of Landscape and History*. 1st ed. New York: Knopf, 1988.

Casaus y Torres, Ramón Francisco. *Carta del Illmo. Sr. Dr. D. Fr. Ramon Casaus y Torres, Obispo de Rosen, y Arzobispo Electo de Guatemala, á todos los Diocesanos de su iglesia Metropolitana*. Tapana, México, 1811.

Castleman, Bruce A. *Building the King's Highway: Labor, Society, and Family on Mexico's Caminos Reales, 1757–1804*. Tucson: University of Arizona Press, 2005.

Catholic Church. Archdiocese of Guatemala (Guatemala). Archbishop (1767–1779 : Cortés y Larraz), Pedro Cortés y Larraz, and Benito Monfort. *Instrucción pastoral sobre el método práctico de administrar con fruto el S.to sacramento de la penitencia*. Valencia Spain: Por B. Monfort, 1784.

Chamberlain, Robert S. *A Report on Colonial Materials on the Governmental Archives of Guatemala City*. Cambridge, Mass.: Harvard University Press, 1937.

Chardon, Roland. "The Linear League in North America." *Annals of the Association of American Geographers* 70, no. 2 (June 1980): 129–153.

Chartier, Roger. *Forms and Meanings: Texts, Performances, and Audiences from Codex to Computer*. Philadelphia: University of Pennsylvania Press, 1995.

———. *The Order of Books: Readers, Authors, and Libraries in Europe between the Fourteenth and Eighteenth Centuries*. Stanford, Calif.: Stanford University Press, 1994.

Chartier, Roger, Alain Boureau, and Cécile Dauphin. *Correspondence: Models of Letter-Writing from the Middle Ages to the Nineteenth Century*. Cambridge, UK: Polity Press, 1997.

Chevalier, Maxime. *Lectura y lectores en la España de los siglos XVI y XVII*. 1st ed. Madrid: Turner, 1976.

Clanchy, M. T. *From Memory to Written Record, England, 1066–1307*. London: Edward Arnold, 1979.

Claxton, Robert H. "Miguel Rivera Maestre: Guatemalan Scientist-Engineer." *Technology and Culture* 14, no. 3 (1973): 384–403.

Clifford, James. *Routes: Travel and Translation in the Late Twentieth Century*. Cambridge, Mass.: Harvard University Press, 1997.

Colegio de Escribanos de México. *Estatutos del Real Colegio de Escribanos de México, aprobados por Su Magestad en real cédula de 19 de junio 1792*. México: D. Felipe de Zúñiga y Ontiveros, 1793.

Cortés Alonso, Vicenta. *Archivos de España y América: materiales para un manual*. Madrid: Edit. de la Universidad Complutense, 1979.

Cortés y Larraz, Pedro. *Descripción geográfico-moral de la Diócesis de Goathemala hecha por su arzobispo*. Guatemala, 1958.

Cortés y Larraz, Pedro, Julio Martín Blasco, and Jesús M. García. *Descripción geográfico-moral de la Diócesis de Goathemala*. Madrid: Consejo Superior de Investigaciones Científicas, 2001.

Cosgrove, Denis E. *Apollo's Eye: A Cartographic Genealogy of the Earth in the Western Imagination*. Baltimore: Johns Hopkins University Press, 2001.

Covarrubias Horozco, Sebastián de. *Tesoro de la lengua castellana o española según la impresión de 1611*. Edited by Benito Remigio Noydens and Martín de Riquer. Barcelona: S. A. Horta, 1943.

Cox, Richard J. *Closing an Era: Historical Perspectives on Modern Archives and Records Management*. New directions in information management, no. 35. Westport, Conn.: Greenwood Press, 2000.

Craib, Raymond B. *Cartographic Mexico: A History of State Fixations and Fugitive Landscapes*. Durham, N.C.: Duke University Press, 2004.

Crowley, D. J., and Paul Heyer. *Communication in History: Technology, Culture, Society*. New York: Longman, 1991.

Cuba. *Legislación notarial vigente en Cuba, Puerto Rico y Filipinas. Contiene la ley del notariado, la instrucción general sobre la manera de redactar los instrumentos públicos sujetos á registro, anotada con resoluciones, sentencias y disposiciones aclaratorias*. Madrid: Centro editorial de Góngora, 1888.

Cuerpo Facultativo de Archiveros Bibliotecarios y Arqueólogos (Spain), and Francisco Rodríguez Marín. *Guía histórica y descriptiva de los archivos, bibliotecas y museos arqueológicos de España que están a cargo del Cuerpo facultativo del ramo*. Madrid: Tip. de la Revista de archivos bibliotecas y museos, 1916.

Cuerpo Facultativo de Archiveros Bibliotecarios y Arqueólogos (Spain), Francisco Rodríguez Marín, and Archivo Histórico Nacional (Spain). *Guía histórica y descriptiva del Archivo histórica nacional*. Madrid: Tip. de la Revista de archivos bibliotecas y museos, 1917.

Daniels, Christine, and Michael V. Kennedy. *Negotiated Empires: Centers and Peripheries in the Americas, 1500–1820*. New York: Routledge, 2002.

Daniels, Stephen. *Humphry Repton: Landscape Gardening and the Geography of Georgian England*. New Haven, Conn.: Published for the Paul Mellon Centre for Studies in the British Art [by] Yale University Press, 1999.

Darnton, Robert. *The Great Cat Massacre and Other Episodes in French Cultural History*. Vol. 1. New York: Vintage Books, 1985.

———. "The Library in the New Age." *The New York Review of Books* 55, no. 10 (June 12, 2008).

Davis, Natalie Zemon. *Fiction in the Archives: Pardon Tales and their Tellers in Sixteenth-Century France*. Stanford, Calif.: Stanford University Press, 1987.

Delbourgo, James, and Nicholas Dew, eds. *Science and Empire in the Atlantic World*. New York: Routledge, 2008.

Derrida, Jacques. *Archive Fever: A Freudian Impression*. Chicago: University of Chicago Press, 1996.

Deza, Elena. *Dictionary of Distances*. Boston: Elsevier, 2006.

Downs, Roger M., and David Stea. *Maps in Minds: Reflections on Cognitive Mapping*. New York: Harper & Row, 1977.

Dubcovsky, Alejandra. "Connected Worlds: Communication Networks in the Colonial Southeast, 1513–1740." PhD diss., University of California, Berkeley, 2011.

Dussel, Enrique. "The "World-System": Europe as "Center" and Its "Periphery," beyond Eurocentrism." In *Latin America and Postmodernity : A Contemporary Reader*, 93–122. Amherst, N.Y.: Humanity Books, 2001.

Dym, Jordana. "'More Calculated to Mislead than Inform': Travel Writers and the Mapping of Central America, 1821–1945." *Journal of Historical Geography* 30, no. 2 (2004): 340–363.

Dym, Jordana, and Christophe Belaubre. *Politics, Economy, and Society in Bourbon Central America, 1759–1821*. Boulder: University Press of Colorado, 2007.

Edney, Matthew H. "Bringing India to Hand: Mapping an Empire, Denying Space." In *The Global Eighteenth Century*, edited by Felicity A. Nussbaum. Baltimore: The Johns Hopkins University Press, 2005.

———. *Mapping an Empire: The Geographical Construction of British India, 1765–1843*. Chicago: University of Chicago Press, 1999.

Eisenstein, Elizabeth L. *The Printing Press as an Agent of Change: Communications and Cultural Transformations in Early Modern Europe*. Cambridge: Cambridge University Press, 1979.

Elliott, J. H. *Imperial Spain: 1469–1716*. New York: Penguin, 2002.

Escriche, Joaquín. *Diccionario razonado de legislación y jurisprudencia*. 3rd ed. Madrid: Viuda e hijos de A. Calleja, 1847.

———. *Suplemento al diccionario razonado de legislación y jurisprudencia*. Madrid: La Ilustracion, 1847.

Fals-Borda, Orlando. "Odyssey of a Sixteenth-Century Document-Fray Pedro de Aguado's 'Recopilacion Historial.'" *The Hispanic American Historical Review* 35, no. 2 (May 1955): 203–220.

Fernández de Mesa y Moreno, Tomás Manuel. *Tratado legal, y politico de caminos publicos, y possadas. Dividido en dos partes. La una, en que se hable de los caminos; y la otra, de las possadas: y como anexo, de los correos, y postas, assi publicas, como privadas: donde se incluye el Reglamento general de aquellas, expedido en 23. de abril de 1720*. Valencia: J. T. Lucas, 1755.

Floyd, Troy S. "The Guatemalan Merchants, the Government, and the Provincianos, 1750–1800." *The Hispanic American Historical Review* 41, no. 1 (1961): 90–110.

Foronda, Valentín de. *Carta sobre lo que debe hacer un príncipe que tenga colonias a gran distancia*. Philadelphia: s.n., 1803.

Foucault, Michel. *The Archaeology of Knowledge*. Vol. 1. New York: Pantheon Books, 1972.

Francaviglia, Richard V., and David E. Narrett, eds. *Essays on the Changing Images of the Southwest*. 1st ed. College Station: Published for the University of Texas at Arlington by Texas A&M University Press, 1994.

Fundación Histórica Tavera., Anunciada Colón de Carvajal, Ignacio González

Casasnovas, Daniel Restrepo, and World Bank. *Los archivos de América Latina: informe experto de la Fundación Histórica Tavera sobre su situación actual.* Madrid: Fundación Histórica Tavera: Banco Mundial, 2000.

Garay Unibaso, Francisco. *Correos marítimos españoles.* Bilbao: Ediciones Mensajero, 1987.

García Mainieri, Norma. *Situación archivística actual de Guatemala.* Guatemala, C.A.: Editorial Universitaria Universidad de San Carlos de Guatemala, 1980.

García Oro, José. *Los reyes y los libros: La política libraria de la corona en el siglo de oro, 1475–1598.* Madrid: Editorial Cisneros, 1995.

García, Jesús M. *Población y estado sociorreligioso de la Diócesis de Guatemala en el último tercio del siglo XVIII.* Guatemala, Centroamérica: Editorial Universitaria Universidad de San Carlos de Guatemala, 1987.

Gerhard, Peter. Mastrangelo. *Geografía histórica de la Nueva España, 1519–1821.* Espacio y tiempo; 1;. [Mexico City]: Universidad Nacional Autónoma de México, 1986.

Gillis, John R. *Islands of the Mind: How the Human Imagination Created the Atlantic World.* 1st ed. New York: Palgrave Macmillan, 2004.

Ginzburg, Carlo, Martin H. Ryle, and Kate Soper. *Wooden Eyes: Nine Reflections on Distance.* New York: Columbia University Press, 2001.

Godlewska, Anne. *Geography Unbound: French Geographic Science from Cassini to Humboldt.* Chicago: University of Chicago Press, 1999.

Gómez, Ana Margarita. "The Evolution of Military Justice in Late Colonial Guatemala, 1762–1821." *A Contracorriente* 4, no. 2 (2007): 31–53.

Gómez, Ana Margarita, and Sajid Alfredo Herrera Mena. *Los rostros de la violencia: Guatemala y El Salvador, siglos XVIII y XIX.* Vol. 1. San Salvador, El Salvador: UCA Editores, 2007.

González Cicero, Stella María, and Delia Pezzat A. *Guía para la interpretación de vocablos en documentos novohispanos: siglos XVI a XVIII. Presentación de Stella María González Cicero; introducción de Delia Pezzat Arzave.* Vol. 1. México, D.F.: Secretaría de Gobernación: Archivo General de la Nación-México, 2001.

González Echevarría, Roberto. *Myth and Archive: A Theory of Latin American Narrative.* Durham, N.C.: Duke University Press, 1998.

González García, Pedro. *Archivo General de Indias.* Barcelona: Lunwerg Editores; Ministerio de Cultura Dirección General del Libro Archivos y Bibliotecas, 1995.

González García, Pedro, and Archivo General de Indias. *Discovering the Americas.* New York: Vendome Press: Distributed in the USA and Canada by Rizzoli International Publications through St. Martin's Press, 1997.

González Sánchez, Carlos Alberto. *Los mundos del libro: medios de difusión de la cultura occidental en las Indias de los siglos XVI y XVII.* Sevilla: Diputación de Sevilla: Universidad de Sevilla, 1999.

Gould, Peter, and Rodney R. White. *Mental Maps.* Vol. 2. London: Routledge, 1986.

Grandin, Greg, and Rene Reeves. "Archives in the Guatemalan Western Highlands." *Latin American Research Review* 31, no. 1 (1996): 105–112.

Greene, Jack P. *Peripheries and Center: Constitutional Development in the Ex-*

tended Polities of the British Empire and the UnitedStates, 1607–1788. New York: W.W. Norton, 1990.

Gruzinski, Serge. *Images at War: Mexico From Columbus to Blade Runner (1492–2019).* Durham, N.C.: Duke University Press, 2001.

Guatemala. Dirección General de Caminos. *Guía kilométrica de la República de Guatemala.* Vol. 2. Guatemala: Tip. nacional, 1949.

Gudmundson, Lowell, and Héctor Lindo-Fuentes. *Central America, 1821–1871: Liberalism before Liberal Reform.* Tuscaloosa: University of Alabama Press, 1995.

Gutiérrez Alvarez, Secundino-José. *Las comunicaciones en América: de la senda primitiva al ferrocarril.* Colecciones MAPFRE 1492. Madrid: Editorial MAPFRE, 1993.

Hall, Carolyn, Héctor Pérez Brignoli, and John V. Cotter. *Historical Atlas of Central America.* Norman: University of Oklahoma Press, 2003.

Hamilton, Carolyn. *Refiguring the Archive.* Norwell, Mass.: David Philip; Kluwer Academic Publishers; Sold and distributed in North Central and South America by Kluwer Academic Publishers, 2002.

Harley, J. B. *The New Nature of Maps: Essays in the History of Cartography.* Baltimore: Johns Hopkins University Press, 2001.

Harley, J. B., and David Woodward. *The History of Cartography.* Chicago: University of Chicago Press, 1987.

Harlow, Alvin F. *Old Post Bags; the Story of the Sending of a Letter in Ancient and Modern Times.* New York: D. Appleton, 1928.

Headrick, Daniel R. *The Tools of Empire: Technology and European Imperialism in the Nineteenth-Century.* New York: Oxford University Press, 1981.

Helgerson, Richard. "The Land Speaks: Cartography, Chorography, and Subversion in Renaissance England." *Representations,* no. 16 (Autumn 1986): 50–85.

Helms, Mary W. *Ulysses' Sail: An Ethnographic Odyssey of Power, Knowledge, and Geographical Distance.* Princeton, N.J.: Princeton University Press, 1988.

Henkin, David M. *The Postal Age: The Emergence of Modern Communications in Nineteenth-Century America.* Chicago: University of Chicago Press, 2006.

Herzog, Tamar. *Mediación, archivos y ejercicio: los escribanos de Quito (siglo XVII).* Ius commune. Sonderhefte ; 82. Frankfurt am Main: Klostermann, 1996.

Heyer, Paul. *Communications and History: Theories of Media, Knowledge, and Civilization.* New York: Greenwood Press, 1988.

Higgins, Antony. *Constructing the Criollo Archive: Subjects of Knowledge in the Bibliotheca Mexicana and the Rusticatio Mexicana.* Purdue Studies in Romance Literatures ; v. 21. West Lafayette, Ind.: Purdue University Press, 2000.

Hill, Roscoe R. "Latin American Archivology, 1951–1953." *The Hispanic American Historical Review* 34, no. 2 (May 1954): 256–279.

Innis, Harold Adams. *Empire and Communications.* Oxford: Clarendon Press, 1950.

Irisarri, Antonio. *El cristiano errante: novela que tiene mucho de historia.* 3 vols. Biblioteca Guatemala de Cultura Popular 31–33. Guatemala, C.A.: Ministerio de Educación Pública, 1960.

John, Richard R. *Spreading the News: The American Postal System from Franklin to Morse*. 1st ed. Cambridge, Mass.: Harvard University Press, 1998.

Kagan, Richard. *Urban Images of the Hispanic World, 1493–1793*. New Haven, Conn.: Yale University Press, 2000.

Kamen, Henry. *Empire: How Spain Became a World Power, 1492–1763*. Vol. 1. New York: Perennial, 2004.

Kapp, Kit S. *The Printed Maps of Central America up to 1860*. London: Map Collectors' Circle, 1974.

Kielbowicz, Richard Burket. *News in the Mail: The Press, Post Office, and Public Information, 1700–1860s*. New York: Greenwood Press, 1989.

Kilgour, Frederick. *The Evolution of the Book*. New York: Oxford University Press, 1998.

Kitchin, Rob, and Mark Blades. *The Cognition of Geographic Space*. New York: I.B. Tauris, 2002.

Klein, Bernhard. *Maps and the Writing of Space in Early Modern England and Ireland*. New York: St. Martin's Press, 2001.

Lardé y Larín, Jorge. *El Salvador; historia de sus pueblos, villas y ciudades*. San Salvador: Ministerio de Cultura, Departamento Editorial, 1957.

Lefebvre, Henri. *The Production of Space*. Cambridge, Mass.: Blackwell, 1991.

Lestringant, Frank. *Mapping the Renaissance World: The Geographical Imagination in the Age of Discovery*. Berkeley: University of California Press, 1994.

Little Tools of Knowledge: Historical Essays on Academicand Bureaucratic Practices. Ann Arbor: University of Michigan Press, 2001.

Livingstone, David N. *The Geographical Tradition: Episodes in the History of a Contested Enterprise*. Oxford, UK: Blackwell, 1993.

Lloyd, Robert. *Spatial Cognition: Geographic Environments*. Boston: Kluwer Academic, 1997.

López Gómez, Pedro. *El Archivo General de Centro América: (Ciudad de Guatemala): informe*. Madrid: ANABAD, 1991.

Lovell, W. George. *Conquest and Survival in Colonial Guatemala: A Historical Geography of the Cuchumatan Highlands, 1500–1821*. 3rd ed. Montreal: McGill-Queen's University Press, 2005.

Lovell, W. George, and Christopher H. Lutz. "Anexo o apendices a perfil etno-demográfico de la Audiencia de Guatemala." *Revista de Indias* LXIII, no. 229 (2003): 759–764.

———. "Core and Periphery in Colonial Guatemala." In *Guatemalan Indians and the State: 1540 to 1988*, 35–51. Austin: University of Texas Press, 1990.

———. *Demography and Empire: A Guide to the Population History of Spanish Central America, 1500–1821*. Dellplain Latin American studies, no. 33. Boulder, Colo.: Westview Press, 1995.

Lujan Muñoz, Jorge, ed. *Relaciones geográficas e históricas del siglo XVIII del Reino de Guatemala*. 1st ed. Guatemala: Universidad del Valle de Guatemala, 2006.

Luján Muñoz, Jorge. *El ordenamiento del notariado en Guatemala desde la independencia hasta finales del siglo XIX*. Guatemala: Serviprensa Centroamericana, 1984.

Luján Muñoz, Jorge, and Instituto Guatemalteca de Derecho Notarial. *Los escribanos en las Indias Occidentales y en particular en el reino de Guatemala*. Vol. 2. Guatemala: Instituto Guatemalteca de Derecho Notarial, 1977.

Lutz, Christopher. *Santiago de Guatemala, 1541–1773: City, Caste, and the Colonial Experience*. Norman: University of Oklahoma Press, 1994.

Lynch, John. *New Worlds: A Religious History of Latin America*. New Haven, Conn.: Yale University Press, 2012.

Lynch, Kevin. *The Image of the City*. Cambridge, Mass.: M.I.T. Press, 1960.

MacLeod, Murdo J. *Spanish Central America: A Socioeconomic History, 1520–1720*. Berkeley: University of California Press, 1984.

Mancke, Elizabeth. "Early Modern Expansion and the Politicization of Oceanic Space." *Geographical Review* 89, no. 2 (April 1999): 225–236.

"Mapa de vialidad de la República de Guatemala." [Guatemala]: Dirección General de Caminos, Admon. Gral. Ubico, 1938.

Martín Barbero, Jesús. *Oficio de cartógrafo: travesías latinoamericanas de la comunicación en la cultura*. Vol. 1. Sección de obras de sociología. Santiago, Chile: Fondo de Cultura Económica, 2002.

Martín González, Ma. Jesús. *La evolución de los adverbios de lugar y tiempo a través de la documentación notarial leonesa*. Serie Lingüística y filología; no. 35. Valladolid: Universidad de Valladolid, 1999.

Martínez de Salinas, María Luisa. *La implantación del impuesto del papel sellado en Indias*. Caracas: Academia Nacional de la Historia, 1986.

Massey, Doreen. "Places and Their Pasts." *History Workshop Journal*, no. 39 (Spring 1995): 182–192.

———. "Talking of Space-Time." *Transactions of the Institute of British Geographers* 26, no. 2. New Series (2001): 257–261.

May, Jon, and N. J. Thrift. *TimeSpace: Geographies of Temporality*. Critical geographies ; 13. New York: Routledge, 2001.

McCusker, John. J. "The Demise of Distance: The Business Press and the Origins of the Information Revolution in the Early Modern Atlantic World." *American Historical Review* 111, no. 2 (2005): 295–321.

Meinig, D. W. *The Shaping of America: A Geographical Perspective on 500 Years of History*. New Haven, Conn.: Yale University Press, 1986.

Mignolo, Walter. *The Darker Side of the Renaissance: Literacy, Territoriality, and Colonization*. Ann Arbor: University of Michigan Press, 1997.

Mirow, Matthew Campbell. *Latin American Law: A History of Private Law and Institutions in Spanish America*, Austin: University of Texas Press, 2004.

Monlau, Pedro Felipe, and José Monlau y Sala. *Diccionario etimológico de la lengua castellana*, 1881.

Montáñez Matilla, María. *El Correo en la España de los Austrias*. Madrid: Consejo Superior de Investigaciones Científicas Escuela de Historia Moderna, 1953.

Montoto, Santiago. *Colección de documentos inéditos para la historia de Ibero-América*. Madrid: Editorial Ibero-Africano-America, 1927.

Mundy, Barbara E. *The Mapping of New Spain: Indigenous Cartography and the Maps of the Relaciones Geográficas*. Chicago: University of Chicago Press, 2000.

Muñoz Pérez, José, and Archivo General de Indias. *Documentos existentes en el Archivo General de Indias, Sección de Guatemala*. Vol. 1. León España: VI Congreso Internacional de Minería Departamento de Publicaciones; distribución Cátedra de San Isidoro, 1970.

Nava, Joseph. "Mapa y Tabla Geográfica de Leguas Comunes, que ai de unos á otros Lugares, y Ciudades principales de la America septentrional." Puebla de los Angeles, 1755. Record number 28987. John Carter Brown Library.

New Spain, and Spain. *Cedulario indiano*. Madrid: Ediciones Cultura Hispanica, 1945.

Noguera de Guzmán, Raimundo. *Los notarios de Barcelona en el siglo XVIII*. Barcelona: Colegio Notarial de Barcelona, 1978.

Nussbaum, Felicity A. *The Global Eighteenth Century*. Baltimore: The Johns Hopkins University Press, 2005.

Offen, Karl H. "Creating Mosquitia: Mapping Amerindian Spatial Practices in Eastern Central America, 1629–1779." *Journal of Historical Geography* 33 (2007): 254–282.

Ortiz de Logroño, Juan Elías. *Un formulario notarial mexicano del siglo XVIII: la Instrucción de escribanos de Juan Elías Ortiz de Logroño*. Querétaro: Universidad Autónoma de Querétaro, 2005.

Ostos Salcedo, Pilar, and María Luisa Pardo Rodríguez. *Documentos y notarios de Sevilla en el siglo XIII*. Madrid: Fundación Matritense del Notariado, 1989.

———. *Documentos y notarios de Sevilla en el siglo XIV (1301–1350)*. Sevilla: Universidad de Sevilla, 2003.

Padrón, Ricardo. *The Spacious Word: Cartography, Literature, and Empire in Early Modern Spain*. Chicago: University of Chicago Press, 2004.

Pagden, Anthony. *Spanish Imperialism and the Political Imagination: Studies in European and Spanish-American Social and Political Theory, 1513–1830*. New Haven, Conn.: Yale University Press, 1990.

Palacio Real de Aranjuez. *Felipe II: el rey íntimo: jardín y naturaleza en el siglo XVI*. Madrid: Sociedad Estatal para la Conmemoración de los Centenarios de Felipe II y Carlos V, 1998.

Pardo Rodríguez, María. *Señores y escribanos: el notariado andaluz entre los siglos XIV y XVI*. Sevilla: Universidad de Sevilla Secretariado de Publicaciones, 2002.

Parker, Geoffrey. *The Grand Strategy of Philip II*. New Haven, Conn.: Yale University Press, 1998.

Patch, Robert. *Maya and Spaniard in Yucatan, 1648–1812*. Stanford, Calif.: Stanford University Press, 1993.

———. *Maya Revolt and Revolution in the Eighteenth Century*. Armonk, N.Y.: M.E. Sharpe, 2002.

Pérez Fernández del Castillo, Bernardo. *Apuntes para la historia del notariado en México*. México: Asociación Nacional del Notariado Mexicano, 1979.

———. *Historia de la escribanía en la Nueva España y del notariado en México*. Vol. 3. Biblioteca Porrúa; 91. México: Colegio de Notarios del Distrito Federal: Editorial Porrúa, 1994.

Pérez Valenzuela, Pedro, and Joseph Manuel Laparte. *Memoria de los trabajos del M. N. Ayuntamiento de la Nueva Guatemala de la Asunción en el año*

MDCCLXXVI, conforme a las actas de su escribano D. Joseph Manuel Laparte. Guatemala: Edición Nueva Guatemala de la Asunción, 1970.

Petroski, Henry. *The Book on the Bookshelf.* 1st ed. New York: Alfred A. Knopf, 1999.

Phillips, Carla Rahn. "The Organization of Oceanic Empires: The Iberian World in the Habsburg Period (and a Bit Beyond)." In *Seascapes, Littoral Cultures, and Trans-Oceanic Exchanges.* Library of Congress, Washington D.C., 2003.

Phillips, Mark Salber. "Distance and Historical Representation." *History Workshop Journal* 57 (2004): 123–141.

Portuondo, Maria M. *Secret Science: Spanish Cosmography and the New World.* Chicago: University of Chicago Press, 2009.

Pratt, Mary Louise. *Imperial Eyes: Travel Writing and Transculturation.* 2nd ed. New York: Routledge, 2007.

Pred, Allan. "Place as Historically Contingent Process: Structuration and the Time-Geography of Becoming Places." *Annals of the Association of American Geographers* 74, no. 2 (June 1984): 279–297.

Rabasa, Jose. *Writing Violence on the Northern Frontier: The Historiography of Sixteenth Century New Mexico and Florida and the Legacy of Conquest.* Durham, N.C.: Duke University Press, 2000.

Rama, Angel. *The Lettered City.* Translated by John Charles Chasteen. Durham, N.C.: Duke University Press, 1996.

———. *Transculturación narrativa en América Latina.* Montevideo: Fundación Angel Rama: Distribuido por Arca Editorial, 1989.

Rama, Angel, Saúl Sosnowski, Tomás Eloy Martínez, and Fundación Internacional Angel Rama. *La crítica de la cultura en América Latina.* Caracas, Venezuela: Biblioteca Ayacucho, 1985.

Real Academia Española. *Diccionario de autoridades.* Madrid: Editorial Gredos, 1964.

Real Díaz, José Joaquín. *Estudio diplomático del documento indiano.* Vol. 1. Sevilla: Escuela de Estudios Hispanoamericanos, 1970.

Riles, Annelise. *Documents: Artifacts of Modern Knowledge.* Ann Arbor: University of Michigan Press, 2006.

Rivera Maestre, Miguel. *Atlas Guatemalteco: año de 1832.* Guatemala: Ministerio de Relaciones Exteriores, 2001.

Robinson, Howard. *Carrying British Mails Overseas.* London: G. Allen & Unwin, 1964.

Romero de Castilla y Perosso, Francisco. *Apuntes históricos sobre el archivo general de Simancas.* Madrid,: Impr. y estereotipia de Aribau y compañía, 1873.

Rubio y Moreno, Luis, and Archivo General de Indias. *Inventario general de registros cedularios del Archivo general de Indias de Sevilla, presentado por el autor en el Congreso de historia y geografía celebrado en 1921.* Madrid,: Compañía Ibero-Americana de Publicaciones s. a., 1928.

Ruggles, D. *Gardens, Landscape, and Vision in the Palaces of Islamic Spain.* University Park: Pennsylvania State University Press, 2000.

Russell-Wood, A.J.R. "Centers and Peripheries in the Luso-Brazilian World, 1500–

1808." In *Negotiated Empires: Centers and Peripheries in the Americas, 1500–1820*, 105–142. New York: Routledge, 2002.

Sack, Robert David. *Conceptions of Space in Social Thought: A Geographic Perspective*. Minneapolis: University of Minnesota Press, 1980.

Safier, Neil. *Measuring the New World: Enlightenment Science and South America*. Chicago: University of Chicago Press, 2008.

Sahlins, Peter. *Boundaries: The Making of France and Spain in the Pyrenees*. Berkeley: University of California Press, 1989.

———. "Centring the Periphery: The Cerdanya between France and Spain." In *Spain, Europe, and the Atlantic World: Essays in Honour of John H. Elliott*, edited by Richard L Kagan and Geoffrey Parker. Cambridge: Cambridge University Press, 1995.

Said, Edward W. *Culture and Imperialism*. New York: Knopf, 1993.

Salas M, Oscar A. *Derecho notarial de Centroamérica y Panamá*. San José, Costa Rica: Editorial Costa Rica, 1973.

Sandman, Alison. "Controlling Knowledge: Navigation, Cartography, and Secrecy in the Early Modern Spanish Atlantic." In *Science and Empire in the Atlantic World*, edited by James Delbourgo and Nicholas Dew. New York: Routledge, 2008.

Santamaría, Francisco Javier, and Joaquín García Icazbalceta. *Diccionario de mejicanismos: razonado, comprobado con citas de autoridades, comparado con el de americanismos y con los vocabularios provinciales de los más distinguidos diccionaristas hispanoamericanos*. Méjico: Editorial Porrúa, 1992.

Sapper, Karl. *The Verapaz in the Sixteenth and Seventeenth Centuries: A Contribution to the Historical Geography and Ethnography of Northeastern Guatemala*. Los Angeles: Institute of Archaeology University of California, 1985.

Scardaville, Michael C. "Justice by Paperwork: A Day in the Life of a Court Scribe in Bourbon Mexico City." *Journal of Social History* 36, no. 4 (2003): 979–1007.

Schäfer, Ernst, and Archivo General de Indias. *Las rúbricas del Consejo real y supremo de las Indias desde la fundación del Consejo en 1524 hasta la terminación del reinado de los Austrias*. Nendeln, Liechtenstein: Kraus Reprint, 1975.

Schäfer, Ernst, and John Pilaar. *Communications Between Spain and Her American Colonies and Inter-Colonial Communications*. Los Angeles, 1939.

Schivelbusch, Wolfgang. *Disenchanted Night: The Industrialization of Light in the Nineteenth Century*. Berkeley: University of California Press, 1988.

———. "Railroad Space and Railroad Time." *New German Critique*, no. 14 (1978): 31–40.

———. *The Railway Journey: The Industrialization of Time and Space in the 19th Century*. Berkeley: University of California Press, 1986.

Scott, H. V. "Contested territories: arenas of geographical knowledge in early colonial Peru." *Journal of Historical Geography* 29, no. 2 (2003): 166–188.

Serrera Contreras, Ramón María. *Tráfico terrestre y red vial en las indias españolas*. Barcelona: Lunwerg, 1992.

Short, John R. *Making Space: Revisioning the World, 1475–1600.* Syracuse, N.Y.: Syracuse University Press, 2004.

Silverblatt, Irene Marsha. *Modern Inquisitions: Peru and the Colonial Origins of the Civilized World.* Durham, N.C.: Duke University Press, 2004.

Smith, Carol A. "Origins of the National Question in Guatemala: A Hypothesis." In *Guatemalan Indians and the State: 1540 to 1988.* Austin: University of Texas Press, 1990.

———. *Regional Analysis.* 2 vols. New York: Academic Press, 1976.

Smith, Carol A., Marilyn M. Moors, and Latin American Studies Association. *Guatemalan Indians and the State, 1540 to 1988.* Vol. 1. Symposia on Latin America series. Austin: University of Texas Press, 1990.

Sociedad de Geografía e Historia de Guatemala. "Anales de la Sociedad de Geografía e Historia de Guatemala." La Sociedad, n.d.

Socolow, Susan Migden. *The Bureaucrats of Buenos Aires, 1769–1810: Amor Al Real Servicio.* Durham, N.C.: Duke University Press, 1987.

Socolow, Susan Migden, and Lyman L. Johnson. "Colonial Centers, Colonial Peripheries, and the Economic Agency of the Spanish State." In *Negotiated Empires: Centers and Peripheries in the Americas, 1500–1820,* 59–78. New York: Routledge, 2002.

Solano, Francisco de, Pilar Ponce Leiva, and Antonio Abellán García. *Cuestionarios para la formación de las relaciones geográficas de Indias: siglos XVI/XIX.* Madrid: Consejo Superior de Investigaciones Científicas Centro de Estudios Históricos Departamento de Historia de América, 1988.

Spain, Europe, and the Atlantic World: Essays in Honour of John H. Elliott. Cambridge: Cambridge University Press, 1995.

Spain. *Escribanos y protocolos notariales en el descubrimiento de América: presentación del premio de investigación histórico-jurídica Madrid, 29 de octubre de 1992.* [Guadalajara]: Consejo General del Notariado, 1993.

Spain. *Ordenanzas para el Archivo General de Indias.* Madrid: In la Imprenta de la Viuda de Ibarra, 1790.

Spain. Dirección General de Correos y Telégrafos. *Anales de las ordenanzas de correos de España.* Madrid,: Imprenta Central a Cargo de Victor Saiz, 1879.

Spain. Sovereign (1759–1788 : Charles III), and collection Hubert Howe Bancroft. *Desde que se incorporó en mi Corona en el año de mil setecientos y seis el Oficio de Correo Mayor de España han conocido en primera instancia en todas las causas, casos, y negocios contenciosos del ramo de Correos, y Postas, y de los individuos que dependen de él . . . : Madrid, 1776, 1776.*

Spain. Sovereign (1759–1788 : Charles III), and Pedro Marin. *Real cedula de S.M. y señores del Consejo, por la qual se aprueba el arreglo de escribanos reales en Madrid su distribución y aplicacion en la forma que se refiere; y manda que su numero quede reducido en lo sucesivo al de 150, observandose para ello las reglas y prevenciones que se expresan.* Madrid: P. Marin, 1783.

Steedman, Carolyn, and Rutgers University Press. *Dust: The Archive and Cultural History.* New Brunswick, N.J.: Rutgers University Press, 2002.

Stoler, Ann Laura. *Along the Archival Grain: Epistemic Anxieties and Colonial Common Sense.* Princeton, N.J.: Princeton University Press, 2009.

Suárez Argüello, Clara Elena. *Camino real y carrera larga: la arriería en la Nueva España durante el siglo XVIII*. Vol. 1. México, D.F.: Centro de Investigaciones y Estudios Superiores en Antropología Social, 1997.

Sullivan-González, Douglass. *Piety, Power, and Politics: Religion and Nation Formation in Guatemala, 1821–1871*. Pittsburgh: University of Pittsburgh Press, 1998.

Taracena Arriola, Arturo. *Invención criolla, sueño ladino, pesadilla indígena: Los Altos de Guatemala: de región a Estado, 1740–1850*. Antigua, Guatemala; San José, Costa Rica: Centro de Investigaciones Regionales de Mesoamérica; Porvenir, 1997.

Taylor, William B. *Drinking, Homicide and Rebellion in Colonial Mexican Villages*. Stanford, Calif.: Stanford University Press, 1979.

———. *Magistrates of the Sacred: Priests and Parishioners in Eighteenth-Century Mexico*. Stanford, Calif.: Stanford University Press, 1996.

Teng, Emma. *Taiwan's Imagined Geography: Chinese Colonial Travel Writing and Pictures, 1683–1895*. Harvard East Asian monographs 230. Cambridge, Mass.: Harvard University Asia Center, 2004.

TePaske, John Jay. "Integral to Empire: The Vital Peripheries of Colonial Spanish America." In *Negotiated Empires: Centers and Peripheries in the Americas, 1500–1820*, 29–42. New York: Routledge, 2002.

Torre Revello, José. *El Archivo General de Indias de Sevilla ; historia y clasificación de sus fondos*. Buenos Aires: Talleres s. a. Casa Jacobo Peuser ltda, 1929.

Trueba Lawand, Jamile. *El arte epistolar en el renacimiento español*. Madrid Rochester, N.Y.: Támesis; Boydell & Brewer Distributor, 1996.

Tuan, Yi-fu. *Morality and Imagination: Paradoxes of Progress*. Madison: University of Wisconsin Press, 1989.

———. *Space and Place: The Perspective of Experience*. Minneapolis: University of Minnesota Press, 1977.

United States. *A Modern Archives Reader: Basic Readings on Archival Theory and Practice*. Washington, D.C.: National Archives and Records Service, U.S. General Services Administration, 1984.

Van Oss, Adriaan C. "La población de América Central hacia 1800." *Anales de la Academia de Geografía e Historia de Guatemala* LV (1981): 291–312.

Villagutierre Soto-Mayor, Juan. *Historia de la conquista de la provincia de el Itza, reducción, y progresos de la de el Lacandón, y otras naciones de indios bárbaros, de las mediaciones de el reyno de Guatimala, a las*. 2nd ed. Guatemala C.A.: Tipografía nacional, 1933.

Volek, Emil. *Latin America Writes Back: Postmodernity in the Periphery: (An Interdisciplinary Perspective)*. New York: Routledge, 2002.

Weber, David J. "Bourbons and Bárbaros: Center and Periphery in the Reshaping of Spanish Indian Policy." In *Negotiated Empires: Centers and Peripheries in the Americas, 1500–1820*, 79–104. New York: Routledge, 2002.

Weber, Max, and Sam Whimster. *The Essential Weber: A Reader*. New York: Routledge, 2004.

Webster, Frank. *Theories of the Information Society*. New York: Routledge, 1995.

Whitrow, G. J. *Time in History: The Evolution of Our General Awareness of Time and Temporal Perspective.* Oxford: Oxford University Press, 1988.

Wilkins, David E. "Guatemalan Political History: National Indian Policy, 1532–1954." *Wicazo Sa Review* Vol. 9, No. 1 (1993): 17–31.

Wold, Lillian Ramos, and Ophelia Márquez. *Compilation of Colonial Spanish Terms and Document Related Phrases.* Vol. 2. Midway City, CA: SHAAR Press, 1998.

Woodward, Ralph Lee. *Central America: A Nation Divided.* Vol. 3. Latin American histories. New York: Oxford University Press, 1999.

———. *Rafael Carrera and the Emergence of the Republic of Guatemala, 1821–1871.* Athens: University of Georgia Press, 1993.

Wortman, Miles. "Bourbon Reforms in Central America: 1750–1786." *The Americas* 32, no. 2 (1975): 222–238.

Wortman, Miles L. *Government and Society in Central America, 1680–1840.* New York: Columbia University Press, 1982.

Wright, John Kirtland, David Lowenthal, Martyn J. Bowden, and Mary Alice Lamberty. *Geographies of the Mind: Essays in Historical Geosophy in Honor of John Kirtland Wright.* New York: Oxford University Press, 1976.

Yanna Yannakakis. "Witnesses, Spatial Practices, and a Land Dispute in Colonial Oaxaca." *The Americas* 65, no. 2 (2008): 161–192.

Zeissig, Leopoldo. *Descripción de las principales carreteras de Guatemala.* Guatemala: Tipografía Nacional, 1938.

Index

Note: page numbers in italics refer to figures or tables.